Routine Crisis

CHICAGO STUDIES IN PRACTICES OF MEANING

A series edited by Andreas Glaeser, William Mazzarella, William Sewell Jr., Kaushik Sunder Rajan, and Lisa Wedeen

Published in collaboration with the
Chicago Center for Contemporary Theory
http://ccct.uchicago.edu

RECENT BOOKS IN THE SERIES

Justice Is an Option: A Democratic Theory of Finance for the Twenty-First Century
by Robert Meister

Authoritarian Apprehensions: Ideology, Judgment, and Mourning in Syria
by Lisa Wedeen

Deadline: Populism and the Press in Venezuela
by Robert Samet

Guerrilla Marketing: Counterinsurgency and Capitalism in Colombia
by Alexander L. Fattal

What Nostalgia Was: War, Empire, and the Time of a Deadly Emotion
by Thomas Dodman

The Mana of Mass Society
by William Mazzarella

The Sins of the Fathers: Germany, Memory, Method
by Jeffrey K. Olick

The Politics of Dialogic Imagination: Power and Popular Culture in Early Modern Japan
by Katsuya Hirano

American Value: Migrants, Money, and Meaning in El Salvador and the United States
by David Pedersen

Questioning Secularism: Islam, Sovereignty, and the Rule of Law in Modern Egypt
by Hussein Ali Agrama

ROUTINE CRISIS

An Ethnography of Disillusion

Sarah Muir

THE UNIVERSITY OF CHICAGO PRESS

Chicago and London

The University of Chicago Press, Chicago 60637

The University of Chicago Press, Ltd., London

© 2021 by The University of Chicago

All rights reserved. No part of this book may be used or reproduced in any manner whatsoever without written permission, except in the case of brief quotations in critical articles and reviews. For more information, contact the University of Chicago Press, 1427 E. 60th St., Chicago, IL 60637.

Published 2021

Printed in the United States of America

30 29 28 27 26 25 24 23 22 21   1 2 3 4 5

ISBN-13: 978-0-226-75264-8 (cloth)

ISBN-13: 978-0-226-75278-5 (paper)

ISBN-13: 978-0-226-75281-5 (e-book)

DOI: https://doi.org/10.7208/chicago/9780226752815.001.0001

Library of Congress Cataloging-in-Publication Data

Names: Muir, Sarah (Anthropologist), author.

Title: Routine crisis : an ethnography of disillusion / Sarah Muir.

Other titles: Chicago studies in practices of meaning.

Description: Chicago ; London : The University of Chicago Press, 2021. | Series: Chicago studies in practices of meaning | Includes bibliographical references and index.

Identifiers: LCCN 2020046172 | ISBN 9780226752648 (cloth) | ISBN 9780226752785 (paperback) | ISBN 9780226752815 (ebook)

Subjects: LCSH: Middle class—Argentina—Buenos Aires. | Middle class— Argentina—Buenos Aires—Attitudes. | Crises—Argentina. | Financial crises—Argentina. | Financial crises—Social aspects—Argentina. | Argentina—Economic conditions—Public opinion. | Argentina—Social conditions—Public opinion. | Argentina—Politics and government— Public opinion. | Argentina—Economic conditions—21st century.

Classification: LCC HT690.A7 M845 2021 | DDC 305.5/5098211—dc23

LC record available at https://lccn.loc.gov/2020046172

CONTENTS

Introduction, 1

CHAPTER ONE
Speaking of Crisis, *13*

CHAPTER TWO
A Suspicious History, *39*

CHAPTER THREE
Economies of Loss, *65*

CHAPTER FOUR
Exhausted Futures, *91*

CHAPTER FIVE
Solidary Selves, *117*

Argentine Afterword, 143

Acknowledgments, 147
Appendix, 151
References, 157
Index, 177

INTRODUCTION

In Argentina, the story goes, neoliberalism ended on December 21, 2001, when President de la Rúa fled the presidential palace by helicopter in acquiescence to the demands of a newly cohered national public. He fled amidst a financial crisis that was rapidly becoming the worst economic collapse in Argentine history. The upheaval was marked by a dramatic devaluation of the currency, the largest sovereign default in world history, prolonged negotiations over international loans, and the flight of foreign capital. Massive street protests in the cities and road blockades in the countryside accompanied nationally unprecedented levels of unemployment and impoverishment as well as profound political uncertainty.

The widely shared experience of loss and disquiet that had precipitated the president's flight stood in stark contrast to the bromides offered up by institutions such as the International Monetary Fund (IMF) and the US Treasury, both of which confidently proclaimed the Argentine financial crisis to be a favorable moment for the country to learn from its mistakes and embark on the sorts of modest and prudent policy reforms that would surely usher in lasting prosperity.[1] In vehement opposition to those sorts of proclamations, which bitterly defended the tenets of the Washington Consensus even as they lamented the unforeseen consequences of its imperfect application, many people within Argentina and abroad saw in the crisis the opportunity for profound—perhaps even revolutionary—change. From this perspective, the crisis had finally revealed fundamental, long hidden, but now undeniable problems that far exceeded the scope of mere reform.

Indeed, during the heady days of 2001 and 2002, there was not only the sense of loss but also the sense of optimism that the crisis might mark a definitive end and a new beginning, that the upheaval might grant people a measure of conscious agency as they seized the moment and steered history in a new direction. That sentiment of hopeful historical agency was not confined to the Left, as Argentines across the political spectrum saw in the crisis irrefutable evidence of a bankrupt political, economic, and social system. However, its widespread resonance lent considerable plausibility to long-standing critiques of "neoliberalism," which, however vaguely defined in popular discussions, seemed to nearly everyone in Argentina a now discredited, even fraudulent, mode of governance. As such, the crisis seemed to many to have inaugurated a new historical moment and "a new radical generation" (Munck 2001, 83) capable of taking full advantage of its possibilities.

---

1. "O'Neill está ansioso por ver el plan de Duhalde: Los pasos deben darse 'pronto,' dijo," *La Nación*, January 10, 2002, http://www.lanacion.com.ar/nota.asp?nota_id=365585. See also Anne Krueger, "Crisis Prevention and Resolution: Lessons from Argentina, Address by Anne Krueger, First Deputy Managing Director, International Monetary Fund," July 17, 2002, http://www.imf.org/external/np/speeches/2002/071702.htm (accessed April 25, 2020).

Much of the writing—academic, journalistic, activist, and otherwise—on the 2001–2002 Argentine financial crisis has focused on these years and on this radical potential. Attending to practices such as barter clubs, neighborhood assemblies, worker cooperatives, and street protests, numerous works have argued that the crisis catalyzed new sites of emancipatory, progressive democratic possibility. In this way, analyses of the 2001–2002 Argentine crisis have allowed it to circulate globally as an icon of the crisis logic of finance capitalism but also as a "space of hope" (Harvey 2000).[2]

Those remarkable practices were real, as was the hope they occasioned. However, the most spectacular dimensions of a crisis are not necessarily its most consequential. And, while the story of neoliberalism's end may well be a compelling one, it is a story that requires us to ignore the many profound continuities between pre- and post-crisis Argentina. In fact, for many Argentines, the sense of newly emergent futures that they felt in the tumultuous days of 2001–2002 quickly gave way to a profound sense of disillusion, not only with the promises of the neoliberal 1990s, but also with the promises of crisis itself to serve as the pivot for historical transformation.

In our rush to locate spaces of hope, immanent alternate realities, and emergent possibilities for a renewed future, we risk failing to confront another, countervailing but no less significant social dynamic, that of radical negativity not recuperated by the dialectic of social reproduction (Munn 1986), of the relentlessly fateful quality of historical time (Sewell 2005) and of the all-too-human incapacity to restore that which has been destroyed (Adorno 1994). It is in attending to the lived, ethnographic reality of radical negativity in this sense that we can see how people's ongoing, often conflictual, interpretive engagements with the past create futures that can be uncanny, discomfiting, or ironic, even as they are also unpredictable and essentially open-ended. Such an approach allows us to grasp the import of ethnographic experiences like disillusion and disorientation, failure and self-destruction, and to see how they are produced in the real-time unfolding of interpretive practice. The interminable logic of that unfolding means that we need neither resign ourselves to the conclusion of fated ruin nor demand that history offer us a narrative of hopeful redemption.

Social scientists have long tended to cast Argentina's twentieth-century history of crisis, impoverishment, institutional degradation, and growing inequality as a glaring exception to general historical trends.[3] However, the

---

2. For analyses of the crisis as a space of hope, see Andermann, Derbyshire, and Kraniauskas 2002; Dinerstein 2002, 2003; Faulk 2012; Graeber 2002; Klein 2008; Kunkel 2014; Larsen 2003; Lewkowicz 2002; Negri, interviewed in Gago and Sztulwark 2002; Pérez, Armelino, and Rossi 2005; Sitrin 2006, 2012; and Virno, interviewed in Costa 2002.

3. Summing up that late twentieth-century opinion, economist Simon Kuznets is famously (but perhaps apocryphally) reputed to have declared that there are four kinds of countries:

global proliferation of financial crises over the past several decades allows us to cast that history in a new light. While by no means novel, the paralysis of financial markets and the resulting cascade of social effects has become so routine an event that one can periodize recent political-economic history and sketch the emergent geography of contemporary capitalism simply by following the shifting epicenter of crisis: Latin America's long debt crisis of the 1980s, Japan's 1992 asset price collapse, Mexico's 1994 peso crisis, Asia's 1997 financial crisis, Russia's 1998 ruble crisis, Argentina's 2001–2002 financial crisis, and so on. Thanks to the global financial crisis that began in 2008, academic and lay observers even in relatively buffered locales within the United States and the European Union now recognize crisis to be central to contemporary capitalism. Additionally, scholars from an array of disciplinary and ideological positions have found themselves increasingly compelled to acknowledge not only the centrality of crisis to capitalism but, more disturbingly still, the possibility that crisis need not catalyze progress, whether in its leftist or its liberal guise.[4] Indeed, the widespread contemporary sense of disorientation in the face of the apparently incessant crises of finance capitalism suggests that Argentina is not as exceptional as it once may have seemed.

In surveying the hopscotch of crisis across the globe, it is insufficient to find confirmation of the old Marxist saw that capitalism *is* crisis and to pen eloquent condemnations of its inherently "violent" (Marazzi 2010) logic. That approach, which promises to uncover the reality behind the ideological veil of modernity, no longer has the capacity to grant us the sparks of critical insight necessary to project a different, better future. Our globally— but unequally—shared historical experience of crisis demands a mode of critique that does not proceed according to the logic of suspicion, with its attempt to "clear the horizon for a new reign of Truth" (Ricœur 1970, 32–33). Such an attempt is bound too tightly to an understanding of knowledge and of historical time that is obsolete. Instead, to the extent that we feel ourselves to inhabit a world shaped by incessant crisis, it is incumbent on us to interrogate the emergence of that historical sensibility and to consider its consequences for the ways that we understand what is possible, what is valuable, what is imaginable.

From the perspective of 2020, as I write these introductory remarks, it is somewhat harrowing to see that Argentina is again in the midst of crisis. For about twelve years, under the presidencies of Néstor Kirchner (2003–

---

developed countries, developing countries, Japan (which develops in inexplicable ways), and Argentina (which declines in inexplicable ways).

4. See, e.g., Calhoun 2011; Harvey 2010; Mann 2017; Picketty 2014; Roubini and Mihm 2010; and Sewell 2012.

2007) and, more dramatically, Cristina Fernández de Kirchner (2007–2015), Argentina pursued a set of policies that were avowedly anti-neoliberal, neo-Keynesian, and leftist.[5] Those policies helped rebuild the national economy and improve social welfare in many key respects. However, they depended on a global commodities boom that funneled billions of much-needed US dollars into the country. With the global collapse of commodity prices in 2008, those policies became increasingly untenable and all the familiar features of crisis reappeared: a shrinking gross domestic product (GDP) and a skyrocketing country-risk index; an unpayable foreign debt and IMF-mandated austerity measures; punishing inflation rates and currency devaluations; growing rates of unemployment, poverty, and indigency; street protests and strikes; and dramatic political polarization with allegations of corruption and even coups on all sides. Mauricio Macri, elected to the presidency in 2015 on the campaign promise of reversing economic decline and returning the country to "fiscal responsibility," found himself unable to do so and lost reelection in late 2019. Cristina Fernández de Kirchner returned to power, now as vice president, with Aníbal Fernández (no relation) occupying the office of the presidency. Promises of a renewed progressive agenda are in the air.

Given this recent past, it is not surprising to find that the idea of a country doomed to crisis has, if anything, become even more firmly entrenched in Argentine discourse. There has emerged a new term to sum up the idea: *ciclocrisis*, a "crisis-cycle" of "circular destiny" defined by short-term economic logics and wild swings in the economy (Oliveto 2014; see also F. González 2012). However, the idea of crisis as circular destiny is simply the inverse of crisis as historical inflection point. Neither idea is particularly helpful for grasping how particular experiences of crisis shape social life, economic practice, and political imaginations.

The years following the 2001–2002 Argentine financial crisis were defined neither by radical social transformation nor by predictable social reproduction. It was a period of uneven, contradictory, and ambivalent movements. People wrestled with progressive and reactionary intuitions, both of which were deeply felt. People struggled to define what the past had amounted to and how to imagine the days, weeks, months, and years that were to

---

5. I do not assess the extent to which the Kirchner presidencies deviated, or did not, from neoliberalism. Suffice it to say the administrations were defined in many ways by what one analyst has called a "persistent dualism" between, on one hand, anti-neoliberal rhetoric, increased spending on social welfare, and the prosecution of past human rights abuses and, on the other, an increasingly precarious labor market, the cooptation of social movements, and an expansion of "hyper-presidentialism" (Sader 2008, 22). For more on the contradictions of *kirchnerismo* and on the "Turn to the Left" or "Pink Tide" in Argentina and elsewhere in Latin America, see also Basualdo 2011; Blanco and Grier 2013; Epstein and Pion-Berlin 2006; Flores-Macías 2012; Gago 2017; Riggirozzi 2009; and Svampa 2008.

come. Throughout, they worried about minute issues of daily life, for no matter how banal, everything seemed bound up with large-scale concerns of national identity, macroeconomic developments, and global relations.

Attending to these uncomfortable and irreconcilable dynamics makes it possible to reframe Argentina's rapid oscillation from austerity to social welfare to austerity (and back again?) not as definitive ruptures or fated repetitions but rather as the slow and uneven working out of much longer-term historical dynamics. Those dynamics have no definitive origo or telos, for both origin and endpoint are necessarily changeable, depending on the interpretive frame people impose on them in their roles as analyst or commentator, consumer or employee, activist or pragmatist, historian or politician. The eventfulness and the significance of the event are, in other words, always potentially remade as new, unexpected developments compel us to reconsider their appropriate framing.

Allowing for such a reframing permits us to sidestep the demand to identify a determinate pattern to that history. The analytic demand becomes instead to trace the interpretive practices through which people come to recognize aspects of the world around them either as new or as repetition and to interrogate the grounds on which they—and we—attempt to know the past so as to make their—and our—present and future. In other words, the task becomes to show how the *afterward* of an event is never given or static but always the tentative product of the continually rewritten *afterword* through which we engage with its significance.

Take, for example, my conversation with Diego.

By the time of my interview with Diego, it was late 2005. By then, the sense of incessant emergency had dissipated, having given way to a relatively predictable day-to-day life. Still, the 2001–2002 crisis had a lingering and unsettling presence, forcing its way through the veneer of mundane affairs in an irregular but decidedly charged fashion. If the logistics of everyday practices had become unremarkable once more, larger, longer-term, and more interpretive matters remained vexed. In this context, the crisis stood at the center of seemingly intractable yet irresistible questions about the country's core identity and ultimate future, questions that surfaced in contexts both surprising and predictable and that prompted lengthy, circuitous, and passionate discussions. At the same time, it was often difficult to see where those discussions led; for all the upheaval precipitated by the crisis, there was precious little evidence of profound institutional change to the country's economic, political, or social structures.

I had come to Buenos Aires to study that uneasy aftermath. For my interview with Diego, a thirty-two-year-old unemployed man, we sat in the living room of his parents' apartment in Caballito, a residential neighborhood of Buenos Aires often described to me as "*very* middle-class," with its mix of midsize apartment buildings, modest houses, and bustling commercial strips of groceries, clothing stores, and cafés. Trained as an architect, Diego was telling me about the difficulty of finding steady work. He had come of age at a particularly inauspicious moment, he explained, in the midst of an economic collapse from which the country would "never truly recover" and which had "destroyed the last remnants of the middle class," leaving "the nation in the hands of the corrupt politicians and the economic interests."

The interview lasted nearly three hours, most of which Diego spent soliloquizing while smoking cigarette after cigarette and drinking copious amounts of *mate*, the ubiquitous and caffeinated Argentine tea. He meandered from topic to topic, weaving together opinions about current events, stories of his upbringing, and bits of national history that sounded as if they came straight from a textbook. Throughout, his tone was nearly uniformly critical, often mournful, and frequently outraged as he described and explained the nation's predicament. No detail—from culinary traditions to Spanish colonial law, from his own family's emphasis on education to contingent features of the country's geography and climate—escaped accusations of complicity. (Argentines' "passion for beef" was evidence of a "pathological tie to an agrarian society that rejects modernity" and was epitomized by "the fertile but empty pampas"; the Spanish legal heritage "condemned [the country] to a system of corruption"; and the long-standing national investment in public education "was just a pathetic attempt to pretend we were something we were not.") All the while, the 2001–2002 crisis stood at the organizing center of his remarks, "an event designed by powerful forces, who manipulated our unconscious desires in order to destroy the nation, to destroy the middle class. . . . That's why it was the end of the future and all we can do is talk about it until the next crisis appears."

"It was the end of the future," he insisted. "After that, we finally realized that there is no future in this country, that there never had been a future. The fantasy of the middle class is over. There is no way out of the absurdity of the present."

Of course, Diego did not dispute that time kept flowing, minute by minute, year by year. What he did dispute was the idea that it was possible to hope for a different, better future. He insisted that the promises and dreams of the past would go unfulfilled and that there was no opportunity to construct new visions or plans.[6] All that was left, he wanted me to understand, was a wasteland of ruined potential. Life was possible within that wasteland. But it was a life of endless rumination, ineffectual chatter, and the expectation of further upheaval.

---

6. Diego's comments unintentionally echoed Taguieff's (2000) argument about "un futur sans avenir," which Trouillot glosses as "a future without prospects" (Trouillot 2003, 69).

The historical stance that Diego took up was not unique to him. In fact, it was quite commonplace in post-crisis, middle-class Buenos Aires. The Buenos Aires middle class had long figured within the national imaginary as a figure of cosmopolitanism, progress, and modernity, and associated with a valorization of all things European and nonindigenous. However, depending on a person's age, the 2001–2002 crisis was easily the second but perhaps even the third, fourth, or fifth severe national crisis within living memory, a widely remarked-upon fact that challenged the increasingly implausible promises of middle-class modernity. With the 2001–2002 crisis, then, the Buenos Aires middle class came to figure as the threatened and long-suffering protagonist of national history. And, within that middle class, the widespread sense of foreclosed futures became the grounds on which people grappled with all manner of practical issues, both public and intimate. Whether deciding how to educate children or how to vote in an election, whether considering what is owed to those less fortunate or what to do about an unhappy marriage, people within that embattled middle class began with the sense that, after the dashed promises of twentieth-century progress, they were now living in an afterward in which no new beginnings were in sight.

Neither is this historical stance unique to post-crisis, middle-class Buenos Aires. That stance will be familiar to those of us who slog through sleepless nights and anxious commutes as we worry about a looming economic recession, about the judgment of presidents armed with nuclear codes, or about the now unavoidable climate change catastrophes that lie ahead. Ours is not a time oriented by the possibility of material improvement and moral betterment driven by our critical interrogation of the world. Ours is a time defined by the usually vague but nonetheless forceful sense that we see quite clearly that things are being upended in a manner that is ongoing, tumultuous, unpredictable, and most certainly not for the good.

That this historical stance can be so readily taken up in so many different contexts, both within Argentina and beyond, and with so many contradictory political valences and implications, indicates that the modern configuration of crisis and critique—that well-known conceptual pairing that Koselleck (1988) identifies with the emergence of modern politics, utopian philosophies of history, and moral investments in a better future—is giving way to something new and decidedly ambivalent. This ambivalence is related to Latour's (2004) worry that post-Enlightenment modes of critique may have "run out of steam." So, too, is it bound up with Hage's (2015, 10) emphasis on endurance rather than mobility when, as he says, "crisis today is no longer felt as an unusual state of affairs that invites the citizen to question the given order. Rather, it is perceived more as a normalcy, or . . . a kind of permanent state of exception." Brown's (2001) characterization of the contemporary moment as "out of joint" is salient here, as is Trouillot's (2003) description of the coming undone of our roles as actor, agent, and subject—not to mention narrator—of history.

In order to bring into view and interrogate the consequences of these sensibilities, I focus attention squarely on a time and place where they were especially visible: the Buenos Aires middle class in the years immediately following the 2001–2002 crisis. That attention is motivated by a concern with narrative, and especially with the interplay between the stories we tell and the stories we live out. Across the intersecting traditions of Marxian and linguistic anthropology, analysts use a variety of terms to conceptualize that interplay. However, they all begin with the twin premises that our experiences as social actors shape the worlds we narrate, and that our narratives, in turn, shape our engagements with the world we inhabit. From this perspective, narrative is not a mere reflection or representation of material reality. Rather, narrative is a material practice, through which we can trace the production of particular modes of historical consciousness and dispositions toward historical action.[7]

Throughout, I pay close attention to negativity—that is, to experiences of loss, frustration, failure, and disappointment—but without demanding that we find in them some glimmer of hope, some promise of redemption. I do so not in order to echo the pessimism of someone like Diego, nor to abandon an interest in emergent possibilities. Rather, I aim to hold at bay what Hankins (2015, 2) calls anthropology's "fascination with the new" in order to untangle the often-overlooked salience of the ways things end.

Especially key in this respect are things that don't end easily, tidily, or in a timely manner. Take, for example, Diego's emotional investment in a vision of "the future" defined in terms of the national middle class. He recognizes that vision to be obsolete but holds onto it, allowing its demise to signify the impossibility of any kind of future whatsoever. This book focuses on a time and place full of such obsolete but stubbornly lingering intuitions, desires, and commitments and maps the many ways that people found themselves trapped in a world that seemed to offer no stable ground from which to project a different, better future.

Toward that end, my analysis does not proceed according to the logic of revelation, bound up as it is with understandings of crisis and historical time that no longer hold. Instead, each chapter circles back to key scenes from the crisis of 2001–2002 in order to trace how people retrospectively

---

7. In other words, my approach is grounded in works such as Bakhtin's (1982) theorization of chronotopes as well as Marx's (1994) argument about the ironic rhyming of events as they unfold across linear time, H. White's (1990) analysis of the form of narrative history, and Trouillot's (1997) analysis of how historical events become un/imaginable and in/visible.

reconstituted it as an orienting event signaling an end that refused to open up onto a new beginning. Each chapter also traces the motif of negativity as it manifested in a particular arena of social life. The structure of the book thus mimics the recursive interpretive practices (such as Diego's interrogation of the crisis) that are its central object of analysis. Over the course of its chapters, I show how those interpretive practices are the key sites for understanding the transformations in the logics of crisis and critique, in Argentina and in other places defined by the "passing of mass utopias" (Buck-Morss 2000).

In carrying out research for this book, I lived in Buenos Aires for several years.[8] There, I conducted both formal and informal interviews with people from a wide variety of backgrounds, many of whom contacted me to request an interview after having learned about my project from someone else. Those interviews provide much of the material that I analyze over the course of the book and offered insight into the shared sensibilities about the crisis that cut across so many social differences, including those of generation, gender, income, and political ideology. I also worked as a part-time volunteer at several civil society organizations that offered social services to impoverished communities. That work gave me the opportunity to see how volunteers, employees, and clients wrestled with the economic inequalities that were so remarkable a feature of the social landscape. I attended neighborhood meetings and civic events as well as adult educational events, such as talks by public intellectuals, cooking classes, and other free or low-cost opportunities for self-enrichment and the cultivation of social and cultural capital. Keen to get a taste of what is a clichéd dimension of middle-class Argentina, I also attended weekly sessions with a Lacanian psychoanalyst, an experience that gave me much-needed insight into ways of speaking, listening, and interpreting that permeate everyday critical practices. Finally, I conducted extensive archival research of mass media artifacts including works of popular history and social analysis as well as a systematic survey of the three major national newspapers (*Clarín, La Nación,* and *Página 12*) in order to chart changing patterns in public discourse over a period of seventeen years (1990–2007).

The analysis of these mass media artifacts helped contextualize a remarkable consensus regarding the tragic inevitability of the 2001–2002 crisis. In chapter 1 ("Speaking of Crisis"), I interrogate the emergence of that consensus by examining in some detail the self-reflexive narratives of crisis

---

8. During fieldwork, many of my interactions and interviews involved sensitive, delicate information about people's hopes and fears, their financial states, their intimate relations, their shameful admissions. In what follows, I have therefore rendered anonymous all my interlocutors as well as the institutions where I carried out fieldwork.

offered up by three very different members of the Buenos Aires middle class: a self-described conservative in his sixties, a professed progressive in her forties, and an avowed realist in his twenties. Tracing the surprising ways those narratives converged with one another, I show how critiques of crisis operated as a ritual of belonging and distinction that returned the middle class to a privileged position within the national imaginary, even at the moment when its very survival seemed most threatened. This engagement with critique as ritual sets the stage for the rest of the book.

Chapter 2 ("A Suspicious History") specifies what I mean, exactly, by "the post-crisis Buenos Aires middle class" as an implicitly racialized national public defined by a particular set of spatiotemporal and sociocultural practices. It also provides a genealogy of the consensus described in chapter 1 by charting two century-long histories: Argentina's successive political-economic regimes and the crises that ended each; and the development of a middle-class public culture characterized by suspicious practices of critique. In tracing those two intertwining histories, I show how, with the 2001–2002 crisis, they came together to produce a middle-class social world defined by the chronotope of routine crisis. The subsequent three chapters focus on the ways that people attempted to find ways of living within that chronotopic structure, even as they frequently declared themselves disillusioned with the prospect of doing so. Along the way, the chapters intervene in debates within anthropology and social theory about money, corruption, and civil society.

The third chapter ("Economies of Loss") focuses on the dramatic currency devaluation that stood at the center of the 2001–2002 crisis. Middle-class Argentines frequently described the devaluation as an awakening, when they realized the thoroughly contingent and socially constructed nature of money. And yet, they simultaneously insisted that this revelation did not help them imagine new monetary or economic possibilities. In this chapter, I explore middle-class critiques of monetary and other forms of value as a key site for understanding how a history of successive financial crises has produced a broadly shared orientation to the social world defined by often paralyzing suspicion.

The fourth chapter ("Exhausted Futures") takes up the increasing frequency with which charges of corruption appeared in the years leading up to and following the 2001–2002 crisis. Drawing on anthropological and historical approaches to witchcraft and witch hunts, I map corruption as the key category of moral critique through which middle-class people articulated and grappled with the delegitimation of state and market institutions. Over the course of the chapter, I engage with workers in good governance organizations, apathetic voters, and political activists as they all labored to understand the implications of a widely shared and despairing intuition of "total corruption," a condition of exhausted social and historical possibilities.

The final chapter ("Solidary Selves") interrogates a radically voluntarist form of social engagement—"solidarity"—that promised to refound national belonging and social welfare in egalitarian gifting practices. The inverse of corruption, solidarity figured in post-crisis Argentina as an explicitly utopian disposition through which people would cultivate a harmonious relationship between self and society, the present and the future. In focusing on the differential demands that disposition placed on middle-class Argentines as opposed to their poorer compatriots, I show how solidarity-building endeavors reproduced new versions of the very inequalities they were meant to overcome.

In the concluding section ("Argentine Afterword"), I revisit what has happened in Argentina in the years between the period of this book (2003–2007) and the contemporary moment. I argue that the dramatic processes of political polarization that have defined those intervening years can only be understood by revisiting the underexamined period of post-crisis Argentina and the widespread sentiment of "the end of the future" that Diego articulated. If, as I have already begun to suggest, that sentiment signals that crisis and critique no longer offer the emancipation they once did, we—as scholars and intellectuals, activists and citizens—need to rethink both the form and telos of our critical analysis. How does our globally shared history of repetitive economic crisis transform the nature of the event and of historical time? How can we theorize that historical rhythm and its affordances? How might an appropriate form of critique avoid the threat of paralyzing suspicion and point toward as-yet unrecognized possibilities for the future? The afterword articulates these questions by positioning the middle-class Argentine experience as an especially productive perspective from which to see how the contemporary configuration of crisis and critique forces us to reconsider all our practices and expectations in uncomfortable ways.

1

SPEAKING OF CRISIS

And this lends suggestive force to the wish for a fresh start . . . for a radical questioning—the wish to scrape off the delusions which a culture that had failed was papering over its guilt and over truth.

But yielding to the urge for an unspoiled basic stratum will make that supposed demolition even more of a conspiracy with the culture one boasts of razing.

Adorno, "Dying Today"

RECOGNIZING CRISIS

Having just arrived in Buenos Aires to conduct fieldwork in July 2003, I made my way from the airport to the city center in one of the small black-and-yellow Renault taxis that sped along the city's streets like yellow jackets. My driver was a middle-aged man wearing recently shined black leather shoes, pressed grey slacks, and a black woolen sweater over a button-down shirt and tie. When I entered the cab, he heard my accent and immediately asked why I was in the country. "I'm an anthropologist," I told him, "studying the Argentine middle class and the economic crisis." He said he could tell me all I needed to know right then and there, no need to look any further, and launched into a lengthy monologue that would "explain it all—the crisis, this country, everything." Over the next forty minutes, he spoke clearly and determinedly into my hastily retrieved voice recorder. "We Argentines want to blame others for what happened to us," he said, "but the real blame belongs 50 percent to Argentina and 50 percent to the United States, the IMF, Europe, all of them." He explained that during the 1990s, "the middle class deteriorated and culture evaporated," leaving behind a "crass, materialist, irrational nation" that pursued self-defeating economic policies such as privatization and an ever-deepening dependence on foreign capital. "This eviscerated nation is what exploded in December 2001." He continued:

> It was a crisis, a real crisis, and nothing will ever be the same. When the people went out into the streets and there was chaos. When the president fled and the police lost control. When you couldn't even withdraw your own money from the banks. That's when we all woke up and saw that nothing was right, that so much was unjust and illegitimate, that there was no future for a country like ours. It was a real, profound crisis, and I think we—we Argentines, we middle-class people—we saw ourselves for the first time. And we thought everything would change, but it never will. Nothing will ever change. We have always been chaotic. We will always be chaotic.[1]

This impromptu interview raised a set of questions that I would routinely ask over the course of my research: In what sense did people grasp the events of 2001–2002 as a "crisis," and why did they so often insist that it revealed an essential truth about Argentina? Why did my cab driver and so many others insist on placing the "middle class" at the center of those

---

1. Spanish-language transcripts of all block quotations appear in the appendix.

events? And, how could it be that the crisis seemed at once to change everything and nothing at all?

Heading into the field, I had anticipated illuminating a host of fine-grained social differences by tracing the ways that variously positioned people discussed the nature of the crisis. Presumably, they would define "crisis" in diverse ways, and the evidence they pointed to would undoubtedly reflect a host of socially significant and unevenly distributed habits, commitments, and aspirations. I anticipated that some might even deny that the developments of 2001–2002 amounted to a crisis at all; they might claim that such a categorization merely served the ends of particular social groups. After all, with half the population in poverty and over a quarter unemployed, it was the poorest who experienced the most severe privations.

Quite to the contrary, I found remarkable agreement concerning the nature, causes, and consequences of the crisis. Most people did not question the claim that the developments of 2001–2002 constituted a dramatic national crisis, one that most profoundly affected the middle class. Events that might in other contexts have seemed hopelessly arcane, specific, or exceptional—monetary and fiscal policies, political in-fighting and machine politics, the living conditions of the unemployed—were only comprehensible, everyone told me, as the particular manifestations of a crisis so general and universal that it threatened the grounds of all social belonging and future imaginings. As one elderly woman put it, "We always think now in terms of a before and an after with the crisis, but we can't imagine what this 'after' looks like."

At the same time, people told me that in many ways nothing had changed. Indeed, walking through the streets of Buenos Aires only a few years later, one could easily be forgiven for believing that the city's recent history had been one of relative calm. Storefronts and restaurants in many parts of town exuded sophisticated well-being and whimsical consumerism. Children went to school in their standard white overcoats, and people hurried to and from work. Banks opened and closed on time, and, aside from the occasional strike-induced jolts, the buses, subways, and trains ran more or less according to schedule. But for a few traces of graffiti, occasional protests, and the nightly appearance of children sifting through garbage for recyclables, the cityscape bore surprisingly few obvious traces of the upheavals it had so recently undergone. Confronted with this sort of observation on my part, people told me over and over that "there's only the appearance of order; in reality life is chaos." "Argentina," they repeated, was always this way: "We're always in crisis, so things can seem calm even when they're not. Things will never change. We're always in crisis because we're incapable of change."

For some time, I ignored the seemingly infinite variations of what I came to think of as "the crisis ruined everything but/and everything has always been in ruins" consensus. Eventually, however, I turned my attention toward tracking its emergence and asking what it might say about a society shaped by a century of political-economic crises. By consensus, I mean not the kind of agreement reached through rational deliberation or conscious judgment but rather a common feeling, that is, a shared sense of things that typically dwells on the level of intuition rather than argumentation. The idea of consensus stands in implicit contrast to that of dissensus, the concept Rancière (2009) develops to describe an unexpected break that shatters our assumptions about the world and enables political transformation. The pervasive sentiment about crisis that I found in Buenos Aires was something else entirely, in which chaos was surprisingly legible and the unexpected seemed oddly familiar, even uncanny. Thus, rather than assume clear distinctions between a naturalized order of things and a radical break that would usher in something new, I interrogate the relationships between these categories of experience and the ongoing semiotic processes that produce them. And so, my focus is on the way that learned practices, both linguistic and nonlinguistic in nature—of recognition and distinction, of recalling and representing events, of temporal reckoning, of mapping the social world and signaling one's place in it—construct socially shared sensibilities about what one can expect of the world, what is imaginable, and how to allow those sensibilities to shape the way one lives. The idea of consensus, then, does not denote a static set of cognitive beliefs but a dynamic set of felt intuitions that are continually emergent and open to the play of interaction, including conflictual interaction.

The consensus about the Argentine crisis that I have described emerged through a commonplace set of discursive practices that were remarkable for their relentlessly suspicious, critical perspective on the rapid, unpredictable, and disorienting developments that had characterized the years 2001–2002. A mode of engagement as much practical and logistical as intellectual and theoretical, these critical practices allowed people to comprehend those developments not simply as disorder, but as meaningful disorder: a coming undone of things both national and intimate that held a lesson for all concerned, but especially for the middle class. In this way, the supposedly chaotic was captioned as a *national crisis* at the same time that the middle class was cast as a *national subject*, defined by a stance of epistemological clarity born of material loss. It was this process that allowed for the mutual constitution of an event—the crisis of 2001–2002—and a public—the Argentine middle class. Together, that event and that public ushered in a post-crisis social world with newly drawn horizons, contours, and possibilities, all pieced together out of the interpretive, instrumental, and existential materials that lay ready-to-hand.[2]

ALIGNING HISTORY AND AUTOBIOGRAPHY

I did not initially set out to gather a set of life histories when I began fieldwork. However, I quickly found that my informants repeatedly and insistently offered me variants of that genre. In interviews and casual conversations alike, as people presented their theories about the crisis in the form of partly or overtly autobiographical narratives, I began to realize how important it was to attend to the form those narratives took. Focusing on their formal features allowed me to understand how the narratives rendered particular happenings comprehensible as "the crisis" and, in so doing, identified the individual speaker, the middle class, and the nation as isomorphic subjects, nearly perfectly aligned in their experiences, perceptions, and judgments.

First, however, for those interested, a brief recounting of the developments that came to be known, almost immediately, as "the crisis of 2001–2002."

—

The roots of the 2001–2002 Argentine financial crisis lay in a series of reforms some ten years earlier aimed at restructuring the national economy in order to address a cluster of problems, including soaring poverty rates, crippling hyperinflation, unserviceable levels of public debt, and rapidly declining salaries. By 1989 those problems had become so dire that they had prompted a wave of protests, lootings, and, eventually, the resignation of then president Raúl Alfonsín, who handed the presidential sash and scepter over to Carlos Menem some six months early. These structural reforms, designed by President Menem's economy minister, Domingo Cavallo, included pegging the Argentine peso to the US dollar, privatizing state-owned companies, disempowering unions, deregulating foreign investment, and dismantling state social welfare programs. With the exception of the currency peg, these reforms hewed closely to the so-called Washington Consensus, a set of policy guidelines typically advocated by

---

2. My approach thus brings together an emphasis on the ongoing semiotic constitution of events (as theorized by authors such as Sahlins 1995; Sewell 2005; Tambar 2017; and Wagner-Pacifici 2017), publics (as theorized by authors such as Gal and Woolard 1995; Habermas 1991; Hankins 2014; Warner 2002; and Yeh 2017), and chronotopes (as theorized by authors such as Agha 2007; Bakhtin 1982; Silverstein 2005; and Wirtz 2016).

the IMF, the World Bank, the United States Treasury, and the European Central Bank.[3]

Controversial from the beginning, these reforms brought Argentina into what Menem's foreign affairs minister, Guido di Tella, famously described as "carnal relations" with the United States.[4] Foreign capital flowed into the country, the state resumed payments on the foreign debt, and consumers enjoyed unprecedented purchasing power. By the mid-1990s, however, a deepening recession was leaving increasing numbers of people unemployed and living beneath the poverty line, and it was becoming clear that the economic boom was both superficial and unsustainable. By 1996, groups known as *piqueteros*—former employees of newly privatized state companies—had emerged in the interior provinces, where they protested their poverty, unemployment, and political marginalization by blockading major highways. At the same time, corruption scandals appeared with increasing frequency in the press, casting doubt not only on the rectitude of Menem and his administration but also on the legitimacy of his political-economic model (see Munck 1997).

In 1999, Fernando de la Rúa handily won the presidency on the basis of a campaign opposing the increasingly unpopular and discredited Menem. However, de la Rúa proved unable to fulfill his promises to end political corruption and rebuild the country's economy. Barely a year later, his own vice president resigned amidst a bribery scandal. Meanwhile, the economic recession steadily worsened. By 2001, unemployment rates of 18 percent and poverty rates of 25 percent had become the undeniable proof that what Menem had called his "economic miracle" had been an illusion.[5] Foreign investors increasingly withdrew capital from the country in a self-reinforcing process of disinvestment that generated a continual increase in the nation's "country risk" (a number calculated by international credit agencies such as Standard & Poor's and Moody's to indicate a country's overall political-economic stability). Faced with spiraling economic decline, de la Rúa replaced his economy minister with Cavallo, the very same minister who had designed Menem's policies ten years earlier. Although Cavallo promised to solve what he euphemistically described as the "economic

---

3. On IMF and World Bank conditionality in general, see Anders 2008. On the contentious role of institutions of global economic governance in the 2001–2002 Argentine crisis, see Blustein 2005; Teunissen and Ackerman 2003; Kedar 2013. On privatization in Latin America more generally, see Aguiar de Medeios 2009. I address the currency peg in greater detail in chapter 3.

4. "Di Tella: pasó la etapa de las 'relaciones carnales,' *La Nación*, May 24, 1997, https://www .lanacion.com.ar/politica/di-tella-paso-la-etapa-de-las-relaciones-carnales-nid69539.

5. Menem himself frequently referred to the economic boom of the early 1990s as his "economic miracle," a term subsequently taken up widely both within Argentina and internationally. For socioeconomic statistics concerning this period, see Beccaria 2002 and Seoane 2003.

situation,"[6] his efforts were for naught. Capital flight left the provincial and federal governments without the currency to pay civil servants, much less service the foreign debt. De la Rúa and Cavallo nonetheless reaffirmed their commitment to the currency peg and issued emergency bonds (a kind of temporary, complementary currency in the form of an IOU) as a stop-gap medium of exchange.

Currency became even more scarce when the IMF withheld a scheduled loan of US$1.3 billion in early December 2001.[7] The national economy seized. De la Rúa limited bank withdraws to $250 per week in an effort to protect the solvency of the banks until the foreign debt could be restructured and confidence restored to the nation's financial system. Cavallo argued that the decree, popularly named the *corralito* ("the little corral") was "a defensive policy against the speculative attacks [carried out by] those hoping for a devaluation" and insisted that the measure would "preserve Argentines' savings and maintain the convertibility" between pesos and dollars.[8]

The *corralito* immediately backfired. Far from restoring confidence in the security of the currency, it prompted a nationwide run on the banks, as small-scale savings account holders and large-scale investors alike anticipated a complete collapse of the financial system and attempted to salvage what they could. In an overwhelmingly cash-mediated economy, the sudden lack of currency meant that salaries could not be paid and everyday economic transactions like grocery shopping became nearly impossible.[9] While the measure most directly affected predominately middle-class savings account holders, such as salaried employees and pensioners who received their pay through direct deposit, the sudden lack of liquidity left informal workers—estimated to be over 50 percent of the urban workforce in 2001 (Sabatini and Farnsworth 2006, 51)—with even fewer options. Over the next three weeks, tips for navigating the increasingly complex world of banking regulations and anxious prognostications about the near future

---

6. Quoted in Daniel Juri, "Se fue Murphy y Cavallo manejará la economía," *Clarín*, March 20, 2001.

7. Throughout the book, "$" refers to Argentine pesos and "US$" refers to United States dollars.

8. Silvia Naishtat and Marcelo Bonelli, "El nuevo paquete de Cavallo: Restricciones al retiro de fondos de los bancos por 90 días," *Clarín*, December 2, 2001.

9. Salaried employees routinely received their pay through direct deposit into savings accounts, from which they would then withdraw cash. Although debit cards had become increasingly common in Argentina, the rarity of stores capable of processing debit card payments meant that their use was almost entirely restricted to withdrawals. Some 11 million cards were the medium for US$36 billion of annual transactions in 2001. Only 0.9 percent of that sum went toward debit-card purchases; ATM cash withdrawals accounted for 99.1 percent (Natalia Muscatelli, "El nuevo paquete de Cavallo/Escenario: Lanzan campaña de promoción," *Clarín*, December 2, 2001).

circulated in the forms of rumor, neighborly advice, official declaration, and televised commentary. Occasional protests and acts of vandalism by savings account holders sprung up in the long lines outside banks in major cities. Generating particular outrage was the widely circulating suspicion that word of the banking restrictions had been leaked to wealthy investors so that they could extract their funds before the official announcement, leaving only small, individual investors trapped in the *corralito*. Outside the city centers, poor residents participated in sporadic lootings of supermarkets while *piqueteros* blocked major highways with increasing frequency.

By the morning of December 19, 2001, a sustained wave of lootings and road blockades was underway across the country, including neighborhoods within Buenos Aires and other major cities.[10] Crowds spray-painted epithets like "shitty politicians" on the walls of looted supermarkets, and violent clashes broke out between crowds and the proprietors of small stores. As President de la Rúa dashed to a hastily called cabinet meeting, an angry crowd hurled insults, eggs, and rocks at his car. News of the lootings and protests filled the airways, and those who didn't participate stayed home to watch events on their televisions and to wonder what it meant that police and other security forces had yet to intervene. That night, de la Rúa appeared on television to declare a state of emergency that suspended constitutional rights and gave himself broad discretionary powers to use federal forces to "put limits . . . on those looking to sow discord and violence" (quoted in Natanson 2001).

Once again, the measure immediately backfired. Instead of obeying the curfew in effect because of the state of emergency, hundreds of thousands of residents of Buenos Aires and other cities poured into the streets, banging pots and pans and chanting, "Down with all of them! Don't let a single one remain!" (¡Que se vayan todos! ¡Que no quede ni uno solo!) The protests, dubbed *cacerolazos* ("pot-bangings"), flowed toward major street corners, public buildings, and plazas. The largest *cacerolazo* formed in the Plaza de Mayo, which stands in front of the presidential palace in Buenos Aires and has long been the symbolic center of the nation and the site of regime-changing mass mobilization. In the early morning, after listening for hours to a crowd that had formed outside of his Buenos Aires home, Cavallo resigned. The next morning, police forces attempted to clear the Plaza de Mayo with increasingly aggressive measures, televised images of which prompted another massive outpouring of people into the streets and plazas. Senators and representatives barricaded themselves in Congress, unwilling to face the angry crowd pelleting the building with rocks, lighting bonfires, and preparing Molotov cocktails.

---

10. See Auyero and Moran 2007 for an analysis of these lootings.

Again, around 4 p.m., de la Rúa addressed the nation on television. Refusing to resign, he urged "national unity" and rededicated himself to preserving "institutionality and governability."[11] In response, a nationwide general strike, organized by the major trade unions and in direct contradiction to the state of emergency, went into effect at 6 p.m. The strike quickly solidified the sense of a nation united in the wholesale repudiation of de la Rúa's presidency and, indeed, of the entire political class. Just an hour later, amid continued police violence in the streets, de la Rúa resigned and fled the presidential palace by helicopter. By the end of the evening, at least twenty-six people were dead and scores injured at the hands of security forces in Buenos Aires and across the country.

Over the next two weeks, four more men shuffled in and out of the presidency, none willing to assume responsibility for what was being called the "social explosion" (*el estallido social*). Congress finally selected Menem's former vice president, Eduardo Duhalde, as interim president. Having assumed the presidential sash and scepter, Duhalde addressed the nation as conspiracy theorist in chief, blaming the country's predicament on "an alliance between the political powers and the financial powers." He pledged to lift the *corralito* and preserve the currency peg so as to counteract the "liquidation of the middle class."[12]

It quickly became clear that Duhalde could not make good on his pledge. Congress agreed to pass the "Law of Economic Emergency," which granted him broad discretionary powers to "reorder the financial, banking, and exchange systems," "reactivate the economy . . . and improve the levels of employment and income distribution," and "create conditions for sustainable economic growth that is compatible with the restructuring of the public debt."[13] Within a month, Duhalde had issued three sweeping decrees that put a definitive end to the political-economic model of the 1990s. The first decree defaulted on Argentina's foreign debt; the largest sovereign default in world history, the measure further strained relations with the IMF and international creditors and dramatically limited access to international loans and investment for a decade and a half. The second decree decoupled the Argentine peso from the US dollar, allowing it to float on international currency markets; over the next several months, the peso lost approximately three-quarters of its value. Finally, the third decree instated the *corralón* (the

---

11. "De la Rúa no renunciará para preservar la 'institucionalidad' del país," *La Nación*, December 20, 2001.

12. Quoted in "Duhalde adelantó que la devaluación 'está descontada,'" *La Nación*, January 4, 2002.

13. National Law 25561, 2002, http://infoleg.mecon.gov.ar/infolegInternet/verNorma.do?id=71477.

"big corral"), which converted all US dollar bank deposits into the newly devalued peso. Thus, even in late 2002, when the *corralito* officially ended and people had access to their previously sequestered bank deposits, three-quarters of the value of those deposits had simply disappeared.

Throughout 2002, these upheavals compelled Argentines to treat the logistics of everyday life as an ongoing economic, political, and social experiment. In doing so, they developed a new repertoire of practices that inspired many people both within Argentina and internationally to imagine a future not defined by the constraints of the global neoliberal order. The unemployed reclaimed abandoned businesses as worker-owned cooperatives. In the absence of monetary currency, people developed nationwide barter networks that amounted to an alternative national economy. Neighbors formed associations that provided spaces for debate, mobilization, and material aid that sidestepped the paralyzed political party machines and bankrupt state coffers.[14]

These experiments in the arts of daily life were essential to many people's survival as well as to the widely shared sense that—whatever else was going on—Argentines were living through momentous times. However, by the end of 2002, living conditions had become even worse than they had been during the dramatic days of the *cacerolazos*. Unemployment had reached 25 percent, and, when combined with severe underemployment, came to 50 percent. Poverty had also enveloped over half the nation. Recently well-employed and even college-educated people found themselves scrounging city streets for recyclables and selling off their belongings—worth less each day amid a suddenly flooded informal market of used goods. People watched, mouths agape, as news programs documented children dying from malnutrition on land renowned for its agricultural riches. By 2003, when I began fieldwork in earnest, the situation had improved somewhat for many. However, the developments described above stood out in popular discourse, as people returned again and again and in all manner of contexts to reexamine the significance of this still fresh event, *the crisis of 2001–2002*.

—

Recall now the consensus I described earlier: the paradoxical sense that the crisis was nothing new, even as it was also a shocking rupture that brought this middle-class nation to a definitive end. That consensus did not simply

---

14. I return to the above sets of practices, and the often-unrealized hopes that so many invested in them, in subsequent chapters. An excellent survey of their legacy can be found in Epstein and Pion-Berlin 2006.

inhere in the unfolding developments I have recounted, and it was by no means the only way people could have come to understand them. There was nothing necessarily middle-class about either the institution or the failure of the currency peg as a monetary policy; in fact, unlike other components of Menem's political-economic reforms, it had enjoyed widespread support. Similarly, the social upheaval that led to President de la Rúa's hasty resignation involved people from all sectors of society in a truly broad, if hastily assembled and ultimately temporary, coalition. What is more, the longer-term privations caused by the economic collapse were by no means singularly middle-class; if any group can be said to have suffered the most severe effects, it was certainly Argentina's rural poor, among whom deaths from malnutrition soared.

Nonetheless, within Argentina and abroad, among observers and participants, the developments I have described were immediately glossed as a "crisis" of which "the middle class" was the undisputed protagonist, both hero and victim of a national tragedy. This consensus was particularly pronounced in forums associated strongly with an educated urban public, such as newspaper editorials, for example, and conversations in cafés. But it was also ubiquitous in other media, including television and radio newscasts. Perhaps more surprisingly, it figured prominently in the appraisals of people who described themselves as resolutely *not* middle-class: as one resident of a shantytown outside of Buenos Aires told me in 2003, "We were never middle-class, my family. We've always been poor. With the crisis, the middle class suddenly lost its fantasy of living in a country apart from us. Suddenly, they realized that maybe they're poor too."

In what follows, I describe the accounts of three people, all of whom used the context of an open-ended anthropological interview to offer me detailed narratives that wove together personal and national histories that revolved around the character of the Argentine middle class. There was nothing especially unusual about their accounts, except the fact that they offered such different sociological profiles. One was a small businessman in his midsixties, a child of immigrants, and an avowed political conservative. Another was a woman in her midforties, a devotee of social theory, the proud daughter of politically progressive teachers, and an activist in local queer politics. The third was a young man just starting his career as a graphic designer and determined to avoid what he considered the ideological battles of previous generations. All three situated their personal tales at the very heart of the national event, as if they were not merely the incidental victims of bad economic policies or unjust global markets but the tragic protagonists of a morally charged historical drama. However—and this is what is most remarkable about them—far from generating a diversity of opinion, this process of personalization resulted in a consistent and robust consensus.

The Traditionalist

Manuel was sixty-five years old in 2001. That September he had retired and passed along his hardware store to his eldest son with the hope it would "support his descendants for years to come." The son of Italian and Spanish immigrants, Manuel had been the first in his family to go to college, studying economics at the University of Buenos Aires but never completing his degree. He had always lived in the neighborhood near his store, an area he described as "middle-class and lower-middle-class, peaceful, quiet, and beautiful," living a life that was far more geographically circumscribed than that of his two younger children, a daughter who practiced law in the United States and a son who was a medical doctor living in a more fashionable section of Buenos Aires. Describing himself repeatedly as "a traditionalist" and "very middle-class," he told me that he "had always believed in education and hard work and the Catholic faith."

From the vantage point of 2006, Manuel looked back at 2001–2002 as "the greatest trauma of [his] life" because of "the complete lack of order. It was total chaos. You couldn't buy anything. There was no money. There was incredible anger. It seemed like the end of the world." Manuel and his wife lost most of his family's life savings, about US$40,000 in saved cash and an equivalent amount in government bonds, and his son was forced to close the hardware shop in July 2002. To get by, they found themselves compelled to sell or barter away their belongings and to sell homemade snacks on the streets until, a year and a half later, he and his wife found regular but informal work as a handyman and a cleaning woman, respectively. Alternately animated and reserved, engaged and withdrawn, angry and ashamed, Manuel conveyed his experiences with a series of partial narratives that revolved around the theme of moral rectitude and the problem of appearances. The crisis, he told me, stemmed from a "contradiction between what we seem to be, what we want to be, and what we really are." He described that contradiction as a "mental illness," which he suffered from as much as did his countrymen, and which had made possible the collusion of "corrupt politicians and the big economic interests, who together stole our money, middle-class money." That "great conspiracy," Manuel insisted, had succeeded because the middle class had temporarily and mistakenly thought that Argentina could be something other than "a blind, complicit, abnormal country" in which "the next crisis is always there, waiting."

"There's nothing to be done," he snorted. "This trauma has no end."

The Progressive

Ana was forty-one in 2001. When we met in late 2004, she was eager to show me that her family history "offers the true story of the Argentine middle class." She began speaking quietly but intensely as soon as we sat down in the back of a café in a bustling strip of downtown Buenos Aires. The granddaughter of "poor, uneducated, but hardworking Italian immigrants," Ana grew up the bookish child of two "very middle-class, very progressive" high school teachers in a quiet residential neighborhood of a Buenos Aires suburb. In August of 2001, she lost her job as a secretary at a real-estate brokerage. Unable to find another position, she relied on the income of her partner, Cecilia, a successful lawyer in a private firm until, with the *corralito*, "everything stopped." Unlike Manuel, Ana had no savings to lose in the banking freeze. Nonetheless, the crisis marked a personal turning point. "The stress and the trauma of the crisis" eventually proved too much for her relationship with Cecilia, and they separated in late 2002. Even so, Ana insisted that the crisis had one identifiable benefit: "It woke us up to what had been going on in this country during the 1990s and it woke me up to what my relationship had really been." Like so many others, she repeatedly and meaningfully drew this sort of parallel between the national and the personal, insisting that with the crisis, "we all realized that we had fooled ourselves and allowed corruption to destroy our country. And I realized I had been with Cecilia only for stability, for material reasons—that I had been corrupt even in the most intimate things."

Like Manuel, Ana made frequent recourse to motifs of suspicion and hidden forces in an effort to discern the causes, consequences, and significance of the crisis. However, for Ana, these motifs appeared in a markedly intellectual style, peppered with specific references to theorists like Marx, Negri, Freud, and Lacan. Nonetheless, her citational style was breezy, and she did no more than Manuel had done to explicate terms like "trauma." Her mobilization of these intellectual terms articulated a perspective that ultimately shared a great deal with that of Manuel, for both were grounded in an agentive, characterological approach in which individual personality and biography explained more than macrostructures or wider economic systems. Full of self-reproach, she held that the crisis had been the self-inflicted wound of "a selfish, deluded people" who had succumbed to "a materialist, conservative point of view that had left the country without protection from its own greed." In these ways, although Manuel and Ana positioned themselves on opposite poles of the Argentine political spectrum, they relied equally on an assumed contradiction between selfish materialism and ethical values, a contradiction that the crisis forcibly resolved by revealing to Argentines their true, venal character.

The Realist

My third narrative comes from Eduardo, who was only twenty-four in 2001. At the time, he was working intermittently as a freelance graphic designer and living at home with his parents, a businessman and housewife who owned an elegant apartment in a neighborhood just inside the border between the city of Buenos Aires and its suburbs. Before 2001, Eduardo told me, his "family, like everyone else, was always a typical middle-class family that worked hard and believed in education and constructing a future for the children, for the next generation." This middle-class investment in education, hard work, and future generations implied "traditional" values for Manuel and "progressive" values for Ana. For Eduardo, by contrast, the middle class stood resolutely apart from specific ideological commitments and was defined by a supposedly straightforward commitment to material prosperity and "realism." Despite finding full-time work early in 2003, he described the crisis in stark terms: "The idea that my parents, after a lifetime of hard work, couldn't use the money they had saved, it was ridiculous; it was completely traumatic." Using the interview to indulge daydreams of a youthful consumerist utopia in some elsewhere, he asked me repeatedly to describe the lifestyles of his European and North American peers and admonished me to "understand the true character of this nation, which can never be more than a failure."

By 2006, when our interview took place, Eduardo had decided to join the estimated 800,000 Argentines who left the country in the wake of the crisis.[15] He was intent on moving to Barcelona and was working to obtain dual citizenship based on the Spanish heritage of a grandparent and two great-grandparents. Contemplating returning to the country of his ancestors, he told me, "All I want is to escape this place. Things will never get better. This country is a disaster. Even my parents, who had always believed in the dream of the middle class, know this now." Echoing themes familiar from others' narratives, he traced the causes of the crisis to a "plot" between US and Argentine politicians, but insisted that "we allowed ourselves to be fooled" and that "this country can never be without crisis." Only a few months later, I learned through a mutual acquaintance that he had followed through on his plan. He emailed me from Barcelona, where he was sharing a small apartment with five other young men, all of whom were working low-paying jobs in restaurants. He was "exhausted," he told me, "homesick," and working "harder than ever before." Still, he was "happy" and "finally felt at

---

15. Evangelina Himitian, "Los hijos de la crisis: El desafío de retornar a la propia tierra," *La Nación*, September 13, 2015, https://www.lanacion.com.ar/sociedad/los-hijos-de-la-crisis-el-desafio-de-retornar-a-la-propia-tierra-nid1827514.

home, despite all the difficulties," because "Argentina is a country in exile, a place where you cannot be what you truly are. Leaving was the only solution."

RITUALS OF CRITIQUE

It would be imprecise to assert that Manuel, Ana, and Eduardo offer more or less identical perspectives on the crisis. Their narratives are respectively of a piece with entrenched positions in the realm of Argentine politics, and all three insist on the irreconcilable nature of those positions.[16] Their protestations notwithstanding, the similarities in their accounts are stunning. They exist at both the most general level of structure and at the most specific level of phraseology. They are as evident in the theses being propounded as in the evidence marshaled and the metaphors employed. For all the ways the three speakers diverge—generation, gender, political commitments, cultural capital, and economic position—their stories converge in key ways.

Viewed from this perspective, the differences among Manuel's, Ana's, and Eduardo's narratives are akin to harmonic variations within an overarching thematic structure. That is not to say that these convergences and resonances are evidence of an ordered, generative schema undergirding a contingent series of articulations, as Lévi-Strauss (1968) might insist. Neither are the differences evidence of their status as ideal-typical instantiations of sociological categories, as Weber (1949) might propose. Rather, the thematic convergences and the self-conscious claims to middle-class typicality served as key operations in a ritualized practice of critique that redefined middle-class belonging as a category of interpretive authority grounded in material loss.

Consider the following excerpts from Manuel's, Ana's, and Eduardo's narratives; key shared themes (marked by subscript numbers) are woven through each:[17]

Manuel

The 1990s were a time of well-being. Of productivity.$_6$ Of confidence and hope. We were finally part of the first world.$_5$ Well, almost. . . . We, the middle

---

16. In other words, the speakers used these narratives to articulate and enact three instantly recognizable voices (Bakhtin 1986) that occupy privileged positions within the Argentine middle-class public and that emerged out of a series of contrastive indirect quotations (Vološinov 1986) of other stereotyped voices, such as those of "the poor," "the politician," "the first worlder," etc.

17. These excerpts have been lightly edited for readability. Spanish-language transcripts appear in the appendix.

class, were working hard for the future. And for our hard work we travelled and lived well. . . . Of course, there was a lot of corruption on the part of the politicians. And all that became apparent in 2001, when the banking freeze went into effect. That was the greatest corruption. They wanted to destroy the middle class, to steal everything from us for the politicians and the big businesses here and abroad.[2] . . . We had no choice but to demand our rights. The middle-class protests didn't occur because they [the politicians] "touched our pocketbooks"' as everyone says, but to demand our rights, to demand the principle of law. To make us a country of laws. The middle class, we wanted to defend the country against such impunity. But it didn't matter. It was the middle class that the crisis really hit hard.[3] We suffered terribly. It was an unbelievable trauma.[7] But there will never be justice. The country is ruined and there is no remedy.[4] We are a terribly selfish people. We have a deep contradiction between our egoism and our values, and that's why we can't overcome this. Now we know. Such a thing couldn't happen in "a serious country." It couldn't happen in the US, could it? It's very Argentine, this inability to see things as they are.[1]

Ana

During the 1990s everyone went to Miami, bought fancy electronics and clothes, pretended like we were in the first world.[5] But it was a dream, an illusion.[1] And it was because millions of Argentines were being marginalized and impoverished. . . . And we were complicit in that. The politicians controlled the whole thing. But we, the middle class, were all complicit[2] in allowing it to happen, because we wanted to go to Miami, to malls, to eat out and pretend that we were in another world. . . . We thought we were building something, growing, but the country was losing everything.[6] It was only the banking freeze that woke people up and made them see what had happened during the 1990s. People went out to the streets because they had "touched their pocketbooks." . . . The poor have always been poor, but this was a real trauma for us.[3] But we also went to the streets because we, the middle class, realized we had allowed something horrible to happen. Because we wanted to end a culture of impunity and corruption, to create "a serious country," to build solidarity instead of selfishness. But that was a dream too; we're too selfish to construct a real future.[4] One must go on to build what one can, but this country is founded on lies, corruption, and greed. And that's almost impossible to change, because at base we don't want to. We've been taught for too long to care only for ourselves. It's an induced pathology, like an abused child that, when grown up, abuses himself and doesn't think of others.[7]

Eduardo

I grew up during the 1990s, during the 1:1, and it never occurred to me that it would change. It was the law. . . . We didn't make as much as people in the first world, but . . . we thought we were sharing the same world.[5] That Argentina was finally going to be what we learned in school it was supposed to be: a middle-class country. Well-being and productivity and peace and, slowly, bit by bit, progress that would leave behind the ugliness of the dictatorship and the shitty cars and the slums.[6] . . . We were all wrong. The politicians knew it. The businessmen and people with a lot of resources knew it. The US and the EU knew it. But we, normal people, middle-class people, were dreaming. We dreamed our deepest dream, the unconscious attachment to the first world.[1] A dream that was induced by anesthesia, by the ruling class that kept us asleep throughout the 1990s, while things were slowly falling apart.[2] . . . The crisis, the freezing of the bank accounts, was like the sudden disappearance of the anesthesia. All of a sudden, we all woke up and saw that we had been robbed.[3] But it was too late. . . . Some say we've learned from all this, that we don't dream anymore about the first world, but I don't know. I think we still have a deep unconscious commitment to the fantasy of belonging to the first world.[7] This has always been true of Argentina, of the middle class here. It's what has impelled middle-class well-being but it's also what caused us to lose everything. I don't think we can let it go. . . . That's why I'm going to Europe. Maybe there I'll dream something else.[4]

Even a cursory perusal of the above excerpts reveals a host of thematic commonalities, which all hang together in a general argument about the nature, causes, and ultimate import of the events of 2001–2002. The speakers all employed freely the metaphors of dreams, fantasies, and illusions as they attempted to convey the sense of awakening and a coming-to-recognition that accompanied the crisis (marked in each of the excerpts with subscript #1). They all insisted that those dreams were engineered by powerful actors who cleverly exploited the self-serving desires of an immature middle class (subscript #2), which they portrayed as the central but complicit victim of the crisis (subscript #3). Despite recognizing the problem, however, they identified no foreseeable path forward; indeed, the only speaker to articulate anything resembling a solution was Eduardo, whose return to the country of his ancestors further underscored the impossibility of building a future in Argentina (subscript #4). Forever both promised and denied inclusion in the first world, Argentina appears in these accounts as an abandoned territory, perpetually left behind and denied a future (subscript #5). Thus, while the 1990s may have seemed to embody possibility, progress, and productivity, the era appears retrospectively to have been simply the latest and most devastating example of those illusory promises (subscript #6). Finally, for all the material damage that the crisis caused, the psychological injuries are the most keenly felt, particularly given that, in these accounts, the individual speakers—as self-proclaimed exemplars of the Argentine middle class—are doomed to repeat the process of self-deception and disillusion (subscript #7).[18]

As an overarching theory of the crisis, this consensus reappeared again and again over the course of my fieldwork. Relatively coherent, it was nonetheless flexible enough to accommodate speakers from a range of socioeconomic positions and political ideologies. Across contexts, the same motifs continually reappeared as people—both public figures and ordinary citizens—drew heavily on the genres of psychoanalytic and conspiracy theories. Presidents de la Rúa and Duhalde, for example, were disposed to proclaiming themselves the targets of elaborate conspiracies on the part of domestic and foreign financiers and "political powers" who hoped to devalue the currency, "sow discord and violence," and "liquidate the middle class."[19] Other politicians bemoaned "the falsehoods and fictions" bequeathed by the dictatorship of the 1970s; left unconfronted, unnarrated, and hence unresolved, they argued, the legacy of violence had prompted the nation "to flee forward, inventing chimeras that masked what we are, what we want to be" (Carrió 2002). Public intellectuals disparaged "a culture of self-flagellation" and "self-degradation" while simultaneously criticizing the "voyeuristic" relationship of the middle class to the poor and "Argentines' immature relationship to politics" (Seoane 2005, 21, 27, 148, 149). Meanwhile, journalists searched for "the murderers of the middle class" while censuring the "collaboration of the media in the construction of a distorted image of violence," a fantasy with "concrete psychological consequences" and reactionary political ramifications (Barros 2005, 70, 81). My fieldnotes are similarly full of words like *dream*, *destiny*, and *nostalgia*;

---

18. These themes reappear in subsequent chapters, for they were prominent not only in my own interviews and conversations but also in public media ranging from newspaper editorials to nongovernmental organization mission statements. Chapter 3, for example, considers the language of dreams and awakenings as part of an analysis of people's relationships with their lost money. The tropes of blame and victimhood, especially as parsed through the category of social class, are central issues in chapter 4, where I discuss the practices and discourses of corruption. The wholesale condemnation of the neoliberalism of the 1990s and the attempt to engineer social bonds that would undo the damage of that decade are the subjects of chapter 5.

19. "Duhalde adelantó que la devaluación 'está descontada,'" *La Nación*, January 4, 2002; Silvia Naishtat and Marcelo Bonelli, "El nuevo paquete de Cavallo: Restricciones al retiro de fondos de los bancos por 90 días," *Clarín*, December 2, 2001; José Natanson, "De la Rúa entre el desconcierto y la negación del estallido social," *Página 12*, December 20, 2001.

trauma, pathology, and *paranoia*; *Manichaeism, schizophrenia*, and *manic depression*. Out of the mouths of friends, acquaintances, and even accidental companions in cafés and subway cars, they appeared alongside other terms like *plot, conspiracy*, and *cabal*; *secret, shadow*, and *invisible*; *powers, forces*, and *criminals*.

To be sure, given the history of psychoanalytic and conspiracy theories as popular modes of critique in Argentina, it is not altogether unexpected to encounter a certain amount of terminological and thematic convergence. As I argue in the following chapter, their opposed but complementary perspectives—with psychoanalytic theories offering a resolutely cosmopolitan self-critique and conspiracy theories articulating a decidedly populist condemnation of nefarious outsiders—were ideally suited to the interpretation and critique of the financial crisis, in which the behavior of arcane actors wielding esoteric technologies disrupted everyday social life in such profound ways. In the context of post-crisis Argentina, the formal features of psychoanalysis and conspiracy (their phrases, themes, and interpretive frameworks) melded into one another and flowed fluidly with other ways of speaking. Here, psychoanalytic and conspiracy theories did not stand as discrete interpretive practices set apart from everyday talk. Rather, both genres circulated freely, as relatively unremarkable, ready-to-hand tools that quickly and casually indexed an idealized (but rarely actualized) practice of fastidious critique.

Nevertheless, in beginning my research, I had no reason to expect that people from vastly divergent backgrounds and political intuitions would deploy these interpretive tools in such similar ways, much less to arrive at such similar conclusions. Following Latour's (1988, 23) methodological injunction to follow "controversies," I had planned to structure my fieldwork around the circulation of competing theories of the crisis. By uncovering points of contention, I had imagined tracking the relationship between processes of knowledge production on the one hand and the consolidation of social categories on the other. Frustrated with the overwhelming unanimity that I in fact encountered, I found myself probing my interlocutors, contradicting their assertions and asking them to defend their claims. Eventually emboldened, I even attempted to provoke controversies. Yet friends, acquaintances, and informants alike stubbornly rebuffed my challenges as abundant proof of my inability, as a foreigner, to grasp the truth about Argentina: "To me, Argentines don't live a life of greater fantasy or illusion than anyone else," I told Ana in exasperation. "It's impossible for you to believe," she responded, "because you're not from here."

So what sort of a consensus was this? What kinds of knowledge were people offering me when they attempted to describe the experience of living in a nation doomed to crisis? How could the same themes and metaphors, the same causal mechanisms and cast of characters appear time and again in the narratives of such a wide variety of people, changing so little over time and across social categories? What happens when the erstwhile dramatic unveiling of the reality lying behind appearances becomes an everyday and unremarkable practice? In sum, what sort of critique purports to unveil the shocking reality behind the world of appearances but operates so much like a regime of common sense?

As a repetitive, stereotyped, and formally reticulated social practice, what I came to think of as "crisis talk" operated as a ritual of belonging and critique, or rather, belonging *through* critique. Here, linguistic anthropological approaches are particularly helpful, for they frame rituals as privileged sites in which claims about the world are authorized and naturalized through the poetics of the performance (Silverstein 1998, 2003). Those claims then circulate as prototypes for interaction in other, less ritualized contexts. In this way, rituals serve as the "poetically dense" (Stasch 2011, 160) organizing centers of entire social worlds because they enact and model what Bakhtin (1982) calls "chronotopes," recognizable orders of space and time, of stylized modes of interaction, and of cultural categories of identification, value, and personhood.[20] In the succinct formulation of Wirtz (2016, 344), a chronotope "is not simply a synonym for framework, orientation, or ideology [but is] far more fundamental, productive of subjectivity itself in grounding our experience of temporal and social relationships, which themselves structure our experience of being and sociality." In this sense, the notion of chronotope allows us to see how it is that we come to feel ourselves denizens of a particular social world, populated by a set of recognizable social types and regimes of values and demarcated by a specific horizon of possibilities.

We should dwell for a moment on the particular, even peculiar, chronotope called forth and exemplified by the repetitive, nearly incantatory ritual of crisis talk. Of course, one could understand the financial crisis as an objective, impersonal event; after all, the discipline of economics tends to presume a realm of systemic laws that guide and periodically correct markets through mechanisms such as crises. Clearly, nothing could be further from my informants' portrayals, which positioned crisis firmly in the realms of motive and morality. Crisis talk established, over and over again, a world of mysterious actors and hidden meanings. Here, the crisis was inherently a matter of ethics, subjectivity, and historical destiny. Even more fundamentally, it was a matter of epistemology: Argentines, we

---

20. For fuller elaborations of the concept of chronotope, see also Agha 2007; Blommaert 2015; Kockelman 2010; Parmentier 2007; Silverstein 2005; and Wirtz 2016, as well as the collections of essays on chronotopes introduced by Lempert and Perrino 2007 and Rutherford 2015.

are told, failed to understand the world—or, crucially, themselves—and allowed misperceptions, delusions, and fantasies to lead them into crisis. In the aftermath, the story goes, the world was suddenly laid bare, visible and knowable for the first time. And yet the critical work that necessarily followed the crisis was revelatory without being efficacious; the crisis would surely return, for it was of a piece with the national character. Here, then, the chronotopic logic of national history operated as a peculiar sort of morality tale, one in which the ethical and the epistemological were welded together in such a way as to produce tragic and mournful heroes who were defined by knowing their unavoidable fate and recounting it time and again.

If this description captures the structure and texture of the world that crisis talk conjures, then these heroes—at once tragic and pathetic, discerning and incapacitated—are key to understanding how the narration operates. In this regard, psychoanalytic and conspiracy theories played a crucial role. They have an elective affinity for one another in that they both purport to unveil the underlying forces shaping a seemingly chaotic world. From opposite and complementary perspectives, they render commensurate the structural and the agentive, the systemic and the personal. Together they posit a knowing, reflexive subject who continually examines the interior self and the world at large with an eye toward producing ethically significant knowledge. So, for instance, when Ana likened the events of December 2001 to an awakening—"we all realized that we had fooled ourselves and allowed corruption to destroy our country"—she immediately reflected on how that coming-to-consciousness played out in her personal life as well—"I realized that I had been with Cecilia only for stability, for material reasons, that I had been corrupt even in the most intimate things." In this small but crucial moment of Ana's narrative, the interpretive genres of psychoanalytic and conspiracy theories operated side by side, with very little to mark them off as different: She asserted almost simultaneously that they (she and the nation at large) were duped by foreign interests and that they were ultimately responsible for allowing it to happen. Perhaps even more remarkably, at this crucial point in the plot, both genres worked together to elide the differences between the "we" of the first assertion and the "I" of the second. It is as if the failings of the collective were borne totally and absolutely by each individual contained within it. The motifs of awakening, unveiling, and understanding were particularly key here, for they wedded the genres of psychoanalysis and conspiracy to the rhetoric of personal experience and epiphany.

Simultaneously the hero and the narrator, the "I" that Manuel, Ana, and Eduardo employed was never unitary; it was alternately narrated and narrating, evidentiary and interpretive, national and personal. This "I" served as the point of inflection for these varied dimensions of the narrative, transitioning it, for example, between the historical and the autobiographical.[21] Thus, for example, Manuel spoke on behalf of Argentina when he lamented the inescapable fact of being "a terribly selfish people." In the same way, all three speakers employed an "I" that was not merely the everyday, self-referential pronoun, but also a "theatrical" (Urban 1989) self-construction in which they fashioned themselves as nearly perfectly representative of broader cultural patterns. The speakers thus all established themselves as prototypical members of the nation, a relationship that allowed the speaker to stand as both evidence and interpreter of the crisis. However, the arrogation of interpretive authority by which Manuel, Ana, and Eduardo claimed the right to explain the crisis took place by virtue of a third category, that of the middle class, which mediated the relationship between the speaker and the nation.

All three emphasized that their interpretations—of the crisis, of contemporary Argentina, of politics and morality, of nearly any matter, but especially matters concerning the public good—were properly situated as belonging to the middle class. Even more strongly, it was as specifically middle-class interpretations that these accounts stood as more than mere opinion, but rather as authoritative, insightful, and meaningful statements about a society that was once oriented toward "construct[ing] a future," but that was now structured retrospectively, defined by the future it had lost. Toward this end, all three speakers insisted not on their mere membership in the middle class but on their prototypicality: they are "very" or "typically" middle-class. Their family histories, which traced arcs of suddenly interrupted upward social mobility and emphasized tropes of immigration, work, and education, instantiated, they claimed, the "true story" of the middle class and, therefore, of the nation itself. In response to my broad and open-ended questions about where they grew up, they offered detailed descriptions of themselves, their families, and their neighborhoods, insisting on their decidedly middle-class character by making the sorts of nuanced distinctions that belie a carefully calibrated social sensibility. Here again, psychoanalytic and conspiracy theories offered particularly appropriate tools, for together they indexed an idealized, middle-class synthesis of elite sophistication and populist cunning. An extraordinarily broad social category, poorly defined in terms of income, occupation, educational level, or ideological commitment, middle-classness figured in these stories as something one explicitly and anxiously claims—not by virtue of the future

---

21. For related analyses of self-narration, see, e.g., Bauman 1986; Chatman 1978; Crapanzano 1984, 1996; Hill 1995; Oakdale 2002; Ochs and Capps 1996; and Wortham 2000.

it aspires to, as is typically the case in other contexts (Heiman, Freeman, and Liechty 2012; see also Heiman 2015), but by virtue of the future it has lost.

That anxiety had deep roots. After years of recession and rising unemployment, a new category had become current in the Argentina of the late 1990s: "the new poor," former members of the middle class who found themselves beneath the poverty line but who "maintain[ed] middle-class social and cultural values" (Minujin 1995, 158). With the crisis of 2001–2002, the ranks of the new poor had swollen, and middle-class lifestyles had become ever more unattainable, even for those who retained a nominal income above the poverty line. The Argentine nation-state was, from its very inception, a racial project of "modernization" and "civilization," in which policies concerning immigration, education, and labor revolved around the explicit goal of making the country as culturally European and as racially white as possible (Alberto and Elena 2016). Beginning in the mid-twentieth century, that project became inextricably bound to the proposition that Argentina was an essentially middle-class country, a status that allegedly distinguished it from the rest of Latin America (Adamovsky 2009). Given these dominant national mythologies, the unattainability of a middle-class lifestyle threatened not only people's hopes for themselves and their families but also the very identity of the nation. In such a context, people struggled with what it might mean to be middle-class and, by extension, Argentine. As one young man posed the question to an Argentine journalist writing about this issue, might it be possible to define middle-classness and Argentineness in terms other than income and material welfare? Might it be possible instead—and here, this young man invoked, as people often did, a profoundly racialized global cartography defined by the two imagined poles of African dysfunction and European modernity—to define the category of the middle class in terms of attitude, a "resistance to sinking, something that doesn't exist in African countries" (Barros 2005, 132–33)?[22]

At the level of propositional content, my informants answered those questions by responding that the middle class no longer existed, that Argentina could not be a middle-class country, and that they themselves could no longer be truly middle-class. Thus, Manuel told me, "The crisis was the end of me, of the middle class, and Argentina has always been a middle-class nation." Similarly, Ana proclaimed, "Today the dream of the Argentine middle class doesn't exist anymore . . . and we see that we are more like

---

22. It is worth emphasizing not only the blatant racism of this comment but also its utter divorce from the socioeconomic reality of contemporary Africa, where the middle class in many countries has been growing in recent decades. The inability of so many middle-class Argentines to imagine such a fact underscores the ongoing strength of the racialized and classed commitment to identify Argentina as a "failed developing nation" (Salvatore 2008).

Bolivia than France." Eduardo, meanwhile, insisted he could only truly be middle-class if he left the country, for "Argentina is . . . a place where you cannot be what you truly are."

However, the narrative act itself offered a very different, even paradoxical answer, one that reconfigured the grounding of middle-class belonging, all the while maintaining its presumption of a racialized national and global topography of modernity. At the level of performance, that is, in the real-time process of a speaker addressing an audience, the ritual of crisis talk reestablished the speakers as essentially middle-class subjects not because of their occupations, incomes, or ability to invest in the future—all those markers were framed as things of the past—but precisely because of the clear-eyed judgment they offered on themselves and the nation. Insightful, critical interpretation thus became the grounds of middle-class belonging, and the middle class thus came to figure as a category of epistemological clarity born of material loss.

AN AUTOBIOGRAPHICAL PUBLIC

Decades ago, Bourdieu (1987) cautioned social scientists against what he called "the biographical illusion," in which the generation of a life history presumes continuity between the chronological order of events and the logical order of the narrative. In my interviews, this narrated commensurability was not (merely) an illusion but rather the very point of the practice: not only did speakers render the chronological order of events continuous with the logical unveiling of a richer and truer picture of reality, but both of those orders proceeded apace along at least three scales—those of nation, class, and individual.[23]

My interviews offered particularly serendipitous opportunities for people to theorize about the crisis and to configure middle-class belonging in just this way. After all, I explicitly asked people to "tell me about the crisis" or to describe their "experience of 2001–2002" and thereby invited them to take up the role of knowing subject and self-conscious cultural exemplar. As a white, educated person from the United States (and from the University of Chicago, with its infamous economists, no less!), I could similarly be harnessed to the role of cultural exemplar and made to stand in for the United States, for "serious countries," and even for something as abstract as

---

23. In aligning individual biography with class and national histories, crisis talk thus does the work of scalar alignment. The scalar function of self-narration reappears throughout the chapters of this book. For more on scale as essential to the construction of "distinctions about power, agency, authority, and validity [as they appear in] vertical—hierarchical orders in meaning making" (Blommaert 2015, 110), see Carr and Lempert 2016.

modernity or material prosperity.[24] Insofar as the interviews proceeded with this sort of a dyadic structure, I held the authority to recognize my interlocutor as a middle-class subject capable of offering the sort of legitimate interpretations that could circulate and be comprehensible in the first world.

This sort of structure does much to explain not only why people offered quasi-life histories in response to my rather open-ended questions but also why they agreed so eagerly to my interview requests, many of them going so far as to contact me to request an interview, in a reversal of the usual order of things. Explaining their interest, they would step back from the back-and-forth of the interview and expound on its usefulness. "It's good you're here to study the crisis," one man told me, "because you can go back and make public what the US did." Or, as another exclaimed, "I think it's great that you're studying the crisis, because what happened to us was traumatic . . . and we haven't dealt with it yet." These metalevel commentaries on our interviews reproduced, once again, the sort of cosmological order depicted in the practice of crisis talk—a world in which the first world had purposefully conspired with Argentina's national weaknesses to devastate the country, leaving it behind to stand as an abandoned, paralyzed, and ghostly presence, capable only of narrating its lost possibilities.

My presence allowed people to engage in an especially full instance of crisis talk. However, the same sort of practice occurred regularly in other contexts, as we will see throughout the subsequent chapters of this book. Lengthy expositions of the crisis were common in the pages of newspaper editorials and even lengthier arguments circulated as bestselling books.[25] Take, for example, the titles of contemporary popular works of social critique, which partook so easily of the same interpretive language found in my interviews: *The Terrible Charm of Being Argentine* (Aguinis 2001), *Reality: Waking up from the Argentine Dream* (Grondona 2001), *Argentina: Empire of Deception* (Landaburu 2001), and *Stolen Argentina* (Cafiero and Llorens 2002). Consider as well the many titles that, like my informants' narratives, depended on an ambiguous first-person pronoun that ran together and aligned national, middle-class, and personal perspectives on the crisis: *What Are We?* (Ulanovsky 2004), *We Were: Adventures and Misadventures of the Middle Class* (Barros 2005), and, mostly simply, *We* (Seoane 2005). Even in casual conversations, a sort of telescopic version of crisis talk could successfully caption any number of quotidian events, such as when a dispute over a parking space elicited from an uninvolved passerby a muttered com-

---

24. Through much of Latin America, the University of Chicago is famous for having trained a number of economists who helped implement neoliberal economic policies across the region in the 1970s and 1980s.

25. For a discussion of these best sellers, see Fiorucci 2005.

ment addressed to no one in particular: "This is why we'll never amount to anything in this shitty country; even we supposedly respectable people have been transformed into psychotics."[26]

In each instance—whether the addressee was a foreign anthropologist, a presumably educated reader, or a supposedly well-mannered pedestrian—speakers established relationships of resemblance between the narrated and narrating events.[27] In this way, parallels and identifications emerged across the wildly different categories of nation, class, and individual, with the speaker claiming to instantiate a uniquely authoritative position with respect to all three. As privileged genres of hermeneutic critique, psychoanalytic and conspiracy theories were crucial to this narrative feat, not because speakers engaged in rigorous psychoanalytic or conspiracy theorizing, but because they mobilized formal features of those two genres as evidence of their interpretive authority as middle-class subjects.[28] By the same token, their mode of address—speaking to and on behalf of a presumed middle-class audience—allowed the Argentine middle class to emerge out of the narrative as a public defined by its ability to offer a critical interpretation of its own crisis.

---

26. The speaker used the phrase *gente decente*, a phrase laden with connotations of class-based manners and morality, typically racialized as white.

27. On the relation between narrated and narrating (or narrative) events, see, e.g., Jakobson 1990.

28. In other words, generic features functioned as evidentials of second-order stances of authority, group membership, and status. See Kockelman 2004 for a discussion of the relationship between evidentiality, first- and second-order stances, and subjectivity, and see Goodman, Tomlinson, and Richland 2014 on the role citational practices play in establishing personhood.

2

A SUSPICIOUS HISTORY

The time is out of joint: O cursed sprite,
That ever I was born to set it right!

Shakespeare, *Hamlet*

OUT OF JOINT

"**W**e are defined by crisis, by our inability to construct normality. It is at once the problem of all countries in an imperialist system and yet uniquely Argentine, this inability that we always lament," Mabel said to the elderly man at the table next to me. He nodded and repeated "Yes, just so!" several times as she continued, "With the end of the middle class, there is no longer even the fantasy of constructing the norms that would allow us to cohere as a nation."

Mabel, the always-friendly waitress at my neighborhood café, was disposed to offering me short, pithy, and sometimes poignant remarks on topics ranging from haircuts and dress styles to parenthood, friendship, and national belonging. Taking her cue from whatever news magazine or novel I happened to be reading that day, she would deliver her comments quickly and then hurry off to her other customers, scarcely giving me a moment to respond. After months of half-made plans and last-minute cancelations, I finally managed to conduct a proper interview with Mabel in May 2007. Sitting down to croissants and coffee at the end of her shift, she began with a diagnosis, articulated so concisely and swiftly it suggested that she had formulated it long ago and had simply been waiting for the appropriate moment to share it. "We used to believe Argentina had a future, but it never did. Our culture, our psychology, our economy—it all condemned us to this fate, and we, the disappointed and disillusioned middle class, finally understand that. We see our fate clearly now. And we cannot look away."[1]

In post-crisis middle-class Buenos Aires, people routinely employed this fatalistic frame of ruined hopes as they took the most trivial of disappointments—dinner plans canceled at the last minute, coworkers avoiding their fair share of the work, broken sidewalk tiles tripping a pedestrian—and harnessed them directly to large-scale interpretive narratives about national life. These were not just any interpretive narratives, but ones that employed a particularly suspicious mode of inquiry that proceeded from a set of premises familiar to students and practitioners of critical theory and interpretive social sciences: Beneath the veneer of the everyday lie powerful structuring forces. Seemingly trivial phenomena are symptoms of those forces. With the right interpretive framework, those symptoms can point the way toward understanding the mysteries, and especially the disappointments, of history. However, far from generating

---

1. Mabel used the term *decepcionada*, which connotes both "disillusion" and "disappointment." I return to this term in the final section of the chapter.

insights that could empower a sense of historical agency, here these premises tended toward a near-paralyzing sense of disillusion.

Throughout the following chapters, I explore the practical import of disillusion across a range of contexts in post-crisis Argentina. In what immediately follows, I interrogate the conditions of possibility for the emergence of this "structure of feeling" (Williams 1977). In part, it emerged out of the long-term Argentine history of repeated political-economic crises for which the country has become notorious, in the minds of its own citizens as much as for students of global political economy. However, disillusion was not the automatic byproduct of that history. Rather, it was entirely mediated by the interpretive frameworks through which people actually grasped that history. Particularly important in this respect were everyday suspicious critiques, which commingled freely and animated casual conversation, political invective, and intellectual debate. Far from constituting a realm of abstract, removed commentary, these critiques were an active mode of practice in their own right that infused and shaped people's lives from the inside out, grounding the post-crisis Buenos Aires middle class in the experience of historical tragedy.[2]

THE PROBLEM OF THE MIDDLE CLASS

Social scientists have long argued over the question of how to conceptualize, define, or measure the middle class, in Argentina and just about everywhere else.[3] For some, "middle class" refers to the relatively straightforward demographic question of earned income and amassed wealth. However, the analytic utility of such a narrow definition is hindered by issues of social and cultural capital as well as generational and intergenerational social mobility. Additionally, there is the question of how to deal with the many ways that individuals identify or refuse to identify with the middle class in descriptive or aspirational terms. Finally, an added difficulty is that, in practice, "middle class" operates as a highly charged social, economic, and political term, with a contextually shifting indexical range. A few words are in order, then, regarding what I have been referring to as the "post-crisis Buenos Aires middle class."

I use "post-crisis" to refer to the years 2003–2007, the period immediately

---

2. In Bourdieu's (1989, 21) terms, this work of constitution would be a "theory effect," in which theoretical language regiments, authorizes, and organizes specific fields of social interaction.

3. On the middle class, both in Argentina and in general, see Bourdieu 1984; Minujin and Anguita 2004; O'Dougherty 2002; Schijman and Dorna 2012; Visacovsky and Garguin 2009; and Wortman 1999.

following the dramatic financial crisis narrated by the speakers in chapter 1. Those years align, quite conveniently, with the presidency of Néstor Kirchner, who was elected with only 22 percent of the vote on the vague campaign promise to make Argentina *un país en serio*, a "serious country."[4] In looking at this post-crisis period, I am interested not in the happenings of 2001–2002 in and of themselves. Rather, I foreground the question of how those happenings were retrospectively reconstituted and reinterpreted as an orienting event. Important in this respect is that the years of 2003–2007 were characterized, for most Argentines, by the gradual but steady shift from a focus on day-to-day survival to the question of how to build a medium- and longer-term future for one's self, one's family, one's community, and the country at large. It was equally characterized by the sense that things had not, in fact, changed as much as people had expected during the nadir of the crisis. The economy remained unpredictable and devoid of steady employment for large sectors of the population. Party politics continued to be defined by labyrinthine networks of favors and alliances, apparently cut off from the exigencies of most people's lives. And still-shocking poverty statistics made social inequality the constantly remarked upon evidence of a divided nation.

As for the second part of the phrase, I mean by "Buenos Aires" the capital city of Argentina. Its busy streets contain a mix of architectural styles, from eighteenth-century homes and beaux arts palaces to postmodern apartment complexes and shantytowns (*villas*) of semilegal, autoconstructed homes. Its infrastructure, parks, and shopping corridors are also highly varied, rooted in a range of historical periods and oriented toward people of all incomes and tastes. This is the city where matters of national import often take center stage, for it houses the country's federal government, headquarters its largest financial and economic interests, and produces its farthest reaching mass-mediated cultural products, from television and radio shows to music, art, and literature. However, by "Buenos Aires," I also mean the periurban surroundings of the capital, where one can drive through ring after ring of settlements and see gated communities, small towns, and squatter settlements, all standing cheek to jowl with one another. All together, *Gran Buenos Aires*—the capital and the broader metropolitan region—was home during this period to about one-third of the country's 35 million people, who routinely traversed its jarringly discordant

---

4. To readers familiar with Argentine politics, I would emphasize that the book is therefore concerned with the period *prior* to the full consolidation of "Kirchernism" and the assemblage of left populist policies that came to define Cristina Fernández de Kirchner's two terms as president.

landscapes as they commuted to and from work, ran errands, and visited friends and family.

Because of its unrivaled political, economic, cultural, and demographic clout within the nation, Buenos Aires can seem as if it amounts to Argentina as a whole. Indeed, within national and international fields of journalism, scholarship, and the arts, not to mention politics and economics, it is frequently treated as a microcosm of the nation. In the aftermath of 2001–2002, that paradigmatic figuration came under some scrutiny and strain, as many turned their attention to the extreme material privations of farther-flung regions of the country. Nonetheless, the decentering of *Gran Buenos Aires* proved transitory and the region was quickly recentered as the privileged site for understanding the significance of the crisis and, more broadly, of national history. That Buenos Aires came to seem, once again, the paradigm of Argentina is one of the many continuities that stretch across the pre- and post-crisis periods and that call into question the utility of considering the crisis as a moment of rupture.

Finally, a few words about the third, and most contentious, part of my formulation: "middle class." I use the term advisedly. I do not use it as an analytic category to describe a determinate demographic group, defined by income, education, job status, aspiration, cultural and social capital, or any other variable. Rather, I treat "middle class" as a folk category in Argentina, and a particularly important one at that.[5] It is a thoroughly racialized category that usually connotes whiteness and an aspirational identification with Europe.[6] However, what it means and who it refers to both vary enormously depending on context. Some uses of the term foreground cultural capital, others economic or social. Some uses emphasize a rather staid, conservative ideological disposition, and others a cosmopolitan progressivism. It typically, but not always, stands in contrast to the competing figure of "the people" (*el pueblo*), as a referentially vague but emblematic figuring of the nation.[7] Here, it is worth emphasizing that particular individuals may understand themselves to be addressed by both terms at different moments and in different registers. For this reason, it is helpful to consider the middle class—like the people—not as a determinate set of individuals whose

---

5. Within anthropology, the terms "folk" or "emic" are distinguished from "analytic" or "etic" when discussing concepts, categories, and classifications.

6. On the co-constitution of categories of racial, class, and national belonging in Argentina, see Delaney 2002; Gordillo and Hirsch 2003; Guano 2003; Ramella 2004; Salvatore 2008; and Sutton 2008.

7. Argentine politics have hinged, since the mid-twentieth century, on the usually agonistic relationship between these two national emblems (Adamovsky 2009).

membership in that set is established by one or some combination of variables but rather as a continually shifting community of interpretation and interpellation: as a public.[8] "The middle class," then, is the locally reified and nominalized image of a public that only exists in perpetual emergence, through people's attention to circulating signs, both written and oral texts, as well as nonlinguistic signs, bodily gestures, and other social practices.[9] In so far as people attend to this constantly shifting circulatory regime, they participate in that public. And in so far as they are hailed (Althusser 2001) by the nominalized reification, they identify as members of "the middle class."

The dispositional capacities and material resources required to attend to that circulatory regime and/or to be hailed by that term were, of course, unevenly distributed and varied dramatically by context within post-crisis Buenos Aires. Nonetheless, even during the period this book covers, after decades of eroding incomes and standards of living, those capacities and resources were broadly distributed (see also Minujin and Kessler 1995). As a result, "the middle class" could include people like Jorge, the owner of a used record shop in the capital who struggled to make ends meet but got by because he lived in a house that his factory-worker father had bought in the late 1960s, when work was plentiful and wages good. It also included Paulo and Julia, the chronically unemployed parents of two children. Themselves the children of factory workers, they had attended a few years of college, and called themselves in 2004 "middle-class in orientation" despite living in a house without running water on a mud road in one of the capital's periurban rings. It included Elisa and Marcos, a husband and wife who worked in midlevel office jobs and were saving up to renovate their cramped three-room concrete house in a residential neighborhood in the southern part of the capital. It included the single, thirty-something woman who worked in nongovernmental organizations devoted to social justice issues and who lived in a spacious two-bedroom apartment bought by her parents. It also included the real-estate developer and his homemaker wife who sent their two teenagers to expensive private schools, employed a maid who came daily, and (they told me without chagrin) saved money in Swiss bank accounts hidden from the Argentine government.[10]

---

8. For more on this approach, see Muir and Villavicencio 2015.

9. In conceptualizing the middle class as a public, I am drawing on the work of linguistic anthropologists who have developed the concept of publicity in ways that extend Habermas's (1991) formulation and Warner's (2002) reformulation in order to attend to dynamics of belonging and authority (Gal and Woolard 1995), of populism and crowds (Cody 2015; Tambar 2009), of coercion and inattention (Hankins 2014; n.d.), of secrecy and perfectibility (Debenport 2015), and of corporeal aspects of race and class (Fennell 2015; Yeh 2017).

10. See Abelin 2012 for more on the cultural politics of taxation and tax avoidance during this post-crisis period.

Despite their wildly varying living conditions, income and education levels, terms of employment, political ideologies, and tastes, all these people attended regularly to written and broadcast mass media addressed, implicitly or explicitly, to the middle class. They debated policy proposals, current events, and matters of civic import. They considered the opinions of public intellectuals regarding the national past, present, and future. None of these practices originated with the crisis; each is a long-standing feature of the Argentine middle class, which has been rendered as an "intellectual public" (Warner 2002) since the early twentieth century (Franco 2002; Goldberg 2016; Herzovich 2015). What shifted with 2001–2002 was that those engagements with public life were no longer oriented by the aspiration for a better future typically associated with the "global middle classes" (Heiman, Freeman, and Liechty 2012). Rather, people such as the ones I describe above did so by taking up a disillusioned orientation to the past. They saw in the 2001–2002 crisis the culmination of individual, family, and national histories of repeated economic crisis and loss, the betrayal of promises that were never going to be fulfilled, and proof of the need to inquire relentlessly into uncomfortable truths about self and society. In sum, the problem of the middle class in Argentina is not only one of economic, social, and cultural capital, of identification and aspiration, of futurity and a privileged place within the national imaginary. The problem of the post-crisis Buenos Aires middle class is also one of the practices of talking and listening, of interpreting and theorizing, that have developed in relation to a history of material loss and foreclosed futures.

ROUTINE CRISIS

The concept of crisis is a very, perhaps even overly, familiar one. As such, the idea carries with it a host of often taken-for-granted premises about the structure of society, the rhythm of history, and the nature of critique. The idea dates to ancient Greek medicine, in which "crisis" referred to the turning point of an illness, when the patient either begins to recover or deteriorates further until death (Beckett 2019; Habermas 1975). However, suturing this idea to a thoroughly moralized conception of history is a distinctive and ubiquitous feature of modern social philosophy that, Koselleck (1988, 168) argues, dates to seventeenth-century England and the bourgeois critique of the absolutist state that inaugurated a new calculus of political legitimacy.

Marx, of course, long ago identified economic crises as an essential feature of capitalism (1978, 447–452). In his analysis, crisis instantiates the dual process whereby the forces and relations set in motion by the pursuit of Value necessarily generate contradictions that forcibly change the system's basic structure, propelling capitalism toward its inevitable end. For theorists who take seriously that diagnosis, economic crisis has therefore been a key site for understanding both the logic of capitalism and the possibilities of its overcoming. Benjamin (1968), for example, sees crisis as the moment when the true picture of the past can be grasped in a revolutionary movement that would redeem history. In a related vein, Lukács (1971) argues that crises reveal the violent irrationality of capitalism as a totalizing but contradictory system. Even the supposedly pessimistic Adorno (1967–68) insists that in crisis we see more clearly the paradoxically irrational self-destruction that defines not only capitalism but reason, as such. Incorporating in their different ways an attention to symbolic power and discursive logics, both Bourdieu (1984, 1991) and Habermas (1975) develop further the concept of crisis so as to account for the normative judgments that inhere within the experience of crisis and that are essential to its potential to spur social transformation.

Across this varied tradition and beyond, theories and intuitions of that potential have relied on three crucial premises. First, since the earliest critiques of the absolutist state, the notion of crisis has privileged the perspective of the "bourgeoisie," or, later, the "middle class." This is even the case for Marxian and post-Marxian theories, which figure the proletariat as historical protagonist while simultaneously arguing that crisis awakens the nonlaboring classes to the violence of capitalism that workers know all too well. Second, all these accounts treat that process of producing a historically conscious and agentive subject as the lived, concrete, and traumatic version of the ideology critique that theorists carry out in abstract and formal analysis. Third and most fundamentally, these first two premises rest on the even more fundamental assumption that people experience crisis as a singular, shocking moment of rupture. These premises have received their clearest explication within the tradition of critical theory. However, as Roitman (2014), following Koselleck (1988), insists, they are extraordinarily widespread as tacit assumptions.

All this is in keeping with the sorts of interpretive and temporal ruptures ethnographers have encountered in contexts of both sudden and prolonged economic collapse. Describing the situation of Cameroon in the 1980s, for example, Mbembe and Roitman (1995, 323, 338) describe the peculiar everyday temporality of crisis as that of the "immediate present," a temporal stance that goes hand-in-hand with a popular understanding of the situation as "incomprehensible." In a very different context, Morris (2000a, 2000b) recounts how the Asian financial crisis of 1997 upset Thai regimes of monetary representation, magical mediation, and historical narration. Consider, too, the way that boom-and-bust cycles of the Nigerian oil economy produced what Apter (1999, 299) describes as a disconcerting mix of irreality and devaluation that culminated in "a national crisis of represen-tation." Similarly, Ferguson (1999) argues that the collapse of the Zambian copper economy eviscerated ideologies of modernity and progress, leaving behind a lived experience defined by the lack of decipherable historical meaning. As Lomnitz (2003, 134) argues in his analysis of the Mexican crisis of the 1980s, these sorts of economic cataclysms present a bewildering and constant flow of unpredictable events, the experience of which produces "a feeling of living in historical times" and "an increased hunger" for narrative explanation. They therefore induce a sort of "present saturation," the sense of living in an indecipherable moment cut off from both the past (with its now-defunct expectations) and the future (which can no longer be projected with any meaningful certainty).

At first glance, the 2001–2002 Argentine crisis might seem to fit this model quite well. After all, both during and after the fact, people described it as a moment of revelation, when they woke up to the injustice of the neoliberal model of the 1990s, which had promised a consumerist paradise but delivered unprecedented levels of poverty and disenfranchisement. In its wake, millions poured into the streets for the first time, demanding accountability, social and economic justice, and substantive democracy. "Down with all of them! Don't let a single one remain!" was the uncompro-mising and revolutionary slogan of a radicalized and impoverished middle class primed—finally—to seek common cause with the poor and marginal-ized. These were "the days Argentina stood still," in the words of one recent analysis (Visacovsky 2018; see also Goddard 2006 and Guyer 2007), when the capacity to imagine the future hung in the balance. In the years that fol-lowed, people returned again and again to this moment, in recursive acts of interpretation that echoed the compulsive return demanded by the trau-matic senselessness that characterizes crisis as the moment of maximally heightened contradiction.

And yet.

The middle-class Argentine experience of 2001–2002 was not really one of indecipherability. Rather, as I argued in the previous chapter, it was one of overdetermined meaning, in which a widespread consensus about its significance arose with remarkable ease. Accounting for that overdetermi-nation requires seeing how the historical logic of crisis in the Argentine case differs from that presumed by the traditions of modern social thought mentioned above. Above all, it requires taking seriously the fact that, in this case, crisis did not figure as singular event, nor even as a one in a series (Smart and Smart n.d.), but as repetition.

Consider the following quotations:[11]

---

11. Spanish-language transcripts appear in the appendix.

"All of a sudden, no money even to buy milk. That's when I realized there had never been a future in this shitty country. . . . Before, we acted as naïfs. But even after the deepest of all our crisis we, the middle class, still can't abandon our attachments to consumerist fantasies. . . . We'll always be in crisis."
Leticia, a forty-five-year-old secretary in the office of a government agency

"Seeing the country risk index go up and up and up every day . . . I woke up and saw that we were never going to be the country we had thought we would become. We've been through so many crises, but we finally woke up to that truth. But we, the middle class, we still refuse to renounce our dreams of the first world. And that's the problem."
Héctor, a twenty-four-year-old occasionally employed architect

"It was a shock. We, the middle class, lost a lot, but the good thing is that we understood that we had never been on the path to a future. But then, it wasn't really a shock, with our history of crisis after crisis. . . . We all knew what it was when the lootings happened. . . . We're a false people. A counterfeit nation. We live in a perpetual crisis of our own making. But then, what else is capitalism?!"
Marta, a seventy-eight-year-old Lacanian psychoanalyst

In each quotation, the narrated events take place in the past, but that past is not a seamless or uniform one. Rather, in the present of narration, each speaker articulates a relationship across multiple, distinct past moments. There is the anchoring moment of an "I" suffering a loss, and thereby awakening to the truth. Next, there is a remembered moment prior to loss and realization, a moment defined by the obsolete practice of projecting a future. Finally, there is the moment of that previously projected future, a future that not only will not be, but never could have been. Across these three moments, the speaking "I" morphs into a national and classed collective "we" that experiences events over the lifetime of the nation. Thus far, all the familiar features of crisis are present: the destructive capacity of crisis has nullified a longed-for future, thereby disrupting the "homogenous, empty time" (Benjamin 1968) of modernist progress and waking the speaker up to the truth of that destruction.

Nonetheless, the crucial difference here is that the above speakers framed all this as itself a repetition. In their telling, the entire configuration of crisis as destruction and awakening has already happened multiple times over. The present of narration therefore supervenes the nested set of moments above as the speaker asserts the capacity to survey multiple crises and recognize that they resembled one another to the point of constituting historical repetition. The narrated history thus takes on the form of a nested set of citations in which qualitative features of each moment of crisis (no money to buy milk, the skyrocketing country risk, the lootings) recall and quote those of a previous moment of crisis.[12] In this way, speakers knit together these events as evidence that crisis will not—indeed *cannot*—produce the longed-for emancipatory social transformation that it once seemed to have offered.

Of course, my Argentine interlocutors were by no means the first to identify the repetitive logic of capitalist crisis. Whether conceptualized by Schumpeter (1983) as the "creative destruction" of the business cycle or by Postone (1993, 289) as the "treadmill effect" of the dialectic of Value, theorists have long understood capitalism to be defined by a paradoxical logic in which crisis serves as the mechanism of social reproduction. In this sense, as Sewell (2012, 314) puts it, writing in the aftermath of the 2008 global financial crisis, an economic crisis in and of itself does not function as an "event" in the sense of a turning point when an "interlocking sequence of happenings . . . durably transforms structures." The people I have quoted were articulating a historically and culturally particular version of this more abstract point. However, in so doing, they insisted on identifying the "hyper-eventful but monotonously repetitive" (Sewell 2008, 527) temporality as a specifically Argentine (rather than generally capitalist) dynamic from which there was no escape.

Here, call to mind the rhythms of Argentine political-economic history as narrated in dominant popular, political, and academic discourse. In the early twentieth century, we are to understand, Argentina was the seventh-richest country in the world. Wealth was distributed unequally, but there was considerable social mobility, processes of political democratization, and massive flows of European immigrants, all contributing to processes of urbanization and so-called modernization. World War I, however, precipitated a global drop in commerce and Argentina's export-led economy suffered. Worse, in 1930, the global Great Depression brought economic strains that precipitated a minor economic crisis and a military coup. Then, 1955 saw dramatic falls in global commodity prices, precipitating Argentine inflation rates of 40 percent and another military coup. The year 1976 saw inflation rates of 600 percent and social unrest, and another coup. Another

---

12. In characterizing the narrative form as a nested set of citations, I am emphasizing that the judgment of repetition was what Nakassis (2016, 6) calls a "total semiotic fact," that is, an "open-ended, non-esssentialist center of gravity of multiply intersecting processes." In other words, the judgment of repetition did not simply inhere within the events themselves but hinged on the material, interactional unfolding of semiosis. More specifically, that judgment required processes of rhematization, entextualization, and cross-chronotopic dialogics as they treated particular facts as portable and replicable from one context to the next. For more detailed discussion of the logics of these semiotic processes, see Bauman and Briggs 1990; Gal 2013; Inoue 2004; Lempert and Perino 2007; Silverstein and Urban 1996; Swinehart and Ribeiro 2019; and Wirtz 2016.

economic crisis occurred in 1989, when annual inflation reached 5,000 percent and lootings, general strikes, and intimations of a coup abounded, prompting the president to resign before his term concluded. All of this brings us, at last, to 2001–2002, the crisis that everyone called "the worst in national history."

Accounting for this century-long history of relative economic decline lies outside the scope of this book, and the problem has generated a cottage industry of analyses in Argentina and beyond in journalism, public scholarship, and academic disciplines of all sorts as people attempt to account for "one of the most puzzling stories in the annals of modern economic history," (Della Paolera and Taylor, 2003b, 1; see also García-Heras 2009; Glaeser, Di Tella, and Picketty 2018; and Della Paolera and Taylor, 2003a). Some of that literature trades in varieties of Argentine exceptionalism, placing responsibility, for example, on Peronism's supposedly unique dysfunctions or, contrarily, on the allegedly unparalleled refusal of Argentine capitalists to invest in national development. More nuanced are histories that focus on Argentina's long-standing position in the global capitalist system as a primary commodity-export-driven economy (or, what Coronil [1997] calls a "nature-exporting economy"). That defining characteristic has allowed Argentina to occupy a stable, "semi-peripheral" (Wallerstein 2004) position in the global political economy for well over a century, despite concerted efforts by multiple political projects to move toward a more industrial and, later, postindustrial economy. Paradoxically, that international positional stability has generated remarkable domestic instability, as the national economy is extremely vulnerable to global rises and falls in dollar-denominated commodity prices, as too are the fates of political regimes (Rock 1985, 2002). Notably, this dynamic continues to structure post-crisis twenty-first-century Argentina, which has shifted from a Washington Consensus model to a slightly revised "commodity consensus" (Svampa 2013; see also Munck 2003).

This reliably unstable history has materially transformed the possibility of experiencing "crisis" in several important ways. First, since the mid-1970s, economic crises in Argentina and elsewhere have tended to occur in response to the speculative dynamics of global finance rather than the dynamics of overproduction and underconsumption theorized in the Marxian tradition (LiPuma and Lee 2004). While these financial crises are not novel (Kindleberger and Aliber 2005), they have occurred with increasing frequency and intensity over the past several decades, and their repercussions are exacerbated by the contemporary system of global reserve currencies, which renders countries like Argentina especially vulnerable to capital flight (Germain 2009; Harvey 1990; Painceira 2012). Additionally, across the past century and a half of political-economic instability in Argentina, state institutions could only be successively and partially captured by competing interests, leaving behind a "palimpsest of half-completed projects" (Corradi 1985, 111; see also Halperín Donghi 1964, 1994; O'Donnell 1973, 1988). As a result, the Argentine state does not enjoy the kind of hegemonic authority that could be punctured by crisis as concrete ideological critique; people regularly experience the state as a conflictual terrain of dubious legitimacy, even in moments of relative calm (Levitsky and Murillo 2006). Modernity, progress, and prosperity have therefore come to figure in Argentina as ideologies not of the future-oriented present but of a past when historical time had appeared pregnant with possibilities for personal, familial, and national well-being (Anguita and Minujin 2005).

However, the ease with which people discerned such a clear and determinate pattern in national history should give us pause. In her work on the semiotics of resemblance, Gal (2013, 34) reminds us that "similarity . . . never simply inheres in objects" but requires a relevant interpretive frame. The question therefore becomes, how did people learn to pick out particular features so as to recognize similarity between 2001–2002 and what came before?

They learned to do so through a host of mundane pedagogical rituals (Gal 2013) that articulate a thoroughly perspectival history of middle-class laments about failure and denied promises. Take, for example, the charts and graphs of a history of economic decline that pepper the history books of Argentine schoolchildren, as they do national newspapers and mass media broadcasts, and that appear regularly in international journalistic accounts, policy papers, and the white papers of institutions of global governance like the IMF and World Bank. Looking at these images, one can apprehend a sort of punctuated equilibrium, with each crisis delivering the nation to a new economic low, especially when contrasted with the plotlines of other countries. One discerns the same general plotline when perusing the titles of bestselling novels and works of popular history and sociocultural critique (Fiorucci 2005), and one cannot but stumble across the same themes in national newspapers and magazines, which are ubiquitous in cafés and restaurants, where they lie about, ready for common consumption alongside the constantly airing TV news and triggering neighborly conversation and complaint. This work of historicization can also take place in less public domains, as when the forty-year-old man who inherited a dry goods store from his father, a Syrian immigrant, remarked casually to the elderly lady ahead of me in line, "It's impossible to know how much to order. When will the next catastrophe happen? What are we doing to ourselves, we Argentines? How to plan in a place where plans are pointless?" Or, as when a young woman declared to me in the midst of airing her doubts about her upcoming nuptials: "The anxiety, the refusal to see what is happening until the worst has happened—that's my very Argentine partner. Maybe we're all like that. Do we repeat in our own lives the national history? Or, does our national history reflect our psychic traumas? What does it matter? It's how things are." Or, again, as the young economics major who insisted that I use my research to "show the world how this conspiracy of vested interests has impoverished one of world's richest countries."

This material history and the ubiquity of its rendering in public life ensured that the 2001–2002 crisis was experienced not as a unique moment but as a token of a general type.[13] However, as these latter comments suggest, there is another dimension at work. Not only did people see a resemblance between the contemporary moment and prior crises, they also felt compelled to account for that similarity in a very particular way. In the course of what Gal (2013, 34) calls "the active ideological, hence semiotic, process" of recognizing similarity across historical moments, people did not stop their interrogations by simply concluding that history repeats itself, as if it were an incomprehensible and brute fact of nature. Rather, they plumbed the depths of their own psyches and the obscure reaches of the global order in order to identify the mechanisms that produced that repetition.

SUSPICIOUS CRITIQUE

In Argentina, psychoanalysis has enjoyed such a peculiarly successful history that the middle-class Argentine analysand has achieved the status of national cliché. Buenos Aires has the highest per capita concentration of psychoanalysts in the world, with perhaps half of them operating according to the principles of Lacanian analysis.[14] Introduced in Argentina in the midst of the depression of the 1930s, psychoanalysis initially enjoyed only a limited audience of medical professionals. However, over the 1950s and 1960s, it became the dominant model of psychiatric education in the psychology departments of major universities and the primary therapeutic

---

13. In Kockelman and Bernstein's (2012, 332) terms, the crisis was thus reckoned to be a "replica" rather than a "singularity."

14. "Ya hay 56,000 psicólogos en la Argentina," *La Nación*, October 15, 2005, https://www .lanacion.com.ar/747686-ya-hay-56000-psicologos-en-la-argentina. According to this 2005 study, Argentina had 1 psychologist (mostly psychoanalysts) for every 649 people, compared with the United States, which counted 1 for every 2,213. For the following brief history of psychoanalysis in Argentina I am especially indebted to Ablard 2003; Bass 2000; Caimari 2003; Dagfal 2009; García 2005; Hollander 1990; Klappenbach 2003; Lakoff 2006; Plotkin 2001, 2003a, 2003b, 2009; Russo 2009; Vezzetti 1996, 2002, 2004; and Visacovsky 2009a. For a comparative history of psychoanalysis, see Burnham 1982.

approach to mental health in hospitals. At the same time, psychoanalytic concepts began circulating among the broader reading public, and analysts took on their now well-established position as public intellectuals in women's magazines and current events publications, commenting on the changing social relations brought about by large-scale rural-to-urban migration, liberalized gender roles, and an expanded and relatively prosperous middle class. During this period, psychoanalytic therapy became a standard component of the urban middle-class lifestyle with long-term, even lifelong, analysis standing as a practice of discerning self-knowledge rather than only a short-term treatment for specific disorders. While the military dictatorship of the 1970s targeted psychoanalysis alongside communism as one of the two greatest threats to Western civilization, psychoanalysis (especially in its Lacanian guise) thrived even as it was forced into a semi-underground existence. Offering a relatively free space for conversation in the midst of state violence, analysis remained a central component of middle-class life, and it emerged in the democratic era with a particularly strong antiauthoritarian, free thinking, and critical reputation. While the 1990s saw the introduction of psychotropic drugs such as Prozac (see Lakoff 2006), such treatments and their biomedical framework have by no means supplanted psychoanalysis as a way of understanding subjectivity, mental illness, and social relations.

As a result of this history, psychoanalytic ideas circulate far beyond their therapeutic context and provide a powerful idiom in Argentina for the explanation of the personal, social, and cultural consequences of national uncertainty (Hollander 1990, Plotkin 2003a, 2003b, 2009). Many people learn psychoanalytic concepts and interpretive frameworks through their own experiences with clinical analysis, with roughly one-third of the inhabitants of Buenos Aires having undergone analysis.[15] However, by circulating through friendly conversation, television shows, advice columns, academic classrooms, and other forums, psychoanalytic ways of speaking—and listening (Marsilli-Vargas 2016; see also Inoue 2004)—are familiar even to those who never lie down on an analyst's couch, and just about anyone can play the part of analyst or analysand in everyday interactions. The far-reaching impact of psychoanalysis on Argentine society has prompted many to claim the existence of an Argentine "psychoanalytic culture" (Plotkin 2001) in which psychoanalysis operates not only as an institutionalized mode of therapy, but also as a form of widely disseminated "common sense" (Visacovsky 2009b) and practical knowledge (Vezzetti 1996) upon

---

15. "Los porteños valoran el aporte del psicoanálisis," Universia, September 20, 2006, http:// noticias.universia.com.ar/en-portada/noticia/2006/09/20/369346/portenos-valoran-aporte -psicoanalisis.html.

which people rely in their attempts to grapple with everyday adversity. At the same time, the decidedly French mode of Lacanian psychoanalysis that is most common and most valued in Argentina is part of a far more general tendency to generate cultural capital through the appropriation of highly valued, Western European signs of sophistication.

What sets this interpretive strategy apart from many other forms of cultural capital is that in post-crisis Argentina, it provided a way for debates over the past, present, and future of the nation to examine the recurring "problem" of Argentine identity. Psychoanalytic theories of the 2001–2002 crisis typically performed this analysis by diagnosing an inescapably destructive contradiction constituting the national middle class, especially the tension between materialist individualism on the one hand and the desire for meaningful social engagement on the other. In this way, psychoanalytic readings of the nation-state often converged with diagnoses of an essential flaw at the core of a perduring Argentine psyche, and the entire twentieth century could appear as a cycle of crises, summed up in the resigned adage, "the past is a predator" (Feitlowitz 1998, 255).

If psychoanalysis has served as a form of cultural capital that simultaneously diagnoses a contradiction at the core of Argentine identity, conspiracy theories have long operated as a less prestigious but equally enduring way of diagnosing a hidden source of national problems. Adept at explaining the world in terms of mysterious actors, they have often surfaced when social and political tensions strained the limits of political institutions, and allegations of conspiracies have helped define political stakes since at least the first mass elections of 1912 (Romero 2002). At times, they have decried the power of elites to wield outsize influence on public affairs and motivated initiatives to democratize politics and redistribute wealth. However, at least as frequently, conspiracy theories about alleged civilian subversives have legitimated military coups, state violence, and extralegal machinations on behalf of those elites.

In a history shaped by actual conspiracies not only on the part of military cadres and guerrillas but also among politicians, businessmen, and bureaucrats, allegations of occult plots are not necessarily unreasonable (H. González 2004). Neither are they far removed from the claims of institutionally authoritative accounts of economic and political power, such as a recent article in the *Fletcher Forum of World Affairs* in which a prominent political scientist argued that decades of both democratic and military governments had intentionally orchestrated "profit-generating chaos" and a "massively regressive transfer of income" on behalf of "a powerful segment of the local bourgeoisie" (Escudé 2006, 127–28). In other words, what distinguishes conspiracy theories is not the veracity of particular truth claims but rather their overarching style of analysis. As a number of political theorists and anthropologists have argued, conspiracy theories approach conditions of uncertainty with a metaphysics of good and evil (see Dean 1998; Faubion 1999; Marcus 1999; Melley 2000). In so doing, they link systemic patterns directly to the actions of individual agents, overlooking the mediations and complications of social institutions (Hofstadter 1979). They therefore offer the potential to carve out an anti-elitist space for the construction of a form of knowledge that can "resurrect agency and the sense of a privileged community 'in the know'" (Stewart and Harding 1999, 292), especially in moments where agency and knowledge feel most imperiled (Briggs 2004) or when the parameters of national belonging are in question (Gürpinar 2013).

Addressing themes of financial ruin, political corruption, and violent crime, conspiracy theories in post-crisis Argentina took on a decidedly populist valence, accusing domestic and foreign powers of having colluded in bankrupting the nation, destabilizing the government, and sowing popular unrest. Nonetheless, like the psychoanalytic theories I described above, the conspiracy theories of post-crisis Argentina questioned the efficacy of the very knowledge they offered, for they frequently interpreted contemporary instability as only the most recent instantiation of a plot against the nation that stretched back almost a century. In this way, they exposed truths that should have already been known and that should have helped prevent the current crisis. As one conspiracy theorist lamented, the crisis suggested "the eternal return of the same [as] . . . the condition of a society that finds it difficult to retain experience, a country that accumulates misfortunes but does not accumulate a memory of the origin of those misfortunes."[16]

Clearly there are important distinctions to be made between psychoanalytic and conspiracy theories, whether in post-crisis Argentina or elsewhere. Whereas psychoanalytic theories stood as a form of elite, quasi-scientific knowledge that emphasized introspection and complicity, conspiracy theories offered a form of popular, conjectural knowledge of the external, malignant forces. What is more, while psychoanalytic theories focused on structural determinations of the national psyche, conspiracy theories insisted on a resolutely intentional understanding of agency in order to explain the global order and Argentina's place in it.

Nonetheless, there is a deep affinity between these two genres, usefully conceptualized, following Bakhtin (1986, 60), as "relatively stable type[s] of utterance" characterized by unique combinations of thematic content, style, and compositional structure. Post-crisis Argentine psychoanalytic and conspiracy theories were characterized by the elaboration of themes of

---

16. Enrique Valiente Noailles, "El clamor de los argentines," La Nación, September 18, 2002. For a more academic articulation of the idea of the "eternal return" of crisis in Argentina, see Novarro and Palermo 2004.

national degradation through a revelatory structure and a recognizable style of unending melodramatic exposition. Additionally, both genres routinely oriented themselves toward a presumed urban middle-class addressee, an idealized and discerning figure capable of grasping the import of the truths therein revealed, and they both constructed present-day Argentina as a time and place decimated by a history of repeated crises. They thus provided opposed yet complementary perspectives on the jointly diagnosed problem of national loss.[17]

The jointly constructed, highly adaptable framework of psychoanalytic and conspiracy theories is especially well suited to the interpretation of crisis. Both portray a world that presents itself as profoundly inchoate, confronting the subject with the unfathomability of one's own actions or the inscrutability of the nation's sudden financial collapse. Both scour that phenomenal world for evidence of a deeper order lurking behind apparent contingencies, and they thereby uncover the signifying chains that structure the unconscious or the agentive networks that dictate the global political economy. In that process of discovery, they look beyond proximate causes and mechanical processes, focusing attention instead on ultimate, justificatory causes and meaningful relationships. As a result, the sense made of a mysterious world is never merely descriptive or abstract. Rather, the epistemological and the ethical are inextricably linked in a form of knowledge that is avowedly constitutive of an active engagement with the world. That knowledge tends to be synechdotal in structure, as both psychoanalytic and conspiracy theories identify forces that work similarly at different levels and on different types of actors. In this way, psychoanalytic and conspiracy theories are antinomically linked interpretive genres that engage self and society, the particular and the general, the subjective and the objective, and explain each category in terms of its opposite in an interminable back-and-forth. It is this capacity that allowed them, together, to stand as critiques, commentaries, and alternatives to other highly visible modes of understanding recent events—such as the proliferation of statistics on suffering, the economic models of the IMF, or the proclamations of politicians—alongside which they appeared.

Psychoanalytic and conspiracy theories thus enable an interpretive strategy driven by an unrelenting stance of suspicious interpretation, or what Ricœur (1970) calls a "hermeneutics of suspicion," in which one ques-

---

17. In focusing on the role of psychoanalytic and conspiracy theories in the post-crisis Buenos Aires middle class, I do not mean to imply the absence of other critical genres. Sprinkled throughout the book are traces of other interpretive frameworks that circulated through this public. Marxism, anarchism, and Catholicism of various stripes are just some of the most legible. Nonetheless, psychoanalytic and conspiracy theories are far more central to the constitution of this public and so require greater attention.

tions appearances in order to discover the hidden reality of the world. For Ricœur, Freud stands alongside Marx and Nietzsche in the long tradition of a philosophy of doubt that begins with Descartes's radical questioning of the world and culminates in the interrogation of consciousness itself. In fundamental ways, suspicious interpretation presents the possibility of an engaged, questioning public capable of fulfilling the Enlightenment demand to interrogate the world, to uncover its undergirding truths, and thereby enable rational, demystified historical agency (Ricœur 1970, 34–35). That demand is, of course, shared by critical theory and the social sciences more generally, as Boltanski argues in his account of the moral, emancipatory logic of critique (2011) and in his argument about the centrality of an "anxiety about *the reality of reality*" in modern European societies (2014, 15; original emphasis). It is also shared by liberal and radical traditions of political thought alike and variations on it appear in the works of thinkers as different, even opposed, as Tocqueville (1969) and Marx (1972), Habermas (1996) and Spinoza (2007), Montesquieu (1989) and Condorcet (1955), and Rawls (2005) and Hardt and Negri (2001). In practice, however, people invested in the suspicious interpretation of Argentina's history of crises found themselves in a position of profound doubt about the efficacy of the knowledge they themselves produced in an apparently never-ending series of revelations.[18]

During fieldwork, I would often pluck interesting media artifacts out of newspapers, magazines, television shows, and so on, in order to discuss them with friends and interviewees. On one such occasion, I was talking with a young married couple who had suggested that I interview them together. They had invited me over for dinner and a joint interview in the backyard of their tiny, concrete-block house in a modest suburban municipality peopled mostly by low-paid, white-collar and service workers who commuted daily to downtown Buenos Aires. Their two children, four and seven years old, played nearby while we ate, and they described their backgrounds. María was a college-educated social worker. The daughter of a factory worker and a housewife, she had grown up nearby during a period when the local economy still revolved around light industry. Tomás, meanwhile, grew up in the capital as the son of a dentist and a nurse. He dropped out of college in the late 1990s to work in the marketing department of a telecommunications company but had been unemployed since mid-2001.

Intrigued by a recent newspaper article that described Argentina as a

---

18. Dean (2002) makes a related argument about the coalescence of classically liberal demands for a transparent public sphere and the peculiar narrative and temporal capacities of information-age technology to generate a sense of secretive realms of power and to reduce political debate to a never-ending series of revelations.

society defined by mistrust,[19] I recounted the journalistic piece and read aloud a handful of excerpts to my captive audience. The author, a staff writer for the largest-circulating Argentine daily, had interviewed a slew of experts about a recent survey finding that Argentina has "one of the lowest levels of interpersonal trust" in the world. A psychoanalyst explained that in Argentina, "the first to fall was trust in the state, which represents the father." Sociologists argued that institutional mistrust had produced "a perverse effect on interpersonal trust." Shocking acts of criminal violence, a lack of personal and national financial credit, the deterioration of friendship, high levels of stress, depression, paranoia, and heart disease—all these phenomena were the product of a general problem of trust, the article contended.

My interlocutors agreed. Tomás described how, over several decades, "mafias" composed of "the big interests—the politicians and the economic forces—had worked to ensure the dissolution of social bonds." The result of that "conspiracy," he said, was a "diminished" and "individualized middle class" with an "utter lack of social trust." María pointed to the crisis as "the ultimate expression of this strategy of national impoverishment" and described the crisis as an event that she had experienced in the form of psychological and physical symptoms of "depression," "anguish," "headaches," and "fatigue." Tomás nodded vehemently, adding that his psychoanalyst had told him that "many people experienced similar pains, a way of punishing ourselves for our own complicity with the crisis, our willingness to believe the fantasies that the politicians gifted us." We circled round and round these themes for the better part of an hour in a diagnostic project that moved at once laterally and vertically to seek out resonances across discrete social spheres. Paternity and governance, tax evasion and poverty, citizenship, friendship, and social ills: all were linked together in a far-reaching analysis that occluded differences of scale, space and time, and social position. Finally, the discussion petered out when one of the children required María's attention. Tomás turned to me with a shrug, "You see how we are? We cannot find a solution to the country's problems, to the national crisis without end. We only talk and talk, but to what end?"

Ricœur would be surprised that María and Tomás's conversation ended in a shrug. As he was at pains to argue, "interpretation as exercise of suspicion" is not a form of skepticism, but an attempt to "clear the horizon for a new reign of Truth" (1970, 32–33). María and Tomás engaged in just such an exercise of suspicion and they did not arrive at a position of skepticism. They felt that they understand perfectly well the reality of the world but that

---

19. Liliana Moreno, "Argentina, uno de los países con más baja confianza interpersonal," Clarín, May 9, 2005, 28.

they were nevertheless powerless to change it. The "Truth" they uncovered was profoundly disappointing but evidently immutable.

In her study of Lacanian psychoanalysis in Paris, Turkle (1992, 191–92, 206) argues that its appropriability allowed it to lose its critical valence and become merely a faddish subject for elegant conversation. A similar process could be said to have taken place in Argentina, where psychoanalytic and conspiracy theories alike circulate so broadly, ready-to-hand for any manner of appropriation. However, the loss of critical valence—what we might call the domestication of critique—does not stem from any tendency of the masses to deform and misunderstand elite theory. Rather, it has to do with the particular form that psychoanalytic and conspiratorial critiques take. As Freud (1966) suggested and Lacan (1977) argued explicitly, the curative or palliative efficacy of psychoanalysis depends on its position as an inappropriate, counterintuitive, even aggressive mode of revelatory discourse.[20]

The same is true for conspiracy theorizing, which is structured as a fundamentally negative critique, the force of which depends on a positive realm of assumed knowledge and taken-for-granted common sense that resists its intrusive revelations. However, when these very theoretical moves become commonplace, even commonsensical, in their own right, as they have in Argentina, their critiques can easily coalesce with doxic (Bourdieu 1977) intuitions about the nature of the world and of oneself. In such a context, these suspicious practices of interpretation fail to account for their own affinity with the object of their analysis, and potentially critical claims can become readily assimilable truisms.

It is for this reason that practices of self-reflexive, suspicious critique produced such familiar, repetitive analyses. And it is for this reason that

---

20. The curative, revolutionary potential of psychoanalysis is articulated most fully by Lacan (1977, 5–6, 15, 22), who argues that the objectification of the world proceeds according to a process that is parallel and correlative to the narcissistic self-alienation of the subject. Thus, Lacan's *méconnaissance* replaces the Freudian reality principle as the crucial characteristic of the ego in its relations to its "exterior," and the fundamental gap within the subject is structurally identical to the gap between concepts and percepts. Psychoanalysis, then—and herein lies its critical capacity—turns upon a manipulation of this aggressive relation to the world, inducing a controlled paranoia in the analysand not in order to undo the disjuncture but in order to comprehend its form (Lacan 1977, 10, 14, 28). It is this manipulation to which Žižek (1989) and others refer in their demand for a second moment of critique and a particular temporal relation to the symptom. Without the sort of institutional structures and pedagogical lineages of psychoanalysis, conspiracy theorizing clearly has no comparably articulated metalevel explanation of its own methodological assumptions. In practice, however, conspiracy theories similarly hinge upon an assumption of a paranoid, knowing subject whose alienation from society's reigning forces allow him to see clearly and, potentially, to change the world by publicizing his knowledge.

those analyses converged on deeply held and widely disseminated intuitions about national victimhood and the denied future of the middle class. In post-crisis middle-class Buenos Aires, then, the aggressive knowledge production of psychoanalytic and conspiracy theories tended to produce not historical agency but an acute sense of inhabiting a time and place in which "the fully enlightened earth radiates disaster triumphant" (Adorno and Horkheimer 1990, 3), and time itself is stripped of redemptive possibility. Engaging in ongoing critique thus produced a peculiar kind of pleasure by allowing speakers and listeners to bask in that radiance and to enjoy the sense that, while there may be no way to undo that disaster, they at least see it clearly.[21]

DISILLUSION

For much of the twentieth century, in Argentina, as in many places, important dimensions of social life were oriented by a familiar chronotope. That chronotope was most evident in genres of modernizing histories, which cast the nation, identified with the middle class, as the protagonist advancing a plot of progress. Progress could assume any number of guises, from the technological to the territorial, from the economic to the political, but its valence was always moralized: The narrative arc pointed toward the rectification of wrongs and the actualization of promises. In other words, these progressive histories laminated onto one another the logics of moral perfectionism, sociomaterial development, and temporal linearity, and then mapped those logics onto the space of the nation, personified in the collective subject of the Buenos Aires middle class.[22]

With time, however, those narratives had become increasingly unconvincing, especially from the perspective of the increasingly impoverished Buenos Aires middle class. The 2001–2002 Argentine financial crisis marked the culmination of that process, when a century of successive political-economic crises finally rendered uninhabitable the chronotope of progress. In this context, people no longer experienced crisis as a singular event disrupting the normally unquestioned grounds of the everyday. Rather, crisis had become an unwelcome but unsurprising collapse of a social terrain felt to be inherently irregular and illegitimate.

---

21. On the pleasures of even ineffectual critical interpretation, see Kockelman 2016 and Latour 2004.

22. For resonant phenomena in other contexts, see Alonso 1994; Lomnitz 2001; and Piccato 2010. For more on approaches to emplotment, see Brooks 1984 and L. White 1990.

This altered experiential logic of crisis produced self-reflexive and sophisticated social critiques. However, those critiques constructed a space of despair that framed the global order and Argentina's place in it as simultaneously unjustifiable and inescapable. Shaped from the inside out by psychoanalytic and conspiratorial practices of interpretation, they framed crisis not as a momentary rupture but rather as the enduring reality that underlay national life. And so, a new chronotope—one of routine crisis— emerged as a dominant orienting framework for the everyday practices and discourses of the Buenos Aires middle class. Thus, the arc of progress reversed direction and charted an equally teleological arc of degradation. However, one trajectory did not simply replace the other. Suspicious crisis talk in middle-class Buenos Aires held together these two opposed plot lines in a relatively stable but fraught amalgam: a chronotope in which crisis was routine and ruin unavoidable.[23]

It bears emphasizing that this is not the sort of relation to crisis and ruin in which Benjamin (1968) and others (e.g., Avelar 1999; Kunkel 2014; Gordillo 2014; Rose 2003) have found such revolutionary potential.[24] The epigraph of this chapter is Hamlet's rueful lament at his misfortune in living in a "time out of joint" and in being tasked with "putting it right."[25] However, the post-crisis, middle-class Buenos Aires experience of crisis was one that dismissed the project of recuperation, for time seemed permanently and irredeemably out of joint.[26] To be sure, people examined their history in the hope that it might generate some insight into how to confront the lived present. However, more often than not, they concluded that history demonstrated that the progress they continued to long for was a foreclosed future. In other words, their "space of experience" had changed so fundamentally as to render obsolete their "horizon of expectation" (Koselleck 2004). Nonetheless, they found themselves unable simply to divest themselves of that

---

23. The temporality of this amalgam calls to mind Hartog's (2003, 202) diagnosis of "negative presentism," that is, the infinite extension of the present into the past and into the future so as to produce the experience of unending catastrophe. It also recalls the temporal experience Yurchak (2005) describes in the late socialist Soviet Union.

24. Rather, this relationship to crisis and ruin bears a family resemblance to the melancholic and ultimately nonredemptive relation to the past that Benjamin (2003) found in the *Trauerspiel*, the eighteenth-century German dramas that featured everyday members of the bourgeoisie as their tragic protagonists.

25. For more on Shakespeare's formulation of "time out of joint," see Brown 2001 and Derrida 1994.

26. In this sense, the chronotope of routine crisis in post-crisis, middle-class Buenos Aires does not simply produce a call to return to normalcy, as the diagnosis of crisis does in some other contexts, such as the ones that Masco (2017) and Roitman (2014) discuss. Rather, it produces a lament about the impossibility of such a return.

horizon of expectant progress. It continued to orient everyday values and desires, even in its avowed obsolescence. The result was a social world defined by double-binds, self-recrimination, and disillusion.[27]

The sentimental stance of disillusion did not spring fully formed out of political-economic history.[28] It required the interpretive labors of specific genres of self-reflexive critique. Those critical practices allowed people to analyze their participation in an unjust social world that they themselves could not but condemn. And yet, it offered its own pleasures, including a path to claiming a relatively elevated status within that world. What is more, it offered those pleasures precisely to the extent that one could discern the subterranean forces structuring that unjustified world in ways that exceeded individual agency. In this way, critique could reinscribe class distinctions and absolve the analyst from intervening in an apparently overdetermined system.

People were by no means unaware of this ambivalence. Many articulated it quite clearly, as did Mabel, who concluded her interview with me with the following words:[29]

> We try to understand how one crisis after another has defined us. How can we allow this poverty and inequality, this total corruption, to continue!? One must critique everything! But it won't change. I wish we Argentines, we the middle class, could learn. But you can't undo your desire any more than you can undo the Oedipus complex. And so, we go forward, knowingly participating in our own tragedy. The system of global capitalism ensures another crisis. And we are complicit.

Mabel's comments make clear that crisis, critique, and historical time are not what they once were. Crisis has been reconfigured as iterative, one moment in a series of similar moments that stretches indefinitely back into the past and forward into the future. Critique, meanwhile, offers analytic insight into that historical series, but insight divorced from meaningful

---

27. The stance of disillusion that I am emphasizing here thus shares a family resemblance with the "politics of disappointment" Greenberg (2014) finds in contemporary Serbia, the "cynicism" that Allen (2013) finds in contemporary Palestine, and the tragic quality of time that Scott (2004, 2014) draws out of postcoloniality. On the importance of attending to a broad range of "historical emotions," see Gilbert 2019.

28. In conceptualizing disillusion as a "stance," I mean to invoke and build on recent scholarship on the linguistic and nonlinguistic dynamics of evaluation and alignment that go into stance-taking. Those dynamics make stance a key site for interrogating the interactional emergence and articulation of emotion, sentiment, and affect. See, e.g., Jaffe 2009 and Kockelman 2004.

29. A Spanish-language transcript appears in the appendix.

action. Finally, national life has been firmly emplotted as a tragedy of corruption that the middle class narrates and analyzes but finds itself powerless to change.

Post-crisis, middle-class Buenos Aires was stitched together by the resulting sentiment of disillusion, as suggested by a piece of graffiti I happened across in 2007: scrawled in red spray-paint across the façade of formerly elegant beaux arts apartment building, it declared, "NOTHING NEW."

3

ECONOMIES OF LOSS

"The Little Corral"

Money is energy.

To be called Argentina, which comes from *argentum*=cash.

To be a fertile country growing in the shadow of a contraband customs office on the River of Cash: Already, at the origin, ambition and the lack of respect for the law commingle.

Before, there were dairy cows tied up on boats to Paris;

Then, the granary of the world, and now a starving country.

Paradoxes.

The banks steal the money, the police commit crimes, judges lose their judgment, and politicians don't represent their electors.

The value of money and the basic moral contracts are broken in a thousand pieces.

It's strange: We repudiate the empire while we wait in long lines to buy its money.

A version of this chapter appeared in *Cultural Anthropology* (Muir 2015).

MONETARY AND MORAL LIMBO

The poem that stands as the epigraph for this chapter appeared in an artist's book published in late 2002. Entitled *Limbo: Argentina 2002, A Story in Images* (Kovensky 2002, 21).[1] The book's photographs, collages, drawings, and poetic musings attempt to capture a bewildered sense of displacement. A sense of time moving forward before the eyes of a paralyzed citizenry, trapped in a country incapable of finding its footing. And, as this poem insists, money—or rather, its absence—stood at the center of that predicament. Take, for example, the following conversation among friends:

"It was terrible, and it was all summed up in the devaluation," Selene, a forty-five-year-old nurse asserted. "Suddenly, money wasn't what we thought. And we have been trapped by that realization ever since." "That's just it," replied Víctor, a thirty-eight-year-old hardware store owner, "to wake up and discover, all of a sudden, that a peso wasn't worth a dollar. . . . It was incomprehensible. We Argentines are still learning what that meant." "We must do so," Selene interjected, "Those who refuse are clinging to a neoliberal fantasy."

It was 2006, and Selene and Víctor were sitting with me in a placid Buenos Aires café, discussing the crisis of 2001–2002 as it was "summed up," as Selene put it, by the currency devaluation. Unhinged from the dollar for the first time in a decade, the peso floated on international currency markets and promptly lost three-quarters of its value. Recounting those events, Selene and Víctor described "the horror" and "the trauma" of that time: families scrounging for food in garbage bags on city streets; statistics enumerating unprecedented levels of poverty; news stories of malnourished children dying in the rural interior; massive street protests, police violence, and political instability. They also described less spectacular but no less deeply felt "traumas": the impossibility of transforming one's credentials into steady employment; the unpredictability of paychecks; the difficulty of calibrating nonmonetarized exchanges like barter transactions, neighborly favors, or family obligations.

At the center of their descriptions was money: the sudden lack and plummeting value of the peso, to be sure, but also what they considered its suddenly visible but long-standing failure "to reflect the true worth of the

---

1. Although the standard translation of the Spanish *plata* is "silver," it is also a colloquial term for money or cash. Here, I have translated the term in the first and third lines of the poem ("*argentum*=cash" and "River of Cash") as "cash" rather than silver in order to emphasize the wordplay through which the author asserts a nominal and essential link between Argentina and money.

country's wealth," "to encourage a trustworthy community," and "to let us build a real future." In short, they argued, Argentine currency had failed to fulfill the political-economic, sociomoral, and spatiotemporal functions of money. Moreover, they continued, that failure had undermined other stores of value, subjecting alternative currencies and family heirlooms, job titles and educational credentials to "a general and unpredictable process of devaluation . . . [in which] our 'a peso is worth a dollar' revealed itself as a fantasy."

Disavowing that "fantasy" had not proved straightforward. During the heady days of 2001–2002, Selene and Víctor had been convinced that Argentina would never be the same. Yet, some four years later, they described the world in the register of clear-eyed resignation. "We middle-class people now know what the poor have always known," Selene asserted, "Things are fucked."

Anthropologists have long engaged with the capacity of money to mediate not only processes of abstraction and commodification but also concretely meaningful projects of signification, solidarity, and even dissent.[2] Surveying this lengthy disciplinary engagement with money as a pluripotent semiotic form, Maurer (2006, 27) notes, "It is not news . . . that money is a social relation, a symbolic system, and a material reality . . . [just as] it is not news . . . that people freak out when the apparent hegemony of money's fictionality and abstraction is newly revealed." Nonetheless, there is a sort of "news" here, and it lies in the particularities of that "freak-ing out."

In keeping with the logic of crisis that I laid out in the previous chapter, a long tradition of analysis posits that, in revealing the constructed nature of money, financial crises "denaturaliz[e] the taken-for-granted monetary order," thereby opening up spaces for critique and social transformation (Maurer 2006, 28). The Argentine case troubles that postulate. People like Selene and Víctor argued that the crisis had indeed unveiled the "fictionality and abstraction" of money. What is more, they declared that revelation to have compelled them to engage in profound critique. They nonetheless proclaimed that it had not delivered any answer to the old problem of "What is to be done?" To the contrary, they found themselves "trapped" by a mode of suspicious critique that they experienced as compulsory and revelatory, but also interminable and ineffectual. In other words, the devaluation deepened their proclaimed commitment to money's reality as a material form demanding theoretical interpretation while eluding practical control. The revealed fictionality of monetary value strengthened the imperative of

---

2. See, e.g., Bloch and Parry 1989; Coronil 1997; Gregory 1996; Hart 2000; Maurer 2005; Pedersen 2002; Peebles 2011; and Zelizer 1997.

acquiescing to its facticity. This paradoxical stance has implications that extend far beyond a specifically middle-class, early-twenty-first-century Argentine experience. Indeed, it challenges our most fundamental intuitions about the emancipatory potentials of crisis and critique.

I begin by discussing the dispute between *ahorristas* ("savers"), small-scale savings account and bond holders, to regain the money they had lost during the crisis and the highly critical appraisals most middle-class people made of the *ahorristas'* efforts. The debate between the *ahorristas* and their critics reveals a shared middle-class folk theory of money as a sociomoral substance capable of aligning self-interest with collective well-being, past work with future reward.[3] It was the collapse of the peso's ability to serve these functions that transformed a fiscal crisis into a national one, disrupting not only public institutions like political parties and banks but also what Bourdieu (1984, 168) describes as the mutually reinforcing dialectic between subjective orientations and objective circumstances.

In the years that followed, people continued to deal with the peso's failure to fulfill the normative vision of this folk theory of monetary value. In so doing, they returned again and again to the themes of the above poem. They wrestled with the sense that money operates as both material tool and spiritual energy. They grappled with the intuition that money depends both on the guarantee of the nation-state and on the whims of global financial markets. And they traced and retraced the etiology of the crisis, looking at once to national "origins" as well as to relationships with "empire" as the two counterposed but complementary sites for assigning causation and responsibility. By no means were these struggles abstract or removed from the ways people navigated the logistical demands of economic life on a daily basis. To the contrary, this process of continual reexamination was bound up with a series of linked practical reorientations in which people turned increasingly and self-consciously away from material stores of value (such as currency and durable goods) and toward embodied practices of self-cultivation as seemingly more reliable ways of building a stable future.

This process shows money to be a privileged site for interrogating the mechanisms by which the long-term history of crisis and critique I sketched in chapter 2 is converted into subjective orientations to the world. It is through monetary practices that people cultivate habits, dispositions, and commitments with respect to the production, distribution, and consumption of material wealth. Even more fundamentally, it is through these prac-

---

3. For an analysis of the sociomoral frameworks of monetary practice among poor Argentines during this same period, see Wilkis 2018. For a discussion of the regimentation of monetary practices through moral metalanguage, see Keane 2008.

tices that they cultivate sensibilities regarding the politics of value, that is, questions concerning the very rubrics that define what to value and why. This is the terrain where the notion of a *longue durée* defined by crisis and critique becomes a lived, experiential reality grounded in a stance of suspicion regarding all manner of things.

THE "PRINCIPLE OF LAW" AND THE "REALITY OF THE MARKET"

Recall that the height of the crisis—December 2001–November 2002—was marked by three key financial interventions: the *corralito* ("little corral"), which froze bank accounts for a year; the devaluation, which decoupled the Argentine peso from the US dollar and led to its swift depreciation; and the *corralón* ("the big corral"), which converted dollar-denominated bank deposits and bonds into five- and ten-year certificates of deposit denominated in the newly devalued peso.

Aimed at halting a run on the banks and salvaging the country's ability to service the foreign debt in a context of spiraling capital flight and a global market contraction, these three measures failed in both respects. In early 2002, a number of banks went bankrupt and Argentina defaulted on its US$100 billion debt, the largest sovereign default in world history. The measures also temporarily removed more than 37 billion pesos from circulation, thereby exacerbating the plummeting GDP and rising unemployment rates. The suddenly illiquid market compelled federal, provincial, and local governmental agencies to pay their debts in alternative and complementary currencies, all of which also depreciated quickly, thereby intensifying the sense that an entire regime of value had come undone. These measures also meant that millions of Argentines effectively lost three-quarters of their life savings; in a very real sense, their money simply disappeared.

Argentines confronted the widely felt, if highly uneven, experience of economic loss by elaborating a broad repertoire of critical practices. For years, groups of unemployed factory workers had blockaded highways to protest economic precarity during a lengthy recession. With the banking restrictions, middle-class Argentines suddenly protested as well, pouring into the streets and banging pots and pans to form *cacerolazos*. Their refrain of "Down with all of them! Don't let a single one remain!" hinged on the total but ambiguous rejection of the so-called *clase dirigente* (ruling class). They also made audible and visible people's sudden inability to carry out that most fundamental task of social reproduction and transvaluation—cooking and consuming food—in a cash-starved environment. As such, they allowed a bankrupted domestic space to erupt into the streets so as to make public those sufferings that might have seemed merely personal.[4]

In the ensuing months, people forged neighborhood assemblies (*asambleas barriales*) and interclass alliances predicated on a general condemnation of politicians and, at times, an embrace of the principles of direct democracy. Barter networks (*redes de trueque*) sprang up around the country as people struggled to meet their daily needs without monetized exchange. Meanwhile, confronting a cascade of newly shuttered businesses, workers occupied their places of employment and reopened them as cooperatives (*fábricas recuperadas*).[5]

These horizontalist[6] genres of politicking continued throughout 2002 and 2003 but with diminishing intensity as the vertiginous collapse of political and economic institutions gave way, fitfully, to a period of reorientation. The banking freeze abated in early 2003, and the new Kirchner administration increased spending on social welfare programs; both measures allowed pesos to circulate more freely. A boom in global commodities prices coincided with and amplified the effects of President Kirchner's neo-Keynesian economic and social policies. During the next following four years, the GDP grew at over more than 9 percent annually, the Gini coefficient dropped from 0.53 to 0.47, and poverty rates decreased from over 50 percent to less than 24 percent (UNDP 2009). At the same time, unemployed workers transformed themselves into durable and sophisticated political organizations, and worker cooperatives either abandoned or began solidifying their legal and practical claims to their businesses. Meanwhile, neighborhood assemblies stopped convening, middle-class street protests became rare, and barter networks dissolved.

This process of reorientation hinged on the popular acceptance of the devaluation and its attendant economic losses. Nonetheless, a vocal minority denied the legitimacy of those losses, and it is to their claims that I turn first. Calling themselves *ahorristas*, they sought monetary restitution

---

4. Svampa and Pereyra (2003) offer a thorough accounting of the *piquetero* movement during this period. Briones, Fava, and Rosan (2004) provide a compelling analysis of the *cacerolazo* slogan as shifter that captured the ambiguous figure of the *clase dirigente*; see also Armony and Armony (2005). In Spanish, the slogan was, "*¡Que se vayan todos! ¡Que no quede ni uno solo!*"

5. These mobilizations received considerable international attention from journalists, activists, and academics. For discussions of the *asambleas barriales*, see DiMarco et al. 2004; Pérez, Armelino, and Rossi 2005; Ouviña 2008; and Svampa and Corral 2006. On the barter networks, see Bombal 2002 and Bombal and Luzzi 2006. For in-depth analysis of the *fábricas recuperadas*, see Faulk 2012; see also García Allegrone et al. 2004; Hirtz and Giacone 2013; and Pizzi and Icart 2014.

6. The term "horizontalist" emerged within these movements and has since circulated globally (Schaumberg 2008, Sitrin 2006, 2012).

through street protests and lawsuits.[7] Early on, during the days of the banking freeze, *ahorristas* held their own protests in front of banks across Buenos Aires to demand the return of their saved money at its full, pre-crisis value. They conducted *escraches*, demonstrations that operated as public shaming rituals in which people would chant slogans and insults outside officials' homes and workplaces. Because *escraches* originated in response to former president Menem's 1990 presidential pardon of human rights violators, the protests thereby linked the neoliberal politicians of the 1990s to the military officers and politicians of the last military dictatorship (1976–1983). One creative family of *ahorristas* even staged an elaborate protest in their bank's lobby, where they spent days among unfurled beach towels, umbrellas, coolers of food, and the other accoutrements of the instantly recognizable middle-class summer vacation they had been forced to forego. As the years went by, these protests gradually gave way to legal challenges, as individuals challenged the legitimacy of the *corralito* and *corralón* in the courts. Some lucky few eventually received favorable court decisions. However, because the Argentine judicial system does not allow for class action suits, those decisions did not extend beyond the individual claimants. Eventually, most *ahorristas* found themselves unable to muster the financial and other resources necessary to sustain their lawsuits and the movement, such as it was, gradually dissolved.

I conducted scores of interviews with *ahorristas*. They explained their position through constant references to "the principle of law" and insisted that they wanted their money back not for narrowly pecuniary or selfish reasons, but because justice demanded it. Arturo, for example, was a middle-aged man when we met in December 2006. We had arranged to talk in a café at the intersection of two broad and verdant avenues, just across from one of the city's largest shopping malls. I arrived about ten minutes early, sure that Arturo, like most of my interviewees, would arrive late and that I would have at least a half hour to do some last-minute preparations. I was shocked to find him already seated at a table, waiting expectantly with a cup of espresso in front of him. "It's very important to be on time," he said, "like the English. Most of my countrymen never arrive on time." He stirred sugar into his coffee, took a sip of water, assured himself that I had properly turned on my recorder, and started his narration, without so much a question from me.

He proceeded to offer me an economic life history in order to illustrate that "the situation couldn't be clearer. We, the middle class, are the people of the country who worked" and "our government hasn't acted correctly with us." Over the next hour, he offered a carefully structured account

---

7. For a description of the *ahorrista* movement and lawsuits, see Smulovitz 2006.

that began with his first job at eight years of age, continued with his work history during high school and college, proceeded through several career changes as an adult, and eventually described his founding of a successful small real-estate company that bought, renovated, and re-sold apartments. Throughout, he emphasized elements of the stereotypical image of the upwardly mobile Argentine middle class, such as his Italian immigrant parents and the tropes of "hard work" and "sacrifice."

As with the narratives of other *ahorristas*, the arrival of former president Menem on the scene in 1989 marked a definitive pivot point in the plot, transforming narrative tropes of work, savings, and deserved reward into those of financial investment, deceit, and loss. As Arturo put it, "this [hard work] is what I did until that gentleman Menem arrived and started in with his lies and with this one-to-one, where our peso was worth the same as a dollar, and that whole aberration that ended where it did." He explained that beginning in 1991, he and his son, two daughters, and a brother all pooled their savings toward the continual purchase of government bonds in the hopes of generating "a better future." His banker at the time had suggested that he consider Canadian bonds instead of Argentine ones, but Arturo refused:

> Since I'm very hardheaded . . . and I have feelings for this country . . . I said to myself, "I can't do something that goes against my principles. I'm going to put my small savings in Argentina." Because the government told us [in advertisements], "Gentlemen, contribute to the country," and I contributed to the country.

For Arturo and his family, the bonds were the monetary means and embodiment of a personal and familial dream. Given that they were issued and guaranteed by the Argentine government, that dream not only linked them all together as a family but also hitched those personal and familial aspirations to national progress. If Arturo's predictions and the government's advertisements had proven true, then a virtuous cycle of work, saving, investment, and returns would have buoyed them, millions of other Argentines, and the country itself into a prosperous future. Those hopes came to naught with the 2001–2002 crisis. In the years following, he and his wife were barely making ends meet with help from their children, and he described his life as one of "mere subsistence." He had imagined that his past work, congealed in monetary savings and amplified by the alchemy of government bonds, would provide for them all. Instead, his children's intended future was subsidizing his mere survival in the present. He attributed a 2004 heart attack to "the stress, the tension, the anger" caused by this loss, saying:[8]

---

8. A Spanish-language transcript appears in the appendix.

All that makes me sick. It's that [you have here] a person who . . . works his way up from the bottom to the top and this brings you from the top to the bottom. Really, what happened to me happened to many, many Argentine families. . . . I'm not talking about very wealthy people. We are workers. . . . I'm not the same man anymore. It was a lie. It's all gone. Forever. But I won't let it go. It's the principle of justice. The principle of law.

Strikingly, the *ahorristas* never garnered much popular support. Graciela, a lawyer in her midthirties offered a typical appraisal. She had lost tens of thousands of dollars in savings during the crisis, and that pecuniary loss precipitated a cascade of material and interpersonal losses, including divorce and the loss of her home. Sitting in the kitchen of her newly rented apartment in August 2006, she told me of her life and her economic losses in ways that echoed Arturo's narrative. She talked about growing up in a "very middle-class . . . family of immigrants . . . who worked hard and educated themselves." She emphasized themes of upward social mobility: her great-grandparents had left Spain and Italy to find jobs in Buenos Aires as maids, cooks, and factory workers; her grandparents had completed high school; her parents had gone to college and found white-collar work as a real-estate company manager and a legal secretary. As with Arturo, that narrative arc shifted with the 1990s, when she and her husband used their ample income from jobs in a prestigious law firm and an engineering firm, respectively, to deposit money in savings accounts and CDs as well as to buy stocks and government bonds. "We all thought we had finally arrived in the first world. . . . We thought we could save money and invest in a better future. The banks and the government told us it was safe."

With the crisis, her husband's firm was shuttered and the couple was compelled to give up their house and move in with Graciela's parents, along with her brother and grandmother. Over most of the following couple of years, the entire household depended on Graciela's income and that of her mother, a secretary, as her grandmother's pension became nearly worthless and everyone else had lost their jobs. By late 2003, the stresses of their living situation—the financial difficulties, the crowded quarters, the sharing of household duties, and the overall "atmosphere of tension"—precipitated Graciela's divorce. "I lost a lot," she told me, "not as much as others, but a lot for me. But what I had doesn't exist anymore."

At this point in the interview, I asked Graciela why, since she had lost so much, she had been reluctant to attend meetings or protests of *ahorristas* or to launch a lawsuit in an effort at restitution. Incredulous, she furrowed her brow and explained herself in terms that I heard over and over again from other critics of the *ahorristas*. She lamented that she "would never build the future [she] had planned." Nonetheless, she had only harsh words for the *ahorristas*, telling me, "Those people are crazy. They think they can recuperate something that doesn't exist. It's as if they've lost any sense of reality. That money is gone. It never really existed to begin with. It was all based on an illusion."

My interviews with Arturo and Graciela demonstrate that the disagreement between the *ahorristas* and their critics cannot be reduced to the quantity of their material losses: People in both camps lost comparable amounts of money in the crisis. Neither can their disagreement be attributed to readily apparent differences in political ideology or generation: The groups are similarly diverse in their allegiances to political party and their professed beliefs about politics, and, while the *ahorristas* were almost uniformly over the age of fifty, most members of their age cohort were just as critical of their efforts as were younger people. The relative socioeconomic position of the two groups similarly fails as an explanation: the long recession had dramatically swelled the ranks of the poor, creating the category of "the new poor," people with the background, education, and tastes of the middle class but without the means of realizing middle-class lifestyles, while simultaneously benefiting a small swath of middle-class people working in industries that had profited from the 1990s structural adjustments. Nonetheless, the meaning of the *corralito*, *corralón*, and devaluation cut across this "breach."[9] Across all these differences, people described the devaluation in similar ways, employing the tropes of deceit and truth, dreams and awakening.

The justificatory claims of the *ahorristas* and their critics sprang out of a contradiction in the very foundation of monetary value. As Hart (1986), among others, has long reminded us, that contradiction is always present as a potential because money's role as token of credible authority relies on both the state and the market. While it normally lurks unseen in everyday transactions, that contradiction becomes suddenly apparent in contexts such as the 2001–2002 crisis, which forced apart these two grounds of monetary value. Nonetheless, while the debate between *ahorristas* and their critics indicates that the devaluation forced open a contradiction between the state and the market as the basis of monetary value, key questions remain.

As I concluded my conversation with Graciela that blustery, cold day in August 2006, I was putting on my coat to leave when she kissed me goodbye and said, "Never forget, Sarita, those people want to ignore the reality of the market to preserve the neoliberal fantasy of the one-to-one. It's an impossibility."

The delegitimation of the *ahorristas*' claims is striking. Despite the

---

9. For an account of the emergence of this "social breach" (*brecha social*), see Armony and Kessler 2004; Minujin and Anguita 2004; and Svampa 2001.

impressive macroeconomic gains of 2003–2007, major economic indicators had barely returned to the levels of the late 1990s, when impoverishment, inequality, and unemployment had already reached historically unprecedented levels (Svampa 2011, 25). Indeed, the devaluation had amounted to a massive redistribution of wealth away from pensioners, savings-account holders, and the citizenry in general toward large-scale debtors (Lim 1999; López 2005). Nonetheless, the socialization of private debt in a context of persistent economic insecurity was accepted not merely as unavoidable, but, remarkably, as legitimate. What accounts for that legitimacy? And how can we make sense of the paradox of "the reality of the market" being framed as the antidote to a "neoliberal fantasy"?

In the stories of Graciela and so many others, the devaluation did more than deprive individuals of a goodly portion of their personal wealth. It also revealed that past wealth to have been illusory all along. In other words, the devaluation may have been revelatory, but it was not liberatory. For people like Graciela, it did not lay bare a straightforward reality; it did not clear a space for empowered experimentation. Instead, it imposed what Selene had called an "unsatisfiable and paralyzing demand" to interpret its "meaning" and to recognize "the fact that we are not a normal country." In other words, for many, the devaluation appeared as simply the most recent instantiation of a *longue durée* of crisis, in which disruption and abnormality lurked at all times, even within moments of apparent continuity and normality. After all, 2002 was by no means the first time Argentines had seen their country default on its foreign debt or devalue its currency. As a result, they insisted that the crisis disallowed the kind of critique that could be satisfied by either horizontalist experimentation or monetary restitution. It demanded a mode of critique that brooked no satisfaction and opened up a field of interminable interpretive labor folded into a sentimental structure of inevitable national failure.

MONEY AND THE USUAL SUSPECTS

Selene and Víctor responded to the "unsatisfiable and paralyzing demand" of interpretation by employing well-worn discursive elements drawn from psychoanalytic and conspiracy theories and familiar to even the most irregular participant in Argentine public discourse. Selene described the devaluation as "the ultimate victory of the reality principle over the pleasure principle" and argued that the previously overvalued peso had resulted from the Argentine "psyche's" tendency toward self-aggrandizing misrecognition. Víctor agreed but cautioned against overlooking the "systems of power and influence" that had led to the devaluation. "The speculators and the IMF, the US and the EU—they plotted to manipulate the market and subvert the peso for their own interests," he countered. As for the *ahorristas*, Selene declared that although they were "victims of a mentality" imposed by "North American and imperialist interests," they embodied the worst aspects of a "morally depraved nation" and proved that Argentina "will never be a modern country." For his part, Víctor considered the *ahorristas* to be trapped "in a melancholic relationship to their lost money," which they had "perversely incorporated as an essential part of their selves." Continuing in this way for a good half hour, my friends agreed with one another by continually reasserting and intermingling two counterpoised approaches: One explored the contradictory impulses of the national psyche, while the other tracked a conspiracy in the opaque machinations of foreign actors.

It was no accident that Selene and Víctor drew on psychoanalytic and conspiracy theories. (This is fitting, of course, since neither psychoanalytic nor conspiracy theories allow for the accidental.) A financial crisis is structured as a series of revelations in which markets are suddenly understood to have overvalued some good. It therefore conjures the categories of apparent and real value and demands that market actors and news consumers alike participate in the semiotic process by which these two levels are repeatedly reconstituted with respect to one another. Speculative profits (accrued by positing a gap between the apparent and the real) evaporate overnight in a movement of material loss and representational disorder that bears little resemblance to the rational corrections of an efficient market.[10] Opposed in their conceptualizations of agency and in their localizations of responsibility, psychoanalytic and conspiracy theories address that process as antinomically linked genres of interpretation (Bakhtin 1986, 60). Elaborating themes of loss in a style of savvy didacticism, they posit a world bifurcated between the manifest and the latent and unfold through a revelatory structure that frequently upends sociomoral orders.[11]

In this sense, people subverted economistic explanations and offered a self-reflexively suspicious counterknowledge rooted in its production outside the centers of symbolic and financial capital and in its exclusion from their associated regimes of truth.[12] In a context of monetary devaluation,

---

10. For a related discussion of the representational dynamics of financial crisis, see Appadurai 2015. Tellingly, Canetti (1984, 186) describes hyperinflation in Weimar Germany as a "witches' Sabbath," an image that captures nicely the experience of uncontrollable monetary loss in the Argentine case as well.

11. Turkle (1992) and Marcus (1999) offer insightful analyses of these features of psychoanalytic and conspiracy theories, respectively.

12. For an extended analysis of the counterhegemonic dynamics of conspiracy theories in particular, see Briggs 2004 and Faubion 1999.

they constructed a highly valued mode of subjectivity predicated on sophisticated discernment.[13] However, that counterknowledge and its associated mode of subjectivity were decidedly ambivalent. "We have been forced to accept that we cannot control the value of the peso; only the market can do so. We cannot simply declare ourselves part of the first world," Víctor reflected, "but where that leaves us, it's impossible to say." Claiming to reveal the interests and desires that had led to the devaluation, these widely practiced interpretive practices might have seemed to promise some solution to the problem of monetary loss. Yet the vast majority converged in the conclusion that the devaluation must be accepted, monetary loss assumed, and the market acknowledged as the arbiter of monetary value. Those who, like the *ahorristas*, contradicted this conclusion seemed to be clinging to what one of my neighbors called "a neoliberal fantasy that can never come true in this country."

Post-crisis Buenos Aires was a place, it bears repeating, where suspicious interpretation constituted a common social practice, not only in interviews with US anthropologists but also in newspaper editorials, radio programs, dinner party conversations, and all manner of formal and informal settings. Across contexts, discussion routinely sought to uncover the latent structure of manifest phenomena, and this style of critique stood not so much as the rarified analysis of bohemian intellectuals but as a mundane modality of interpersonal interaction, a modality that promised to constitute its practitioners as quintessentially modern subjects—as knowing subjects capable of perceiving the patterns that organize mass society, even when those patterns revealed the speaker's failure to fully instantiate the promises of modernity.

Several years after the fact, when discussing "the crisis," people frequently offered me lengthy narratives like Arturo's and Graciela's, which articulated biography and history as twinned stories and where the personal stood as token of the national type.

Money is, of course, known for its copulative capacity, equating, for example, linen with coats under the sign of Value (Marx 1992). Here, the peso equated the personal and the national under the sign of failure. Speakers most commonly began by gesturing to the early twentieth century, that oft-mythologized era of European immigration and economic growth, and concluded by framing the devaluation as having exposed the impossibility of that era's aspirations. Structured by tropes of futile work, thwarted sacrifice, and downward mobility, these narratives offered a historical account

---

13. On conspiracy theorizing and psychoanalytic theorizing as practices of subject formation, see Boyer 2006 and Hollander 1990, respectively.

of the peso's failure to perform its normative functions. The plot was one of realization, of coming to see that one had misunderstood the nature of money, of Argentina, and even of one's self. They amounted, in other words, to suspicious retrospectives on the illusions of Argentine middle-classness as shaped by the currency peg, which, in Graciela's words, had promised that Argentina "had finally arrived in the first world." Even people like Graciela and Arturo, who vehemently disagreed about the legitimacy of the *ahorristas'* claims, agreed that the devaluation had revealed the illusory nature of the currency peg's promises. His lost money "was a lie," Arturo exclaimed. "It never really existed," Graciela declared.

The currency peg epitomized an era in which a recent history of dictatorship and democratization and ongoing questions of justice and social welfare were "subsumed . . . [by] the overwhelming desire for economic stability" (Munck 2001, 74). Following fifteen years of declining real income levels and standards of living and a searing period of hyperinflation, the newly elected president, Carlos Menem (1989–1999), instituted a slew of structural adjustments, including the privatization of state industries, which threw millions out of work while temporarily flooding government coffers with foreign capital, and the loosening of trade restrictions, which allowed an unprecedented flow of consumer imports while weakening domestic production. While those measures proved controversial, the tremendously popular currency peg constituted the cornerstone of his reforms.

Throughout the 1990s, politicians, economists, journalists, and laymen alike talked of how the peg "ended hyperinflation" (Canitrot 1994, 88), made foreign capital a stabilizing "stakeholder" in the national economy (Treisman 2004, 412), and, in the words of one banker in 2003, "provided a foundation for economic growth and political stability . . . [and] secured Menem's reelection." In Menem's own words, the one-to-one "brought Argentines into the first world."[14] Even at the height of the 2001–2002 crisis, when it was clear to most economists and foreign observers that the country simply could not afford the peg, politicians of all persuasions refused to broach the topic. President Duhalde declared the one-to-one "inviolable" and "an essential part of Argentine law" only weeks before he abandoned the peg.[15]

Upholding the peg had been the simple, if expensive, matter of maintaining dollar reserves equal to the number of pesos in circulation. In this way, the legal stipulation of peso-dollar equivalency constructed that elusive but all-important quality of confidence by treating the dollar as the

---

14. Daniel Muchnik, "Uno a uno, deme dos: Cuando creímos en la fantasía del primer mundo," *Perfil*, July 12, 2009.

15. "Duhalde adelantó que la devaluación 'está descontada,'" *La Nación*, January 4, 2002.

foundational embodiment of value.[16] This was a confidence that had long proved elusive in a national economic history marked by the successive introduction and collapse of currency regimes. Having maintained its neutrality during the Second World War, Argentina was the only Latin American country not invited to participate in the 1944 Bretton Woods Conference and did not become a signatory of the Bretton Woods Accords until 1956. Between 1956 and 1971 (when Nixon abandoned the gold standard and allowed the Bretton Woods system to disintegrate), Argentina attempted to fix its currency to the US dollar.

However, balance-of-payment problems and high inflation rates complicated those attempts, prompting various Argentine governments to adopt crawling pegs, that is, regularly scheduled, small-scale devaluations. During the 1970s and 1980s, efforts to manage the currency exchange rate became even more vexed in the face of changing international interest rates and the massive growth of the foreign debt; those efforts took the form of crawling pegs as well as dramatic devaluations and even the introduction of entirely new currencies. Sweet money and strong money, the Argentine peso and the legal peso, the national coin peso and the national currency peso, the austral and the convertible peso: all were tokens of political regimes that failed to realize the dreams of pecuniary wealth conjured by the very name of the country (Argentina, *argentum* = silver, money, as the poem at the beginning of this chapter reminds us). It was in response to this history that the currency peg was structured in a way similar to the gold standard, in which a government stipulates by law that a currency is grounded in and can be exchanged for a substance that possesses a supposedly essential value—here, the US dollar rather than a precious metal.[17]

Menem's policies did produce a measure of economic growth, if only temporarily and if only for relatively privileged parts of society. The stable value of the peso gave a wide swath of Argentines unprecedented purchasing power over imported consumer goods. Travel abroad suddenly became imaginable for many, with those of comparatively modest means crossing the border to Bolivia or Brazil and those with more resources heading to

---

16. Because of its association with Menem's other reforms, the peg is considered in Argentina to epitomize neoliberalism, despite most orthodox economists' opposition to currency boards.

17. This monetary history points to the limitations of accounts of economic performativity as articulated by inflation-targeting central bankers and modern monetary theorists. In order for the concept of economic performativity to be helpful in understanding the dynamics of monies that do not serve as global reserve currencies, far greater attention to global geopolitical-economic dynamics is essential. While such an account is beyond the scope of this chapter, the Argentine case provides a wealth of materials for that project of reconceptualization.

Europe or the United States. (Disney World was an exceedingly popular destination.) It was the era of *deme dós*, or, "give me two of them," a phrase supposedly uttered by Argentines in stores and duty-free shops around the world.[18] The peg also prompted financial investment in the form of a massive influx of foreign capital, especially through the purchase of newly privatized, state-owned enterprises, from Argentine Airlines to the waterworks of Buenos Aires. On a smaller scale, individuals put their savings in banks and government bonds because, as they explained to me later, the peg "guaranteed it to be safe, guaranteed it to grow" and allowed them "to contribute to the country and its future." Throughout, a largely unremarked but predictable counterpoint to all these investment practices was the massive elevation of the foreign debt, which increased elevenfold during the decade of the one-to-one (Munck 2001).

For the middle-class people who lost so much money in the *corralito*, devaluation, and *corralón*, these investment practices had been driven by government and banking propaganda, as Arturo's story attests. When the one-to-one first became law, its architect, economy minister Domingo Cavallo, became one of the most popular public figures in the country overnight. He actively sold the nation on the notion of monetary equivalence through interviews and television appearances, and photographs of his grinning face hovered above juxtaposed peso and dollar bills.[19] The national government, in conjunction with large transnational banks such as Chase, Bank Boston, and CitiBank, ran an advertising campaign urging citizens to "Save in Bonds: Save in the Country" and describing the soon-to-be-defaulted on bonds as "solid and profitable" as late as 1999. The campaign's website, "www.ahorr.ar," engaged in wordplay by explicitly fusing national belonging, technological progress, and monetary savings. (*Ahorrar* means "to save"; the ".ar" extension is the Argentine extension for websites; and the graphic design of the logo transformed the "o" in "www.ahorr.ar" into the radiant sun of the Argentine flag.) Throughout, the advertisements demonstrated the dependability of bonds and savings accounts by pointing to the one-to-one as the bedrock of "price transparency."[20]

Reiterating the claims of these advertisements, people described for me in the years following the crisis that they had trusted in the promise that

---

18. For a detailed account of similar consumption practices among the Brazilian middle class, see O'Dougherty 2002.

19. Daniel Muchnik, "Uno a uno, deme dos: Cuando creímos en la fantasía del primer mundo," *Perfil*, July 12, 2009.

20. For an archive of these publicity campaigns, I am indebted to the Asociación de Ahorristas de la República Argentina, which compiled a collection of what it considered "deceptive publicity" in these advertisements and published that collection on its website, www.aara .org.ar, which is no longer active.

"the whole country [would] enter, finally, the first world" and that "secure in the present, [they] could plan for the future." They framed these investment practices, moreover, not merely as the means of generating personal wealth but also as a way of forging sociomoral bonds across spatial and temporal divides. An elderly woman spoke of her savings account as "my way of assuring that my children have the lives they deserve." One man described his savings and bonds as "a small contribution to my future, to my children's future, but also to the country's future." In interview after interview, people conjured up images of multiple generations working in tandem toward a more prosperous future, of nationwide pools of funds that would spur economic development and lift the country's most marginalized out of poverty. They said they had believed the government when it promised that the one-to-one would allow, in the words of a young teacher, "my family and my whole country to work toward the future, to achieve finally the future we dreamed of." The peg, a middle-aged housewife explained to me, had offered "the dream of a stable, middle-class country, the country we middle-class people had always worked toward. The dream of prosperity, stability, everything that is modern."[21]

In explaining how that "dream" had come to seem so real, many mined the psychoanalytic premise that consciousness assumes misrecognized forms, the manifestations of an always mediated unconscious logic (Freud 1989). People also availed themselves of Freud's later model (1990) of the psyche as structured by the conflict between the pleasure principle and the reality principle but also, and more fundamentally, by the opposition between this broad orientation toward vitality and the death drive, an aggressive compulsion to return the world to inorganic stasis. In this light, the devaluation figured as the moment when reality finally punctured national fantasies, generating a conflict that had to be managed, lest the country fall prey to the destructive impulses of the death drive.

Importantly, this understanding did not lay the matter to rest. Rather, it allowed people to take up different positions regarding the precise etiology of those fantasies. A retired nurse suggested a relation of Oedipal filiation (Freud 1960) between Argentina and Europe, while the waitress at my neighborhood café identified a disrupted mirror-stage identification (Lacan 1977) with the United States. A real-estate broker speculated about a melancholic (Freud 1957) libidinal investment in early-twentieth-century Argentina's economic promise, and a veterinary student pointed toward the production of capitalist chains of desire (Deleuze and Guattari 1983). Speakers rarely framed their accounts as definitive. As befits a middle-class public in which psychoanalytic therapy is an ongoing "technique of the

---

21. For a discusson of the affective dimensions of financial speculation, see Allon 2016.

self" rather than a one-off treatment of discrete symptoms, the psycho-analytic interpretation of the devaluation was a continual dialogue about Argentine identity through which participants embodied "certain aesthetic values" (Foucault 1992, 11).

Many of the very same speakers described a shadowy world of agents equipped with the arcane knowledge necessary to manipulate the financial system. Leaping across scales, focusing on willful actors, and insisting on direct connections where the social sciences are more likely to emphasize systemic logic and institutional mediation, conspiratorial accounts none-theless drew on a familiar economic model. After all, it is not only conspir-acy theorists who understand financial markets as fundamentally opaque because they "detach the value, cost, and price of money . . . from the fun-damentals of the economy" (LiPuma and Lee 2004, 2). Indeed, financial markets provide particularly fertile terrain for both conspiratorial theoriz-ing and conspiratorial action, given their curtailed accountability and the specialized nature of the field's instruments. Properly positioned individu-als, moving with an air of "alchemical" (Soros 2003) expertise, are indeed quite capable of executing financial maneuvers that exceed the controls of even the wealthiest nations. Especially relevent is the history of intimate relations between authoritarian regimes and international financial inter-ests (see Kedar 2013), not to mention the role of secretive "money doctors" in manging financial crises (see Drake 1994 and Flandreau 2003). Search-ing out the agents responsible for the devaluation, people from across the political spectrum had no trouble in identifying the IMF, the European Union, the United States, "the political class," and "speculators" as the cul-prits. The nurse who identified an Oedipal relation between Argentina and Europe also waxed eloquent about politicians who had secretly moved their money before the banking freeze. The veterinary student so well versed in the works of Gilles Deleuze and Félix Guattari opined expertly about the mechanisms through which speculators and officials may have conspired.

Again, no single theory purported to be the last word. One of my neigh-bors, a widow with an abundance of free time, could often be found just outside our apartment building, chatting excitedly with some local resi-dent or store clerk about the latest exposé of some heretofore unknown detail concerning the devaluation. Instead of falsifying other theories, each account incorporated its antecedents, drawing together bits of evidence in an expanding web of insight. There was, quite simply, always more to know, and the pleasures of these chats lay in the conversational practice itself, not in the prospect of solving a mystery once and for all. As this elderly neighbor characterized it, "It is impossible to know the full truth. And yet, we must critique everything, ourselves included, in order to find a way to live."

It is tempting to view the dominant middle-class response to the devaluation—first protest, then resignation—as the unremarkable reaction to pecuniary loss, but such an assessment merely begs the question: What is the nature of the pecuniary in a context characterized by an understanding of money as an uncontrollable social fiction? Whether elicited by anthropological queries or neighborly remarks, interpreting the devaluation invoked a specific theory of money's normative functions. It was this folk theory that had underwritten the currency peg, which aimed to render the peso a token of the dollar so that it could finally work as money should. It would, of course, serve as a durable store of wealth and a reliable medium of exchange, but it would also serve as a temporal bridge, linking the present to the future, the short-term to the long-term. It would calibrate self-interest and social welfare by constructing mutually reinforcing circuits of economic prosperity and social connections.[22] Tied to the dollar, the peso would, at long last, function as capital, with the "occult quality of being able to add value to itself" (Marx 1992, 255). In this way, the peg had promised to generate a middle-class Argentina, its future grounded beyond the national territory in the stable, prosperous, and expansive space of the US dollar, a space depicted variously as the first world, the modern, and the normal.[23]

Abandoning the currency peg thus involved more than pecuniary losses. To be sure, the devaluation meant that as measure and store of value, the peso became unreliable, and that as medium of exchange, it became unavailable. But more than that, people claimed, the peso ceased to operate as a reliable medium of social, temporal, and spatial commensuration. Instead of securing a predictable future, the devalued peso imperiled daily survival. Instead of harmonizing individual and national interests, it rendered individual claims to monetary restitution detrimental to the financial system and repositioned middle-classness as an impossible future. Instead of allowing for the self-propagation of capital, the devalued peso morphed into a sort of anticapital, cannibalizing its own value as currency markets recalibrated their investments to account for the daily updates in the nation's plunging "country risk" assessments. However, the temporality of my formulations here is not quite accurate. My interlocutors insisted that these failures only *appeared* sudden. In fact, they declared, the peso had never *truly* performed those functions; it had only seemed to be real money because of the currency peg. In fact, they proclaimed, the peso had been false all along.

People thus cast the crisis as an event that refigured the 1990s as a duplic-

---

22. Within economic anthropology, there is a large literature on the functions of money that exceed the definitions of orthodox economists. See, e.g., Bloch and Parry 1989; Guyer 1995; Hart 2000; Maurer 2005; and Peebles 2011; as well as Wilkis 2018 and Zelizer 1997, 2005.

23. On the "culture of growth" in financial speculation, see Allon and Redden 2012.

itous era during which they had been complicit in carrying out neoliberal injustices. A schoolteacher remarked, "In some sense, maybe we wanted the crisis because of our own deep ambivalence about Menemist society. The conflict between fantasy and reality had become too great to bear; only the crisis, which is a form of social death, could resolve that conflict." Similarly, a young, struggling architect told me that the devaluation "forced us to see reality for the first time, to see the injustices that we had committed in the service of neoliberal fantasies." A retired accountant summed up the post-crisis appraisal: "Neoliberalism was a confidence game from the beginning, but the one-to-one blinded us, the middle class, to it all—to the unemployment and the poverty, to the recession, all of it." In other words, they declared retrospectively, the peg had not only failed to serve as a vehicle for national progress; it had also ensured national failure by disguising processes of plunder in a veneer of self-deception.

LOSS AS GAIN

One acquaintance, a psychoanalyst in his midfifties, described the devaluation in a supremely poetic formulation: "We thought we were living in the clouds, but it was a dream. We woke up and realized they were clouds of farts. Our own farts. The IMF had anaesthetized us with our own farts."

In describing that awakening, people framed the devaluation as the manifestation of an all-encompassing process, long ignored but now undeniable. In part, they were capturing a four-year-long recession that, by 2002, had generated unprecedented levels of unemployment, poverty, and inequality (Kessler 2000, Minujin and Anguita 2004).[24] However, they also spoke of the relentless, decades-long devaluation of other stores of value such as educational degrees (which had become less convertible into social prestige) and occupational positions (which had become less reliable indicators of salary, status, and autonomy). These more gradual devaluations had also been masked, they insisted, by the counterfeit prosperity of the currency peg.

In 2002, many people turned out of necessity to barter networks for everyday commodities. However, they made a virtue of that necessity by framing nonmonetized exchange as the means of constructing a national

---

24. In part, they were also describing decades of economic policies that, since the military coup in 1976, had increased the foreign debt to an unserviceable level, eroded social welfare institutions, and seen average real income decline dramatically (Beccaria 2002; López and Romero 2005). For more on the sociocultural dynamics of increasing inequality, see Kessler 2000 and Minujin and Anguita 2004.

community grounded in spontaneous, unmediated, and authentic relationships that would resist devaluation. At the time, they had spoken of "reinventing the market," "even reinventing life," according to principles of "trust and reciprocity" (Bombal 2002, 100–1). Within a year, however, the networks had collapsed under a wave of scandals that, in eerie echoes of the peso's devaluation, alleged that a shadowy conspiracy had induced hyperinflation with counterfeit barter tickets.[25] Somewhat later, many former barter participants told me the movement had been doomed from the start, since, in the words of one, "You can't escape money; the tickets were just like the peso, because they were ours, they were Argentine."

If it proved impossible "to escape money," people nonetheless seized on the sense of awakening to assume a suspicious stance not only with regard to money (which they had precious little of) but also to other stores of value. Scores told me that they "no longer prioritized money or material goods," because "in this country one can't know what will happen tomorrow." Interviewees described people, themselves included, who in the 1990s had "worked like mad . . . and accumulated a ton of money, and never enjoyed it," or who "had such pride and devotion for [their] job[s], which disappeared overnight," or who "had truly believed in education as a way of ensuring a tranquil life, only to find [themselves] impoverished." These sorts of errors, they explained, stemmed "from the fantasy . . . of the one-to-one," from the belief "that Argentina was a normal nation." Countless interviewees proclaimed, as did one bus driver, that the devaluation had allowed him to see that during the 1990s, "this country, this middle class, we abandoned our emphasis on culture; we became materialist and focused on money and status."

This self-conscious antimaterialism unfolded at a moment when, despite dramatic improvements, people had not recovered from the losses of 2001–2002, much less the losses of the years prior. As a result, most people were not (yet) in a position to debate whether or how to invest their pesos (cf. D'Avella 2014). Instead, many explicitly rejected an aesthetic of consumerism, now associated with the currency peg, and emphasized an aesthetic of ethicized culture as the hallmark of what one schoolteacher called "our middle-class values, our morality, our culture." This was also a moment when appeals to precisely those values played a key role in political discourse, as politicians of all stripes sought to locate themselves squarely on

---

25. Although called "barter networks" (*redes de trueque*) and popularly framed as constituting a space of interpersonal trust and solidarity, exchange was mediated by "tickets" (*boletos*), which, like state-issued currencies, became subject to problems of counterfeiting and inflation.

the right side of history by loudly rejecting the currency peg and claiming to inaugurate a more moral social order.[26] Of course, those appeals frequently ran up against a robust suspicion. Nonetheless, the turn to a highly moralized political discourse is in keeping with the overarching frame of crisis and critique.

Whether alongside or in the absence of remunerated labor, my interlocutors juggled seemingly endless activities, from yoga and English lessons to book fairs and theater groups. Advertisements for psychoanalysis appeared constantly in newspapers and even on street signs and garbage cans. Late-night dinner parties in the houses of family and friends, afternoon coffee breaks in neighborhood cafés, and chance neighborly encounters offered routine settings for all manner of convivial conversation, including, of course, suspicious crisis talk. Undergirding all these practices was the insistence that, in the words of one young mother and amateur actor, "With the devaluation, we woke up in this country to the fact that we, the middle class, had trusted in the untrustworthy. Now, it's a moment to find what's really valuable, to turn inwards and develop ourselves." Crucially, that self-development did not typically take on the patina of cheery optimism so common to North American self-help guides; it was more often pursued doggedly but wryly—like crisis theorizing—as a necessary way of confronting Argentine reality. As another young, unemployed actor put it, "I feel the need to better myself since I, too, am a member of this pathetic country." The ethicization of unremunerated activities also propelled an efflorescence of voluntarism and "solidarity-building" initiatives that aimed to construct an interclass national public grounded in the cultivation of individual ethical commitments.[27]

Given the difficulty of converting a particular education into an appropriate job or a lifetime of work into a respectable retirement, it is unsurprising that the devaluation shifted the value of work, education, and money. However, rather than lose their importance, they were refigured as ends in themselves through which people constructed their lives as projects of personal and interpersonal development. In the words of one prominent psychoanalyst and public intellectual (Bleichmar 2002, 90–91), "If we have gained something, it is the loss of the shame of being poor. And that lets us

---

26. It should be noted that, early on, appeals to specifically "middle-class values" were voiced by members of both the newly dominant Kirchner faction of the Peronist party and its opposition. By 2007, however (the end of the period I am discussing), the Kirchner front spoke mostly to "the people," while the many, splintered opposition groups were mobilizing "the middle class" as an antipopulist, anti-Peronist figure (Adamovsky 2009, 475–92).

27. This is not dissimilar from the mode of "ethical citizenship" Muehlebach (2012) theorizes in the roughly contemporaneous context of northern Italy, a resonance I return to in chapter 5.

start to recuperate the dignity of who we are: people who, with precarious means, not only arrived on these shores and survived, but lived in solidarity with our families . . . who continue writing, painting, making film, music, theater . . . trying to know who we are, to produce something new, to open our eyes together." In this way, the crisis was constituted retrospectively as an event composed in equal parts by monetary loss on one hand and epistemological and ethical gain on the other.

Of course, Buenos Aires has always been a city of extraordinary busyness, and its middle class has long pursued embodied modes of cultural distinction (Joseph 1999; Guano 2004). Precisely by recontextualizing these long-standing practices, and by repositioning them over and instead of material stores of value—the peso above all—people were participating in a historically specific process of naturalization and revaluation (Briggs and Bauman 1995, 584). Animated by critiques of the peso as the indexical icon of a failed national history, that process allowed monetary losses to be accepted not as a matter of practicality but of principle. The crisis thus prompted an embrace of practices of individual self-realization that, not coincidentally, reasserted a historically long-standing and geographically widespread mode of middle-class distinction predicated on ineffable morality and cultural discernment.[28]

Popular consensus held that the 2002 devaluation marked the culmination of a decades-long process that had eroded the material grounds—monetary and otherwise—for membership in what my informants variously called the first world, modernity, the middle class, and normality. It therefore prompted a search for other metrics of evaluation (and here, I mean the term in both its monetized and ethicized senses) and other modes of exchange (both material and interpretive). However, the positive revaluation of self-cultivating practices is not evidence of utilitarian maximization or instrumental strategy. Rather, it is evidence of practical reasoning through which people grappled with the logistical and interpretive problems occasioned by the collapse of the currency peg.

In so doing, they generated a post-crisis, middle-class "representational economy" (Keane 2003; see also Keane 2018) linking together the circulation of money and goods as well as words, practices, and other signifying media. Within that representational economy, critiques of neoliberalism, middle-class aspirations, and even the speaker's own capacity for self-delusion were not epiphenomenal commentary. Rather, suspicious crisis talk was a key practice of daily life, organizing and regimenting both the devaluation of material stores of value and the positive revaluation of embodied practices of value. As such, these utterances circulated as a privileged currency within

---

28. See, e.g., Elias 1982; Bourdieu 1984; O'Dougherty 2002; Liechty 2003.

an expansive representational economy predicated on the principle of suspicion. Crisis talk thus turned loss into gain and transformed monetary "failure" into the coin of the realm.

OF MICE AND TRAPS

To conclude here, however, would be to dwell in the interpretive alchemy that transformed monetary loss into the experience of epistemological and ethical gain. Such an emphasis would elide the profound negativity that remained even after that alchemical transformation. I insist on concluding with that negativity, for even Silvia Bleichmar's talk of recuperated dignity unfolded as a contrapuntal response within the overarching affective harmonics of *decepción*, the same word that Mabel used in chapter 2 to bring together the experience of both disappointment and disillusion that the devaluation involved and that Bleichmar's (2002) book, entitled *Country Pain*, invoked.

The acceptance of the devalued peso resulted from all manner of practical considerations. However, it also emerged out from an affinity between the suspicious crisis talk I have described and the logic of monetary value. After all, money is not meant to *be* valuable, but rather, to signify value. When money simply works as measure, medium, or store of value, we may overlook the predicated "gap between its material form and the ground of value it supposedly represent[s]" (Poovey 2008, 62). On the other hand, speculation, capitalization, and arbitrage depend on the shrewd recognition and manipulation of that very gap.[29] In other words, as financial tool—as capital—the monetary form refuses the possibility of definitive grounding in order to open up the possibility of profit through practices of cunning analysis. Crisis, then, is simply the inversion of financial practices predicated on a posited gap between economic fundamentals and the market valuations. As such, the possibility (or, perhaps better, the inevitability) of crisis is built into the logic of the monetary form itself. So, too, is suspicious crisis talk, which intuits the groundless play of monetary value and engages it in a formally similar play of critique.[30]

Maurer (2005, 166) argues that the recognition of money as social fiction "carries with it the moral obligation to reconstruct and remake," as well as a pluralistic imaginary that orients the practices of the anthropologist as much as those of alternative currency practitioners and Islamic bankers. Within that imaginary, he proposes, to work on money is to play with the

---

29. See Marx 1992, 255; LiPuma and Lee 2004, 37.

30. For an extended discussion of the semiotics of monetary value, see Keane 2008.

ideology work of the fetish, conceptualized, following Slavoj Žižek, as the "(unconscious) fantasy structuring our social reality." (Žižek 1989, 33; quoted in Maurer 2005, 114). The point, in other words, is not to dispel monetary illusions but rather to restage money's phantasmatic apparatus, just as *The Mousetrap*, Shakespeare's play-within-a-play, foregrounds "not the revelation of truth . . . [but] the particular staging of truth." (Maurer 2005, 114).

My middle-class Argentine interlocutors would agree with Maurer's appraisal in the abstract. Yet they insisted that they were practically unable to meet that "moral obligation to reconstruct and remake" the peso. They told me that the market-valued peso must be accepted despite its participation in what one young plumber called "an unjust global system that relies on our fidelity to carry out its treachery." Like Maurer, a thirty-year-old veterinarian also cited Žižek (a familiar personage in the Buenos Aires mediascape even before he married his second wife, a fashion model and the daughter of an Argentine Lacanian psychoanalyst): "We all know that money is a fetish, but, as Žižek says, understanding isn't controlling. Our money is part of a global fantasy network. We necessarily participate despite it all." To return to the metaphor of the mousetrap, my interlocutors insisted that we attend to the compulsory as well as the fictional and playful dimensions of the monetary fetish.

After all, a key aspect of the middle-class Argentine experience of monetary value was the diagnosis of the peso's susceptibility to crisis and the supposedly clear-eyed recognition of the material limits to monetary play. As such, people's long-term experiences with the peso and their experience of the peso as a historically and geopolitically located monetary form entailed a suspicion that extended to a host of other value forms, but not to money as such. It was in the peso as a resolutely concrete historical form, and *not* as an instantiation of money in general, that my interlocutors diagnosed national failure. They insisted that market evaluations reflected real and unavoidable distinctions between durable currencies (i.e., the US dollar) and their false counterfeits (i.e., the Argentine peso).[31] The peg's collapse, then, eroded confidence in the peso, but not in the dollar, which continued, for a great many people within the post-crisis, middle-class public, to serve as the ideal type of the monetary form.

Looking beyond the configuration of post-crisis, middle-class Buenos Aires, what are we to make of my interlocutors' laments about the limits of critique? As I have suggested, we would do well to consider the extent to which suspicion inheres within money itself, and not simply in this particular context of so-called peripheral modernity (Sarlo 1988). Keane (2002, 65, 67, 69) argues that the representational economy of liberal capitalist

---

31. For a discussion of more and less durable currencies, see Guyer 2012 and Neiburg 2010.

modernity is predicated on sincerity as a privileged normative ideal. Relying instead on the inverted principle of suspicion, the critical practices I have been discussing illuminate the underbelly of that representational economy. It is through practical, situated engagements with money that people form and reform their economic dispositions, transforming what Bourdieu (1984) calls objective political-economic conditions into subjective dispositions. In post-crisis, middle-class Buenos Aires, those engagements were resolutely suspicious in their logic, foregrounding the fictitious—even duplicitous—qualities of money, but also, by extension, of a far more general representational economy that people judged to be as unreliable as it was inescapable. In this way, these ambivalently critical monetary practices offer insight not only into the experiential dimensions of money and its crises but also into that economy's discomfiting and paradoxical resiliency. And they show that resiliency to have come about not despite but *through* a century of successive financial crises.

It is to that resiliency that so many of my interlocutors pointed when offering me their resounding chorus, "We simply must accept the devaluation. There is no other way." Or, in the words of the acquaintance who so eloquently spoke of clouds of farts, "Now that we have woken up, we can smell all too well what has happened. But we can't sniff our way out."

4

EXHAUSTED FUTURES

> Then every thing includes itself in power,
> Power into will, will into appetite;
> And appetite, a universal wolf,
> So doubly seconded with will and power,
> Must make perforce a universal prey,
> And last eat up himself.
>
> Shakespeare, *Troilus and Cressida*

A version of this chapter appeared in *Comparative Studies of Society and History* (Muir 2016).

BANAL ILLEGITIMACY

Many observers have argued that the 2001–2002 Argentine financial crisis precipitated a crisis of legitimacy (e.g., Grimson 2004). Marked by the largest sovereign default in world history, a dramatic currency devaluation, and nationally unprecedented levels of unemployment and poverty, the crisis also entailed acute political disarray, with five men shuffling in and out of the presidency in two weeks. As the economic model of the 1990s revealed itself to have bankrupted the nation and governmental agencies demonstrated themselves incapable of fulfilling even the most pressing social needs, Argentines from an extraordinarily wide range of social backgrounds and ideological commitments demanded that the regime end.[1]

Only a few years later, the legacy of that repudiation had proved paradoxical. On the one hand, the sense of imminent catastrophe had waned as day-to-day living had become, if not normal, then routine. On the other hand, there lingered a sense of banal illegitimacy, a widely shared sense that the veneer of quotidian routines belied a more fundamental condition of lawlessness and immorality, frequently articulated in the terms of conspiracy and psychoanalytic theory. That sense of illegitimacy found its clearest and most common expression in the idiom of corruption.

Politicians and financiers were the most widely condemned incarnations of enduring but discredited institutions. However, the regular necessity of submitting to those institutions' bureaucratic procedures could generate a sense of complicity whenever people paid their taxes, voted, or visited the bank. Even interpersonal relations could assume a related taint of moral turpitude, as people wondered aloud whether a friend had taken advantage of them or, most surprisingly of all, whether they themselves had taken advantage of a friend. It was to this general sense of mistrust that my acquaintances referred when they spoke of living in an age of "total corruption" in which social virtues had given way to the unavoidable prioritization of egoistic instrumentalism.

The diagnosis of total corruption was productive within the post-crisis Buenos Aires middle class in the sense that it produced social relations, from the interpersonal to the national. However, it was also negative in that it lamented a host of social losses. In other words, "total corruption" operated as a folk category of critique through which people grappled with

---

1. See Habermas 1975 for a pertinent theorization of a legitimation crisis as a series of conflicts beginning on economic terrain and escalating onto the administrative and the sociocultural.

dynamics of mistrust, illegitimacy, and self-destruction, dynamics that they felt to have exceeded all bounds and to threaten sociality itself.[2] The diagnosis of total corruption thus marked a historical stance widely adopted within the post-crisis Buenos Aires middle class. That stance inverted the familiar idea that national history is a teleological progression toward a better future. In twentieth-century Argentina, as in so many places, that generic narrative, with its accompanying civilizational and racial imaginaries, had long posited the middle class as the protagonist of a national project oriented toward the telos of modernity. At the turn of the twenty-first century, the economic collapse seemed to many the death blow to that long faltering project.

In taking up this historical stance, people posited corruption as an internally driven and irreversible process of sociomoral decay that barred Argentina from ever living out its once-projected future. At the same time, for an impoverished middle class, this historical stance constituted the grounds of a conflictual but cohesive mode of quotidian sociality and national belonging. Thus, a particular historico-moral sensibility marked the idea of corruption, which bound together recent events with long-term patterns in order to lament the impossibility of a national future: an alleged condition of historical exhaustion.

Consider a brief excerpt from a 2005 interview with a psychoanalyst who worked with middle-class analysands in Buenos Aires and poor analysands in an exurban neighborhood a two-hour bus ride away. In the midst of a discussion about social inequality, Federico turned his gaze to corruption. First, he criticized the "selfishness" of politicians and their alleged manipulation of poor voters. Both the poor and the politicians, he asserted, were responsible for Argentina's "obscene social marginalization." He went on, however: "It's woven into our social fabric, but even more, the corruption is in our hearts." Asked to clarify, he continued, "We [Argentines] are corrupt in our hearts. . . . In all our relationships we are corrupt. We're corrupt with our parents and our children, with our friends and our [romantic] partners. We always look to take advantage. We have fake relationships. . . . We have the politicians we deserve." Permeating every aspect of social life, corruption was the reason "Argentina cannot mature, can never be—as our dear president aspires—a normal country."[3]

Federico's commentary began in the public realm but moved fluidly

---

2. I have discussed this approach to corruption at greater length elsewhere (Muir and Gupta 2017; Muir 2021).

3. As mentioned in chapter 2, *un país en serio* was Néstor Kirchner's 2003 presidential campaign slogan. My gloss here emphasizes its normative connotations, but one could well translate it otherwise, as "a serious country," as I did in the previous chapter.

into intimate relationships of romance and filiation. In Federico's telling, corruption described an egoistic but ultimately self-defeating orientation to the world. Because, he insisted, that orientation inheres within Argentine subjectivity, it erodes trust not only in public institutions but also in the supposedly pre-political domain where trust should simply go without saying. For Federico, corruption is not a problem to be solved: it is a compulsion toward self-destruction lodged in the interiority of even the speaker himself, whose insightful diagnosis effects no cure.

Federico was not alone in extending corruption in such directions and in bringing together, under a single, self-reflexively critical rubric, questions of interpersonal trust, political legitimacy, and national history. The categorial extension and plasticity of corruption demands that we attend first and foremost to the pragmatics of the term's use and that we treat it as a very particular kind of concept, as a folk category rather than a normative analytic, to be sure, but more specifically, as an evaluative category that inheres within and orients particular practices as well as discourses about those practices. In other words, by resisting the temptation to define the concept, we can illuminate its actual, practical life—its career as an elastic category of critique that, while a "notoriously weak analytic concept" (Elyachar 2005, 113), is nonetheless a notoriously robust folk concept.

This chapter centers on three events; each instantiated a different mode of apprehending, interrogating, and performing the stance of historical exhaustion implicated in that folk concept. All took place in Buenos Aires and its environs between 2003 and 2007 and involved people who assumed a middle-class "footing" (Goffman 1981). The first was an unsolicited confession offered up to me during an ethnographic interview. Here, the speaker framed her own career networking as an instance of a national propensity to exploit unfair advantages. The second took place in my neighborhood *hipermercado* ("hypermarket," the term for an especially oversized supermarket). There, a dispute over line etiquette precipitated collective outrage at the deterioration of civic decency. The third event was a televised spectacle in which Diego Maradona boasted of cheating in the World Cup. That melodramatic revelation allowed the soccer star to celebrate himself as the glorious incarnation of national audacity. In each event, the recognition of corruption, and of the speaker's participation in it, grounded membership in a national public characterized by the putatively uncontrollable transgression of its own norms.

At first glance, the idea of corruption might not seem to pertain to any of these three events. Nonetheless, in each case people seized the opportunity to mobilize the category of corruption in the service of evaluative claims about self and other, individual and nation. While the valence of those claims varied, in each case people denounced corruption in the same breath as they voiced their complicity with it. To return to my earlier formulation, these events were *productive* in that they grounded membership in a national public. At the same time, they indexed a *negativity* that we cannot simply gloss over, for the logic of each event hinged on the historical experience of loss that defined the Argentine middle class.

CORRUPTION AS RADICAL NEGATIVITY

An abiding preoccupation of the middle class, but also a relevant term in the everyday conversations of the poor, corruption figured routinely as the culprit for any number of political, economic, and social ills, from the crisis itself to the nation's rising Gini coefficient, its crumbling transportation infrastructure, and its entrenched political dynasties. As to the term's referent, corruption certainly described former president Menem's alleged embezzlement of US$60 million from prison construction projects. It also easily encompassed his alleged arms-smuggling ring, laundering of drug-trafficking funds, and eagerness to turn the privatization of state companies toward the enrichment of himself and his allies. Indeed, Menem and his neoliberal structural reforms stood in post-crisis Argentina as the very epitome of corruption, all the more so since he had gone unconvicted of his ostensible crimes in a court of law[4] (albeit not in the court of public opinion). However, the category also extended to the often-unspoken favors between lawmakers and business elites and to those between politicians and poor voters.[5] It named not only petty bribes but also tax evasion. It could describe employment secured through personal connections and even the subtle manipulation of loved ones. Popularly understood as a vicious and intractable problem responsible for the disintegration of social institutions ranging from democratic representation to the family, it was a category that, in its diffuse application, might have seemed to risk meaning nothing at all. Nonetheless, a tripartite logic cut across the otherwise sundry acts it encompassed and granted corruption a highly flexible, practical cohesiveness.

First, a decade's worth of bribery and clientelist scandals grounded the

---

4. In 2013 (well after the period I focus on here), Menem was convicted of arms smuggling but not of other alleged crimes. Despite this conviction, he was never sentenced, and the charges dismissed in 2018 due to the lengthy period of judicial limbo that had passed.

5. Although dismissals of clientelism as corrupt are closely associated with the middle class, they are also commonplace among poor people in Argentina. Considerable evidence suggests these critiques are correlated with the speaker's social distance from political brokers, not with socioeconomic status, per se (see Auyero 1999). I return to the issue of clientelism in chapter 5.

concept of corruption in the illegitimate conversion of value between the fields of the economic and the political. That model proved highly iterable, as people commonly extended it to other social fields, such as the domestic, as in the nepotistic abuse of bureaucratic authority and even the strategic manipulation of familial sentiment. A social worker, for example, once described one of her clients to me as "corrupt, she uses her son's success to gain influence over the other mothers": a first feature of corruption, therefore, was the self-serving and unsanctioned conversion of value from one social field to another.

Second, unlike straightforward theft or appropriation, corruption required the graceful imitation of legitimate practices, a requirement people indicated with terms like "fake," "counterfeit," and "dishonest." My interlocutors made clear that euphemisms such as "help" and "favors" were crucial to the felicity of a corrupt transaction. So, too, was the appropriate selection of person, request, and mode of reciprocity.[6] Corruption therefore demanded ongoing interpretive labor to discern the logic of even trivial interactions. "Don't trust anyone," an unemployed daughter of former factory workers warned me, wryly, in reference to a revoked birthday party invitation. Over and again, people corrected my glaring naïveté about the unfathomable depths of quotidian life.

Third, people insisted that false and illegitimate transactions did not merely coexist alongside their true and legitimate counterparts. Because corrupt practices imitated legitimate ones, they had penetrated the social world and consumed it from the inside out. The logic of illegitimate and egoistic instrumentalism had become not merely common, people declared, but unavoidable. As a restaurateur explained to me, "The bribes were absolutely necessary to open the restaurant. If I didn't pay, the situation would be one of unfair competition." The instrumentalization of the world appeared so complete as to compel complicity with its logic, threatening what one sociologist called "the disappearance of society" (Simonetti 2002, 47).

Thus, the logic of corruption granted it a particular historical directionality: Its origin may have been inscrutable (People routinely wavered between culturalist and individualist explanations, often in a single utterance.), but its advance through the body politic was supposedly inexorable.

In considering corruption corrosive to projects of political legitimacy,

---

6. Predictably, delayed reciprocity usually occurred across relatively minimal social distances and further bound the parties together, while prompt reciprocity, usually monetized, both presumed and entailed shorter-lived transactions between parties at greater social distance. See L. Lomnitz 1971 for an especially clear and insightful analysis of these tendencies. See Bloch and Parry 1989 for a theorization of this set of sociotemporal contrasts in terms of two different "transactional orders."

economic welfare, and social cohesion, my interlocutors echoed an understanding consolidated over the past several decades among international governing bodies, nongovernmental organizations, and the academic analyses that inform their policies. That understanding is epitomized in a declaration by the founder of Transparency International (a global monitoring agency) proclaiming that "corruption is one of our epoch's capital sins" (Eigen 2004, 15; see also Goldsmith 1999). Thought to erode civic trust and regime legitimacy and to inflate the costs of business transactions, corruption does not appear in these globally popular accounts as a problem of mere logistics or incentives; rather, it violates universal moral standards. That perspective has found fertile ground in Latin America, where academic and popular analyses alike routinely lambast machine politics and quid-pro-quo relationships between political and business elites. In post-crisis Buenos Aires, such criticisms routinely presupposed a middle-class footing, an implied position of ethical clarity, from which elites and poor alike were allegedly alienated.

By reframing certain favors, prestations, and alliances as culturally attuned forms of sociability, a good deal of anthropological attention to corruption has parochialized the bureaucratic norms that undergird notions of corruption.[7] A related body of literature has resituated corruption with respect to transparency as two "North Atlantic universals" (Trouillot 2003, 36) that have become especially relevant in neoliberal regimes of governance and accountability.[8] These works all share a concern with demonstrating the systematicity of corruption. That emphasis is welcome, because understandings of corruption tend to suffer from both methodological individualism and its inverse, culturalism. Both obscure the reasons corruption has become an object of especially intense academic scrutiny and popular concern around the world in recent decades, when structural adjustments and

---

7. For works emphasizing the disjuncture between bureaucratic-administrative and sociocultural norms, especially in postcolonial contexts, see Gupta 1995; Hasty 2005; Olivier de Sardan 1999; and D. Smith 2008. On the historical and sociocultural specificity of normative frameworks associated with processes of state formation that obtained in modern northeastern Europe, but that were absent in other contexts, including Argentina, see Chakrabarty 2000; Chatterjee 2004; Corradi 1985; Corrigan and Sayer 1985; Mbembe 2001; and G. O'Donnell 2007. All these analyses parochialize bureaucratic norms and reject facile assumptions of criminality, aberrance, and dysfunction.

8. See Jackson 2009; Mazzarella 2006; and Morris 2004 for analyses that frame transparency and corruption as the mutually constitutive poles of a far-reaching regime of visibility, the tensile logic of which undergirds the political and economic projects that corruption's critics seek to safeguard (Blunt 2004; Ferme 2001; Sanders 2003). In Argentina, that regime of visibility was crucial to the historical transition from the last military dictatorship (1976–1983)—marked by state terrorism, arbitrary "disappearances," and authoritarian decrees—to democratic rule, and it has since been integral to pursuits of good governance and human rights (Barrera 2013; Gandsman 2009).

related transformations have destabilized extant political-economic institutions and opened vast extralegal spaces of possibility for appropriation and influence or, even more dramatically, of "state capture" (Escudé 2006) and the wholesale "criminalization of the state" (Bayart, Ellis, and Hibou 1999).[9] As a result of this dialectic, as Morris (2004, 227) has argued with respect to contemporary Thailand, "wherever the discussion of social inequality was once explained by reference to the structural inequities inherent in . . . capitalism, it has been replaced by a rhetoric of transparency and corruption." The discourses and practices of corruption in post-crisis Argentina partook of just these sorts of systematicities (Astarita 2014). However, they also require attention to a rather different systematicity—that of self-destruction.

Claudio Lomnitz has argued that analyzing corruption requires attending to three levels: the functions and interests corrupt practices meet; the circulation of discourses of corruption; and the moral sensibility it occasions or, "how discourses and practices of corruption affect personal attitudes, definitions of self, and how corruption is cleansed or avoided" (1995, 38). I dwell on the last question, for two reasons. First, the problem of normative judgment "has been given surprisingly little attention" in studies of corruption (Granovetter 2007, 166–67). Second, the moral sensibility indexed by corruption was remarkable in post-crisis Buenos Aires. Here, people took up a category normally used to condemn dysfunctions in public bureaucracies in order to name breaches of interpersonal ethics. They mobilized a concept normally reserved for castigating others in order to fault themselves. And they attempted to "cleanse or avoid" that moral taint, but they routinely judged those attempts insufficient in the face of an insidious force that had infected every part of the body politic. Here, then, the practices and discourses of corruption evoked a complex experiential logic in which people understood themselves to be the agents of their own undoing.

Couched in these terms, it is only natural to turn to the study of witchcraft. Within the social sciences (especially within history and anthropology) the vast literature on witchcraft suggests a number of instructive parallels with corruption. For example, as with witchcraft, the discourses, practices, and morality that constitute corruption offer insights into the production and negotiation of normative frameworks, particularly those that orient the fields of politics and economics (Bratsis 2003; Corbin 2004). Also, as with witchcraft, because institutions of trust are at stake, corruption incites

---

9. On these new extralegal spaces of possibility and the new dynamics of political and economic inequality they have set in motion, see Gledhill 2003; Humphrey 2001; Osburg 2013; Roitman 2004; Shore 2005; and Smart 1993. On the role of corruption in exacerbating inequality in such contexts, see Bähre 2005; Gupta 2014; and D. Smith 2008. On the ways that anti-corruption movements have become the culturally appropriate vehicle for combating those intensified inequities, see Ansell 2014; Lazar 2005; and Schneider and Schneider 2003.

the mobilization of tremendous, sometimes frenzied, energies in efforts to counteract it (Eisenstadt and Roniger 1984; Hetherington 2011).[10]

However, there is a third dimension to witchcraft that is especially relevant to corruption as it figured in post-crisis Buenos Aires. This is the logic of what I call, following Munn (1986), "radical negativity." In developing a model of the practices through which people produced and transformed value on the island of Gawa (Papua New Guinea) in the late 1970s, Munn situates the witch as the emblem of intense egoism and secretive rapaciousness. Feeding a boundless appetite, the Gawan witch's predation exceeds simple theft by mimicking the dialectic of food transmission and consumption, that prototypical set of practices that constitutes Gawan self and society. As a result, witchcraft produces a "destructive, subversive value" that emerges out of but exceeds that normal dialectic of positive and negative value (1996, 13). In this way, the witch's limitless greed constitutes a form of cannibalistic reciprocity that threatens to "consume the community's capacity to exist" (227).[11]

Munn's analysis posits a radical negativity that inheres within and threatens to consume sociality itself. Named "witchcraft," that negativity is at once inextricable from and yet destructive of everyday social relations. It does indeed occasion efforts to reassert transgressed norms and reconsolidate social forms, but it exceeds the dialectic of social reproduction. Conjuring a powerful and uncanny realm, witchcraft arises out of, imitates, and threatens legitimate practices of exchange, recognition, and trust. Witchcraft, then, is not asocial; it is a self-destructive mode of sociality, a way of being that imperils its own conditions of possibility.

Like witchcraft, corruption in post-crisis Buenos Aires named a mode of radical negativity. With this concept, people grappled with the intuition that they harbored within themselves an uncontrollable force, at once foreign and yet deeply familiar, that threatened to erode the very grounds of sociality. In the words of Pocock, who reads a remarkably similar narrative in Machiavelli's *Discourses*, corruption refers to an unstoppable process of civilizational ruin in which "virtue itself . . . becomes cannibal—

---

10. On the capacity of witchcraft to display, actualize, and police social norms, see Austen 1993; Evans-Pritchard (1937) 1976; Geschiere 1997; Lévi-Strauss 1963; West 2005; and Wilson 1951. On the terrifying dynamics of witchcraft and witch hunts, especially as they express anxieties regarding trust and fairness in intimate networks of kith and kin, see Behringer 2004; Hutton 2004; Levack 1987; Robischeaux 2009; Piot 2010; Scarre and Callow 2001; and Trevor-Roper 1969.

11. A handful of other analyses have approached witchcraft in congruent ways. See, e.g., Siegel's (2006, 2) conceptualization of witchcraft as "a violence that inheres in the social and that turns against it" and Geschiere's (2013, xv) insistence that witchcraft's "implicit message [is] the warning that seeds of destruction are hidden inside social relations as such, even though these are vital for any human undertaking."

Shakespeare's 'universal wolf' that 'last eats up itself'" (1975, 204). In the following sections, I trace three progressively more robust but incomplete attempts in post-crisis Buenos Aires to, in Lomnitz's phrasing, "cleanse" people of that force.

THE CORRUPTED SELF

Throughout my fieldwork, in casual conversations and formal interviews, friends, acquaintances, and informants offered innumerable—and, at first, utterly surprising—confessions of their own personal corruption. In the midst of parsing blame and victimhood for societal ills, my interlocutors turned their critique back on themselves. Confessing their own wrongdoings and comparing themselves to the very politicians they had just been denouncing, they offered themselves up to me as the morally fallen instantiations of a corrupt society. In so doing, they framed their articulations as the profoundly private unveilings of a painful truth about a society in which basic orienting frameworks had been upended, each individual had become compelled to act counter to the common good, and the very possibility of sociality was in doubt.

One such confession occurred during a 2007 interview with a thirty-seven-year-old woman who worked as a social worker at a foundation that offered cultural activities, a soup kitchen, and other services to poor people in Buenos Aires. Seated in the kitchen of her modest apartment in a comfortably middle-class neighborhood of the city, Alicia was describing the ways the crisis had changed her job: the dramatic increase in the number of people seeking help; the sight of well-educated people unable to buy food, much less find a stable job in their fields; the way each encounter provoked anxiety about her own situation; and the difficulty of realizing the future she had imagined for herself.

All this had an identifiable cause, she proclaimed: "The real problem is corruption. You probably won't understand, because you're from the first world, from the US, but here the political class is completely corrupt, and that's the fundamental problem." Outraged, she went on to explain how illegitimate alliances between big business and the "political class" had sold off the country's "patrimony," destroying the nation's productive potential and throwing millions into poverty-induced dependence on the meager handouts offered by those same politicians. "They destroyed us. They destroyed the country and they don't care. We, the middle class, almost don't exist today," she said plaintively:[12]

---

12. A Spanish-language transcript appears in the appendix.

Only the ruling class and the humble people who sell their votes to survive. They don't understand the true value of the vote. Today, middle-class values don't have importance. I'm from a middle-class family, but not now. It's a shame, but don't pity us. We're the corrupt ones. There's a saying here: "Every country has the president it deserves." We deserved Menem and we deserve the politicians we have now. They come from us. From all of us. They don't exist in some far-off place. They're from here, and they reflect us.

She paused and looked down, took another sip of tea, and then looked up at me again, her jaw rigid and her eyebrows raised, as if challenging me to respond. Fumbling, I asked her what, then, she thought might be done. What kind of change might be possible?

"I don't see any possibility of change," she responded, "because it's impossible not to be corrupt here." She pointed her finger at me, proclaiming, "I'll show you how it is. This will surprise you, but with this you'll understand Argentina: I work in civil society, and even there, where supposedly everyone works to help others, there is a lot of corruption." She went on to decry the personal networks that had allowed her to secure employment and cited them as evidence of a "fundamental corruption" that had warped her most basic values. "I'm from a middle-class family, and I studied hard and I work hard, and I would want to get a job because of that, not through some personal relationship. It's pure corruption."

At this point, Alicia was almost screaming. She paused and proceeded more calmly, "You see, there's no way to get a job without taking advantage of your friends. . . . I can't escape it or I'd be left without a job. But more than that, I don't escape it because we're corrupt. Because the Argentine always seeks to take advantage. We take advantage of each other, of friends, of lovers. It's the famous creole cunning. It's the way we are." She shrugged her shoulders. "It's part of us. We're not a moral people. We'll never have justice. A hundred years ago we were supposed to become as rich as the United States. That will never happen. The Argentine mind can't change. The epoch of middle-class values is gone now. It's as if we have no future."

There are several features of Alicia's confession that warrant attention. Chief among them, for my purposes here, is its discursive structure through which she revealed the alleged "public secret" (Taussig 1999) of corruption and, especially, her own complicity. Drawing attention to its own performance as much as to its content, that revelation took place through the medium of Alicia herself. Simultaneously heroine and storyteller, her "I" was never unitary. As with Manuel, Ana, and Eduardo (in chapter 1), the first-person pronoun was alternately narrated and narrating, evidentiary and interpretive, national and personal, confessional and condemnatory.

Here, too, Alicia's movement across these "I"s established herself as a representative member of the nation, claiming to stand as both evidence and interpreter of its corruption. And, once again, the arrogation of interpretive authority only took place by virtue of a third category—the middle class "we"—which mediated the relationship between speaker and nation. If Alicia's critique mobilized a complex series of identifications and differentiations between herself and the nation, it was her proclaimed middle-classness that explained the fact of her utterance.

Most of the time, people in post-crisis Buenos Aires did not frame activities such as routine career networking as corruption, as if every aspect of life needed to abide by the "artificial virtue" (Hume 2003) of justice. However, an encounter with a US anthropologist constituted an invitation not only to opine about the national predicament but also to assert a very particular mode of distinction. Alicia's narrative was no casual conversation or everyday chat, but a pedagogical event through which she instructed a foreigner who was not only naïve but also a token of the United States and the first world, a token of a society that was supposedly not fundamentally corrupt, the sort of society Argentina should have become, in which both justice and economic welfare prosperity existed. Her confession was therefore an exaggerated performance of the difference between the "I" and the "you," between the corrupt and the noncorrupt, between Argentina and the United States. At the same time, the dismay she expressed served to construct similarities between her and me at the level of presumably shared moral values, which her narrative associated with a middle-class identity that had become impossible to realize in Argentina. Precisely by emphasizing her inability to refrain from corruption, she reasserted her identity as someone who held "middle-class values," who understood the value of a vote, the goals of justice and equality, the importance of hard work, and who was trapped in a country where that identity and those values were present only as the ghostly remainders of a lost era.

Long the most disposed to embracing liberal proceduralism, the Argentine middle class, routinely invoked as the embattled victim of the 2001–2002 crisis, came to occupy a privileged position with regard to post-crisis corruption critiques. This middle-class populism also often mobilized a disdain for the poor inextricable from anxieties about racialized threats to national progress (Guano 2004, Milanesio 2010). All this is quite apparent in Alicia's discussion of "humble people who sell their votes" (a phrase that conjured images of poorer, darker-skinned, marginalized masses—a stereotypical mainstay of Argentine political discourse) and in her eulogy for an "epoch of middle-class values," implicitly white and European, that could have grounded the national project.

However, corruption critiques did not simply offer a mode of social distinction. While that dynamic was essential, it does not fully account for the insistence on a dysfunctional practical logic through which individuals found themselves compelled to undermine the very institutions they valued so highly. That logic is brought into clearer focus when Alicia's confession sits alongside two other genres through which people performed that experience of complicity.

HYPERCORRUPTION

While confessions such as Alicia's surfaced regularly in my interviews, they were by no means a common feature of public discourse. Nonetheless, the sense of a community defined by a sort of negativity did emerge regularly in another guise: in face-to-face condemnations of the sorts of mundane breaches of etiquette one routinely suffers in the course of navigating any busy urban landscape.

In post-crisis Buenos Aires, it was exceedingly common for people to comment on "the lack of norms" when reprimanding one another for failing to abide by the unwritten rules of thumb that enable everyday social coordination. This was especially the case between strangers in public places, whether pedestrians on the sidewalk, motorists on the city streets, or audience members in a movie theater. The repetitive form—the constantly outraged bemoaning of the loss of proper standards of behavior—made it apparent that the point of these interactions went far beyond the content of their message. Everyone already knew that standards had been lost and that society was on the brink of collapse. Constantly articulating this truth was a way for strangers to instantiate a community defined by particular standards of ethics and etiquette—precisely by lamenting their absence.

This was never clearer to me than one afternoon in mid-2003 when I was waiting in the cashier's line in my neighborhood's overcrowded *hipermercado* (a "hypermarket," rather than a more mundane "supermarket"). It was a Saturday, always a terrible day to go grocery shopping, since it was the day that families stocked up on supplies for the week and prepared to host weekend get-togethers for friends and relatives. Interminable, scarcely moving lines snaked around the store, crisscrossing one another and blocking aisles. Exasperated mothers admonished their children not to scamper between the carts. People grumbled to one another about the frustration and absurdity of submitting to the frustrations of waiting in line, as the woman in front of me put it, simply "to give our money to a giant company." Meanwhile, a gaggle of young men, getting ready to watch the evening's soccer game, stood proudly over their carts, which were chock-full of beer and snack food, preening and roughhousing with one another. In sum, the atmosphere was equal parts festive and grouchy.

Behind me in line, a young couple in their midtwenties was debating whether they should go back and get toilet paper and seltzer water. After a tense exchange with one another, they agreed that each would go off in search of one of the two items and that they would meet back at their cart, which they would leave in the line. Having watched all this out of the corner of my eye, I turned my attention to other shoppers, peeking into an elderly lady's cart and wondering what it meant that she was buying only rice, a single steak, and a few containers of yogurt.

Thus lost in thought, I only belatedly noticed increasingly curt voices behind me. I turned around to see that the young woman who had gone off in search of the toilet paper had now returned, but that another couple, who looked to be in their forties, had pushed the cart aside and taken their place in the line. The two women had already passed through any tentative stage of their negotiation and were clearly incensed with one another. The older woman declared, in reference to leaving the cart as a placeholder in the line, "It's not what's done!" and "You can't do that!" The younger woman protested, exclaiming that she had only been gone "for a moment" and only "to look for one little thing." Their voices got louder and louder. The older woman maintained that "it's about a lack of respect," and insisted, "There are norms; there is civilization!" The younger woman, incredulous, shot back, "Where is there a rule like that? Where does it say that?" The older woman, grasping for an ultimate grounding for her declaration, stated, "I'm a lawyer. I know. There are rules. You can't do that." The younger woman was not convinced, and the fight went on. Meanwhile, the younger man had returned with the seltzer and, having looked on somewhat bewildered for a moment, engaged the older man in the dispute.

Everyone within earshot was by now watching the argument, and, every once in a while, one of the four disputants would appeal to the crowd of entranced onlookers, turning to the audience and asking, "Right?" After a few minutes, a man in his fifties from a neighboring line took it upon himself to intervene. Taking the side of the older couple, he began screaming at the younger couple, repeating many of the same phrases: "You can't do this," "You have to respect the rules," and "That's the problem with this country, a lack of respect for norms!" Others discussed the event amongst themselves. Eventually, and for no clear reason other than perhaps fatigue and embarrassment, the younger couple retreated and moved to the back of the line, but not without a fair amount of eye-rolling, muttered insults, and passive-aggressive comments. As the crowd quieted down, people continued to discuss the event and, from what I could hear, nearly everyone took the side of the victorious, older couple, declaring that it was indeed a breach of norms to leave your shopping cart to hold a place for you in line and that, as the woman in front of me put it, "This country will never advance because we refuse to respect decent norms! We live in a complete corruption."

Relating this incident to one of my neighbors, whom I ran into on my way home, she nodded emphatically, agreeing with the last woman's comment and adding, for good measure, "I know you are interested in corruption. You can find corruption everywhere here: if you walk through the streets, if you drive a car, even in supermarkets! Everyone is seeking to take advantage." As she suggested, complaints about people's conduct in public space—pushing and shoving their way through crowds, refusing to clean up after their dogs, cutting others off in traffic—surfaced regularly in conversations and newspaper editorials. Standing as the mundane evidence of a degenerate nation, such acts often prompted strangers to collectively shame the wrongdoer.

Take, for example, a similar incident on a bus when an elegant middle-aged woman pushed an older, somewhat unkempt man in an attempt to get a seat. The wronged man brought the scandalous action to the attention of everyone on the bus by shouting at the woman, who responded by shouting about "chivalry." Soon the entire bus was loudly reprimanding the woman and talking to one another, saying things like, "How will we survive in this country if we can't even be on a bus without drama?" or "These things never used to happen. What has happened to us?"

Not dissimilarly, commercial exchanges were routinely characterized by what one friend called "the continual war for small change." A shortage of coins compelled customers and cashiers to hoard what they could and engage in elaborate rituals of dissimulation, during which both parties would pretend only to have large bills. During one such encounter, in which I was trying to make a purchase with a large bill, the woman behind me in line turned to me and said loudly, "This shitty country! Together we could force her [the cashier] to give us change. The Argentine mind is incredible." The cashier suddenly found that she could indeed complete the transaction.

In each of these encounters, a decidedly ambivalent relationship emerged between the shamed wrongdoer and the ad hoc community of shamers. On the one hand, the act of shaming framed the younger couple in the *hipermercado*, the woman on the bus, and the cashier in the store as the willful perpetrators of illegitimate behavior. Yet, at the same time, by moving from a particular incident to an evaluation of national essences, the shamers implicitly included themselves as objects of critique and underscored the impossibility expelling corruption from the body politic. As with Alicia's confession, this ambivalence inhered within the performative structure of the encounters, which linked individual behavior to an implicitly classed and racialized civilizational rubric of "decency," "chivalry," and "progress."

Unlike the ethnographic confessions I heard, however, these events mobilized not a mode of distinction predicated on identification with a "first worlder," but instead a mode of publicity predicated on the shared recognition of illegitimacy. Public condemnations thus operated similarly to Turner's Ndembu "rituals of affliction." In Turner's analysis, the deeply conflictual Ndembu society emerged as "a transient community of suffering" brought into being in punctuated moments of ritual, "each couched in the idiom of unity through common misfortune" ([1957] 1996, 289, 301).[13] In post-crisis Buenos Aires, a differently conflictual society emerged out of these intermittent shaming rituals—not a community of suffering, but a community of suspicion united in the understanding that the national predicament demanded mistrust. In this way, ad hoc communities of public condemnation instantiated a paradoxical national public, grounded in the recognition of a sustained process of corruption that had rendered the nation a failed and, indeed, impossible project.

THE LEFT HAND OF GOD

The ethnographic confession and the face-to-face condemnation both unfolded in a register of moral outrage. There were, however, instances in which talk of corruption elicited humor and even affection. That was the case in August 2005, when Diego Maradona used his new primetime talk show, *La Noche del Diez*, as a venue to announce that he had cheated in the World Cup some nineteen years earlier.

The event he was referring to was well known: the 1986 quarterfinals between Argentina and England in Mexico City. Only four years prior, the British navy had roundly defeated Argentina in a brief war over the Islas Malvinas/Falkland Islands. The soccer match was thus widely seen in Argentina as a chance to defeat an imperialist bully. Fifty-one minutes into the game, with the score at 0–0, Maradona jumped into the air to intercept the ball. His head did not quite reach, however, and he used his left fist to pound the ball into England's net. The referee failed to see the illegal move and,

---

13. Turner ([1957] 1996) places great emphasis on the internal sources of conflict and suffering that generate Ndembu belonging. That emphasis resonates with Herzfeld's (1997) notion of "cultural intimacy" and contrasts instructively with modes of national belonging based on suffering in war (Gellner 1983) or on the experience of "transient events of collective vulnerability" (Wedeen 2008, 93). Of course, differentiating internal from external sources of suffering is itself necessarily a semiotic process of "fractal recursivity" (see Gal and Irvine 2000 and Gal 2002).

ignoring the protestations of the English team, allowed the goal to stand, putting Argentina ahead 1–0. Minutes later, Maradona scored another goal so astounding that members of the International Soccer Federation later judged it to be the "World Cup Goal of the Century."[14] He intercepted the ball and dribbled it almost the entire length of the field in ten seconds, all the while touching it with only his left foot and eluding the frantic English team with daring footwork and sudden feints.

After the game, reporters flocked to Maradona, seeking a memorable declaration. Maradona complied. In the face of accusations that the first goal was a "handball," he defended it, telling the press that he had made it "a little bit with the head of Maradona and a little bit with the hand of God." This ambiguous statement—which at once admitted the truth of the English team's allegations, declared the goal the miraculous result of divine intervention, and rendered Maradona and God equivalent actors— became belovedly famous in Argentina, where the goal became known as the "Hand of God."

Over the following years, Maradona's status in Argentina only grew. His stunning 1986 World Cup performance grounded his identity as the embodiment of a decidedly non–middle-class vision of the nation: a boy born into a humble family in a poor suburb of Buenos Aires who went on to achieve greatness on the world stage, drawing only on talent, cunning, and a bit of luck (or fate, or divine providence, as it were) to defeat an imperial power. It became commonplace to liken him to a particularly virile Jesus, both of them unlikely heroes, at once fully human and yet fully divine. There even sprang up the lovingly parodic "Church of Maradona," which aimed "to keep alive the passion and the magic with which our God played soccer" through prayers and creeds modeled on Catholic liturgy: "Our Diego, who art on Earth, blessed be thy left hand . . ."[15]

It was, therefore, with a great deal of fanfare that in 2005, having lost 120 kilograms, undergone gastric bypass surgery, and recovered from a debilitating cocaine addiction, Maradona began his primetime talk show. For weeks leading up to the debut, advertisements blanketed the airwaves, retelling the familiar story of Maradona's life, from birth (when "a chosen one came to Earth"), to his first childhood soccer team (for whom he performed feats "that seemed like miracles"), and culminating with the "Hand of God" goal. During the premiere episode, Maradona sang the popular song, "The Hand of God," written several years earlier by Argentine rock

---

14. "1986 FIFA World Cup Mexico." https://www.fifa.com/worldcup/news/video-vault-goal-of -the-century

15. Iglesia Maradoniana. n.d. *La Mano de Dios*, http://www.iglesiamaradoniana.com.ar (accessed April 25, 2020).

star Rodrigo Bueno. The lyrics compare Maradona to Jesus, portraying their births as "the wish of God," describing how the "immortal" soccer player "sowed joy among the people" and "watered the land with glory," and likening Maradona's cocaine addiction to Jesus tripping while he carried the cross. In Maradona's televised performance, the third-person hagiography became first-person testimonial, with Maradona celebrating himself as a gift from God, sent to save Argentina from mediocrity. Gigantic television screens showed highlights from Maradona's career, confetti filled the air, half-naked women danced behind him, and a studio of cheering fans clapped, danced, and sang along.

It was in this ecstatically ironic context that Maradona declared on the air what everyone had known all along: "For the first time I'm going to say that I did it with my hand. . . . It's something that came from deep within me, from having done it in Fiorito [the poor town where he grew up]. . . . Honestly, I meant to do it with my hand and I've never regretted it. My teammates came up to hug me, but as if they were thinking, 'We're stealing.' But I told them, 'He who robs a thief receives a hundred-year pardon.'" Arguing that the goal constituted legitimate revenge against the English for their "theft" of the Islas Malvinas/Falkland Islands in the 1982 war, Maradona thus justified his action while simultaneously framing cheating and trickery as practices rooted within himself as the product of a rough-and-tumble locale.

The next day, Buenos Aires was alive with talk of Maradona's unrepentant revelation. In conversations with friends, people remarked to me, usually registering some wry alloy of amusement, pride, and mild embarrassment, that the confession stood as further evidence that Argentines were "a nation of corrupt thieves." Some acquaintances exclaimed that "corruption can never be justified because [it is] a cancer." Most, however, told me laughingly that "our corruption comes out of our creole cunning," and that, in Maradona's case, "it was a justified corruption," retribution for British imperialist crimes. The discussion proceeded as if Maradona's spectacularized revelation was novel. In fact, however, he had revealed this secret some five years earlier, in his bestselling autobiography, *I Am Diego*, where he stated, "Now I can tell what I couldn't back then, about the moment known as 'The Hand of God.' . . . What hand of God? It was the hand of Diego! And it was like stealing the English team's wallet" (Maradona 2000, 32).

Everyone I spoke to asserted that they had always known that the Hand of God was a handball. Why, then, did this doubly redundant confession precipitate such frenetic commentary? A thirty-year-old doorman told me, "This is why we love Maradona. We love the beauty of the deceit. We love Maradona because he is us. We are him. The confession is just one more level of deceit." According to the owner of my local laundromat, "Maradona's confession gave us the opportunity to talk about something we all know, but which we don't always want to say—the profound corruption of this nation, something we're both proud of and ashamed of." A young banker told me, "We love to have an opportunity to talk about our flaws, but also about the history that denied us a just position in the world. Maradona brings all that together and allows us to have hope for a just position, a glorious position." Or, as a middle-aged cleaning woman put it, "Maradona permits us to argue that our corruption is a divine corruption, even though we know that's not the case. With him, we pretend our corruption is that of a god, although it's really that of a pathetic nation."

I take these reflections to be apt. Maradona's staged revelation allowed people an opportunity to discuss issues of corruption and lawlessness. However, what was essential was the tone of these conversations, a tone made possible because Maradona's "corruption of the game" was understandable as both justified (given Argentina's history with Great Britain) and successful (given that Maradona helped propel the Argentine team to victory in the World Cup). His "theft" stood as a clear-sighted act of daring that "watered the land with glory" and recapitulated an often-asserted Argentine exceptionalism. As a young architect remarked, people enjoyed the revelation "because he is an Argentine god. Because we are that way: an audacious but hardworking nation, deceitful but sincere."

Thus, Maradona's televised revelation offered a rare moment in postcrisis Buenos Aires when the national stereotype of deceitful cunning could be celebrated rather than lamented, an uncommon instance of carnivalesque reversal that actually served "the nation." In no small part that reversal was possible because he had always, quite skillfully, instantiated a decidedly working-class, autochthonous subversion of the "civilizational norms" and "middle-class values" with which Alicia and the lawyer in the *hipermercado* identified so intimately. With Maradona, it was as if corruption were a form of what Bataille called the "left hand sacred," in which a doubled transgression (Maradona's theft from the thieving Brits) did not return the world to the status quo ante but unleashed a potentially glorious but supremely risky form of social energy, capable of unraveling but also of elevating the bonds of national belonging into a transcendent realm of autonomous sovereignty (Bataille 1991; see also Hertz 1974 and Hubert and Mauss 1964). If, after the crisis, acts of egoistic instrumentalism routinely incited harsh and universal condemnation, Maradona offered an exceptional experience in which charming, felicitous, and spectacular forms of corruption could redound upon and be celebrated by the nation as a whole as—in the words of Geschiere, describing witchcraft in postcolonial

Cameroon—"not just something evil . . . [but also] thrill, excitement, and the possibility of access to unknown power" (1997, 1).

CORRUPTION AS HISTORICAL PLOTLINE

Moving across the above three events, each achieved a more expansive, open-ended public and a progressively fuller, more successful attempt to cleanse participants of the moral taint of corruption. We see evidence of that progression in the range of discursive registers and affective tones associated with each event. (We move from Alicia's mournful, self-revelatory fatalism to the frisson of scandalized denunciation in the *hipermercado*, and finally to the wry ecstasy authorized by Maradona's tricks.) In related fashion, the classed and racialized dynamics of the events shift (from Alicia's disdain for the uncomprehending poor to Maradona's self-stylization as an emblem of autochthony). The movement across that trajectory of genres—from ethnographic confession to face-to-face condemnation, and culminating in televised spectacle—was not chronological in nature but interactional.[16] Throughout my research, events such as the *hipermercado* dispute occurred regularly and I received countless ethnographic confessions; meanwhile, opportunities for celebration such as the one Maradona afforded were decidedly scarce. Moreover, even Maradona's divine capacity to "water the land with glory" did not neutralize the radical negativity of corruption. In fact, the joyful embrace of Maradona's supposed corruption was not opposed to, but was of a piece with, the routine insistence that corruption had triumphed definitively over virtue.

The material scaffolding of this understanding of corruption lay in a two-decade-long process that dramatically transformed the nation's political and economic institutions and produced an astoundingly low economic growth rate of .02 percent and a decline in real salaries of roughly 25 percent (Llach 2004). Those two decades began with the transition from military rule (1976–1983) to democracy. The military regime had legitimated its claim to powers and its so-called Dirty War (a campaign of clandestine state terror, forced disappearances, torture, and extrajudicial killings) as necessary to protect the nation from communists and allied threats to "Christian civilization" (see Feitlowitz 1998). It pursued a deregulatory trade policy and oversaw intensified economic woes, including a dramatically increased foreign debt and currency devaluation, but it did not definitively lose its claim to legitimacy until the war over the Islas Malvinas/Falkland Islands (the

---

16. In other words, the relevant axis of comparison across the events is what Goffman (1981) calls the "participation framework."

event that eventually became the backdrop to Maradona's World Cup performance). At that moment, democracy as such came to seem the antidote to the military's many failures. Public debate would allow the will of the people to emerge, journalism and political parties would ensure an open, competitive field for that debate, and voting would hold officials accountable to the general will. These institutions were charged, then, with ensuring the equation of democracy and social welfare. In the words of Raúl Alfonsín, the first president of the new democracy, "With democracy, we eat, we educate, we cure" (quoted in Palermo 2012, 133).

However, the equation of democracy and social welfare proved difficult to realize, and Alfonsín's presidency (1983–1989) was hobbled by economic difficulties, including a plummeting GDP, a crippling foreign debt, and annual hyperinflation rates that reached 5,000 percent. In the face of a series of rebellions by disgruntled sectors of the military and then a wave of supermarket lootings, Alfonsín passed the presidential baton to president elect Menem (1989–1999) some six months early. Menem granted impunity to military officials in exchange for their accepting civilian authority and launched a project of structural reforms; the measures were necessary, he insisted, in order to save the nation from civil war and economic destitution. Over the next several years, those reforms produced economic gains for a few privileged social sectors. They also resulted in the disinvestment of previously robust organs of social welfare such as schools and hospitals, the disappearance of massive numbers of jobs in state companies and bureaucracies as well as small private businesses, and a dramatic rise in socioeconomic inequality (Svampa 2005). Political parties responded to and accelerated that process by shifting from corporatist to clientelist modes of organization, thereby marginalizing already weakened unions and other corporate actors and empowering individual political operatives with heightened discretionary capacities to distribute state resources (Levitsky 2005, G. O'Donnell 1994).

If the popular lesson drawn from Alfonsín's presidency was that formal democracy alone was insufficient, for many it was the *menemato* (Menem's presidency) that clarified the reason for that insufficiency: corruption. Corruption scandals surrounding Menem's reforms began appearing in the press as soon as 1990. By 1994, the opposition's (eventually failed) presidential campaign was prioritizing "moral authority beyond all reproach" and "eliminating corruption at its roots."[17] In the latter half of the decade, scandals appeared with dramatic frequency, and by 1998, *Clarín* (the largest-circulating newspaper) was publishing an average of three articles every

---

17. Campaign publicity for FREPASO (Frente País Solidario), *Clarín*, May 10, 1994, 12.

day about corruption in seemingly every governmental apparatus.[18] However, the notion of total corruption only truly coalesced with the 2001–2002 crisis, when it became commonsensical to talk about not only particular corruption scandals but about corruption in general as "the principal force eroding . . . the normative order" (Sautu 2004, 27).[19]

Coursing through post-crisis Buenos Aires were attempts to develop a self-reflexive understanding of this recent history. Because of their historical role in the consolidation of the Argentine middle class, public schools were a paradigmatic site of those attempts, both symbolically and materially. Whereas previous generations had sent their children to public schools reputed to rival their European counterparts, over the 1980s and 1990s people with means increasingly sent their children to private schools. The most frequently cited reason for that shift was "lack of investment." As the number of children in private schools increased, so too did those schools' government subsidies, and funding for public schools fell further. A newly decentralized regime of accountability, aimed at improving the quality of the schools, created an array of novel encounters between bureaucrats and businessmen, and the system leached money through the new extralegal points of contact. These problems further incentivized parents to seek out private alternatives, even at the height of an economic recession that made those alternatives ever less affordable (Minujin and Anguita 2004).

Thus, middle-class families were both participants in and victims of a self-reinforcing process of disinvestment that progressively eroded an institution that had been crucial to the formation of the middle class in the first place. By the time of my fieldwork, people could capture this dynamic in the idiom of corruption. As one mother of young children put it, "If we all sent our kids to the public schools, they would improve. But you can't because they are abandoned—by the politicians who steal their funds and by the middle class, [for] we have to be selfish and educate our own children however we can. That's what corruption is and that's what will end this middle class, this country."

As this example shows, many in the middle class marked their moment in time as the culmination of a long process through which the pursuit of individual advantage had undermined the fields of practice that enable such pursuits. From this perspective, the cannibalistic logic of corruption meant that particular practices (e.g., educating one's children) did not

---

18. As I mentioned in the introduction, I surveyed the content of the three major national newspapers over a seventeen-year period (1990–2007) in order to chart these sorts of thematic threads. On the role corruption allegations play in Argentine politics, see Balán 2011 and Pereyra 2012.

19. For analyses of the 2001–2002 crisis as bringing about a third, and utterly stark "disillusion" with democracy, see Quiroga 2005 and Romero 2004.

merely fail to fulfill their putative ends (e.g., a cultivated mind, a respectable job, an informed national citizenry), but had actually undermined those goals by weakening the institutions (e.g., the public schools) that were their condition of possibility. In other words, corruption named a historically situated experience of radical negativity, one that played out as a felt complicity with the destruction of the very social institutions on which one depended the most.

Invoking this institutional history and its attendant sentimental education, post-crisis condemnations of corruption drew on but inverted the promises of the 1980s transition to democracy and the 1990s turn toward structural adjustment. Despite the differences between these two turns, both had promised to ensure social well-being through the transparent institutional mediation of individual demands, whether political or economic. In 2001–2002, however, these institutions were paralyzed. Coinciding with Néstor Kirchner's presidency, the post-crisis period was characterized by political stability and economic growth as well as the widespread sense that the crisis had ended the "liberal and neoliberal economics that began [with the military coup] in March 1976" (Llach 2004, 148). Even so, many people were quick to warn me, as did an unemployed bus driver, that nothing had changed except "we have perhaps finally woken up to our own nature, to our inability to progress, to our place in the world."

The category of corruption thus drew on but differed in kind from its precedents in a long discursive history inaugurated by Sarmiento's literary classic, *Facundo or, Civilization and Barbarism* ([1845] 2003), which defined Argentina as riven by those two warring principles—the first associated with Europe, liberalism, urbanity, and prosperity and the second with autochthony, authoritarianism, rurality, and destitution. In many other Latin American contexts, racialized and classed anxieties about national character and civilizational progress generated ideologies of *mestizaje* (see, e.g., Martínez-Echazábal 1998). However, in Argentina, sustained governmental policies aimed at "whitening" (Ramella 2004) the population and "invisibilizing" the indigenous (Gordillo and Hirsch 2003) rendered *mestizaje* nearly inconceivable. Instead, there emerged an ideology of irreconcilable dichotomies, which people have reanimated time and again in order to diagnose alleged national dysfunctions.[20]

The outlines of this discursive history are clearly visible in the category of corruption I have been describing. Yet participants in the above events were describing something else—an Argentina in which that historical

---

20. For examples of the legacy of the Sarmiento schema in Argentina, see Jauretche 1966; Martínez Estrada 1933; and Scalabrini Ortiz 2005. For an analysis of that legacy, see Goodrich 1996. For an analysis of Sarmiento's legacy throughout Latin America, see Skurski 1994.

conflict was all but over, an Argentina in which corruption had exhausted any conceivable opposition. As such, the category of corruption may have provided a potent idiom for the critique of neoliberalism, but it simultaneously mobilized racialized and classed conceptions of national progress in the service of a stance of historical exhaustion.

That stance partook most immediately of an often explicitly voiced impulse to come to terms with the recent past. It also posited the crisis as the definitive end of a frustrated project of national progress. A vast literature attests that, throughout the twentieth century, the teleological orientation of that project laminated civilizational, racial, and class imaginaries onto one another, allowing the middle class to become a privileged national subject, identified with normative ideals of whiteness and modernity.[21] The diagnosis of total corruption declared that project defunct, the victim of an essential and ineradicable national trait—a duplicitous and self-serving cunning that had slowly but unavoidably eroded social life, leaving behind a barbaric hyperindividualism from which no collective future could be projected. For some, this unenviable predicament could be traced to the presence of non-European (or even non–northern European) elements within the body politic. For others, it could be summed up in the idea of "savage capitalism," and its etiology lay in the injustices implicit in the narrative of progress to which I have just gestured. In the broadest of strokes, these two positions characterized "conservative" and "progressive" positions within the post-crisis middle class. Undergirding that opposition, however, was the shared supposition that the nation had from the beginning carried with it the seeds of its undoing.

HISTORICAL EXHAUSTION

When he assumed the presidency in 1989 amidst a hyperinflationary recession, Carlos Menem proclaimed that Argentina's future depended on a linked strategy of radical structural reforms and austerity measures: "major surgery without anesthesia" on the body politic and "carnal relations" with the United States, meaning acquiescence to its every policy demand (di Tella, quoted in Munck 2001, 73). Some fifteen years later, after years of exile in Chile, house arrest in Argentina, and the threat of trial for corruption, he returned triumphantly to Buenos Aires to be sworn in as a newly elected senator and thereby (temporarily) immunized against criminal prosecution. Upon hearing Menem's name, then president Néstor Kirchner reached

---

21. For extended discussing of the racialized dynamics of the middle class as privileged national subject, see Adamovsky 2009; Garguin 2009; and Visacovsky 2009c.

behind himself and, raising his eyebrows, touched the wood of the Senate dais.[22] That evening, as the nightly news recounted Menem's swearing in, millions of Argentines mimicked their president in a more vulgar fashion: with their right hands, men touched their left testicles and women their left breasts. Infuriated by Menem's notoriously corrupt administration and convinced that it had caused the 2002 crisis, they touched wood, testicles, and breasts in an effort—at once sincere and farcical—to save themselves from further devastation at his hands.

Meant to ward off "bad luck" or "the evil eye," the symbolism of these touches was hardly subtle. As people variously explained it to me, wood is "strong," "pure," and "reliable." In a related sense, testicles and breasts are "the essential thing that defines a sex" and the locus of "virility or femininity." Touching these objects whenever someone uttered Menem's name thus "protect[ed] against bad luck" by mobilizing some of this reliable, essential, and pure power at a "threatening moment." In the case of testicles and breasts, the touch also served to shield these potent but "delicate" body parts. The gestures thus pointed up a negative relationship between corruption and sociosexual reproduction and put forth an embodied argument about the falsehood of Menem's early promises: instead of generating a stable and prosperous nation, his carnal relations had made the national body politic complicit in its own evisceration.

From Alicia's confession to the *hipermercado* condemnation, from Maradona's revelation to Menem's uncanny return, these events all exhibited an uneasy tension. On the one hand, in recognizing the erosion of social norms, people performed those very norms, effecting a paradoxical but analytically legible, if popularly denied, mode of sociability. On the other hand, that tidy dialectic of social (re)production does not capture the entirety of these engagements, for it dismisses without interrogating the lived experience of irrecuperable loss, both particular, material losses as well as the loss of the nation as a middle-class project (with the racial and civilizational imaginaries that project had entailed).

In this context, corruption (like witchcraft in other contexts) served as a privileged site for struggles over the grounds of legitimate modes of accumulation and authority. In post-crisis, middle-class Buenos Aires, those struggles articulated a historico-moral sensibility that brought together in an unstable amalgam intuitions of complicity as well as feelings of victimhood; criticisms of inequality, as well as racialized distaste for the poor; not to mention a full-throated repudiation of neoliberalism as well as a fatalistic rejection of political-economic alternatives. In holding those divergent intuitions together, the category of corruption allowed members of the Bue-

---

22. "Kirchner desairó a Menem en el Senado," *La Nación*, November 30, 2005.

nos Aires middle class to articulate themselves as the iconic instantiations of a social world that had exhausted its history. Of course, the post-crisis period was full of what one might understand, from any number of perspectives, as "history." But the widespread insistence to the contrary betrayed a profound suspicion about its possibilities. It is around that suspicion about the affordances for projecting national horizons and social connections that the next chapter revolves.

5

SOLIDARY SELVES

This rich endowment, painfully won, built, fashioned, or invented by our ancestors, must become common property, so that the collective interests of men may gain from it the greatest good for all.

Kropotkin, *The Conquest of Bread*

THE ANTIDOTE TO NEOLIBERALISM

Given the corruption critiques I discussed in the previous chapter, one might wonder how people managed to make their way in a world so resolutely untrustworthy. Indeed, were I to conclude the book here, the reader would be left with the sense that the crisis really did amount to "the end of the future," as Diego insisted in the introduction, and that the years thereafter were an endless present full of pointless chatter. Of course, this was not the case. Social life did proceed and relationships of trust did emerge, despite the popular sense of an often-unbearable set of constraints. In fact, many middle-class people felt that the crisis had prompted them to discover an alternate form of social engagement that was the antidote to neoliberalism, popularly understood as a system defined by selfish materialism, the dissolution of social bonds, and the hollowing out of the nation-state. They called this anti-neoliberal form of social engagement "solidarity."

The term has a long history in syndicalist and related leftist politics, not to mention in the Durkheimian sociological tradition. However, in an avowedly post-neoliberal Argentina, it referred to something else: the ethic of intersubjective commitment animating everything from free medical care, neighborhood associations, and barter networks to fair-trade consumption and even organ donation. The inverse of egoistic materialism and corruption, solidarity described a purified sociality that would transform individual acts of selflessness into a renewed national community of equals. Grounded in civil society and characterized by spontaneity, transparency, and immediacy, solidarity promised to avoid the dynamics of manipulation, deception, and mediation that lay at the heart of the anxieties around money and corruption that I discussed in previous chapters. In sum, the concept of solidarity offered a utopian vision of egalitarian prosperity achieved not so much through institutional transformation or material redistribution as through the cultivation of subjective, voluntarist virtues made manifest in acts of unreciprocated generosity.[1] Solidarity thus emerged partially as a logistical solution to practical problems of material well-being, but more foundationally as a moralized response to the dissolution of social bonds. In the words of the mayor of Buenos

---

1. In his account of East German political culture, Glaeser (2010) explores a similarly idealist understanding of social transformation. There, as in Argentina, that idealist framework was bound up with a robust hermeneutics of suspicion, albeit one that unfolded on the institutional grounding of the *Stasi* rather than on the historical grounding of a disappointed and disillusioned middle class.

Aires, solidarity is a "value" that serves as the "cement" that holds society together.[2]

In a context defined by widespread structural unemployment, gifts epitomized solidarity initiatives. However, gifts also occasioned unavoidable practical and ethical dilemmas for middle-class solidarity builders. Those dilemmas emerged out of a series widely shared judgments: that poverty and inequality posed existential threats to the nation; that state and market institutions were irredeemably corrupt and so could not address those threats; and that unreciprocated gifting within civil society was therefore the only viable way to enable a new national project. As I argue over the course of this chapter, those judgments ultimately led middle-class solidarity workers and volunteers into irreconcilable impasses that threatened to undermine the utopian promise of solidarity.

However, first it is worth considering how poverty and inequality became a matter of pressing concern for the post-crisis middle class. After all, poverty and inequality do not always trouble individual consciousnesses any more than they necessarily stand at the center of public debate. Nonetheless, in post-crisis Argentina, poverty and inequality had become nearly unquestionable scandals of moral import. The process that made possible that sentiment foregrounded questions of motive and interpersonal dynamics over and above material and systemic dynamics, with profound implications for the ways people subjected these problems to interpretive scrutiny and pragmatic intervention.

PROBLEMATIZING POVERTY, INTERPRETING INEQUALITY

In an upper-middle-class area of the neighborhood of Palermo, next to lush botanical gardens and the rather malodorous but celebrated zoo, and in front of a sprawling exhibition center, sits the Plaza Italia. Home to an enormous marble statue honoring the millions of Italian immigrants who streamed into Argentina in the late nineteenth and early twentieth centuries, the plaza is where three major boulevards come together. Surrounded by posh restaurants, shops, and apartment buildings, it is also the site of a dozen city bus stops, a major subway station, and an outdoor used-book market. Buses, cars, and taxis jostle for position as they merge in and out of the traffic circle around the plaza. Diesel fumes fill the air, horns blare, and

---

2. Aníbal Ibarra. 2003. "Ser solidario." In *Pensar, hacer y ser solidario* [program brochure], 5. Buenos Aires: Department of Social Development of the City of Buenos Aires.

pedestrians dart through the traffic, creating a scene that epitomizes the kind of urban hustle and bustle the Italian immigrants sought and helped create. In the midst of this activity, the plaza stands as the point of departure for travels in any number of directions, two of which are particularly salient for a discussion of the dynamics of post-crisis solidarity.

First, during this period, one could walk a few blocks deeper into the neighborhood of Palermo, through tree-lined streets, past restaurants and shops, and alongside residential buildings, some in disrepair and others emanating a sense of placid comfort. In the summer, one would pass people lounging in outdoor cafés, sipping espresso and reading newspapers. In winter, one would surely pass women in furs and men in woolen topcoats, bundled up as they carried out their daily errands. At all times of the year, one would confront families pulling carts full of trash, which they would later recycle and turn into cash, and children performing juggling tricks for passengers in cars stopped at stoplights. Everyone made their way carefully through dilapidated streets, avoiding loose sidewalk tiles, careening automobiles, and aggressive pedestrians. Within this scene stood the Buenos Aires headquarters of the Porón Foundation, one of the three civil society organizations where I carried out ethnographic research as a volunteer between 2003 and 2007.[3] Entering the foundation's building, with its elegant, two-story beaux arts edifice, one would be greeted graciously, offered a seat and some coffee or *mate*—the green tea that figures throughout Argentina as a sign of hospitality and conviviality—and attended to with the utmost civility by one of the foundation's employees, whose work included publicizing and fundraising for projects to help the suburban municipality of Porón, about thirty-five kilometers away. A former single-family home with beautiful, if somewhat worn, parquet floors, intricate plaster moldings, sixteen-foot ceilings, and mahogany woodwork, the building was the kind of space where one could easily imagine the wealth of Buenos Aires' golden age in the late nineteenth and early twentieth centuries.

Second, on any given weekday at the evening rush hour, one could join one of the lines of people in the plaza waiting for the buses that would take them home after a day of work. One of these buses traveled to the town of Porón. The forty-minute bus ride proceeded northwest on a busy commercial avenue, passing through a series of middle-class neighborhoods before hitting the highway that marks the city limit. As it made its way out of the city, the bus would merge on and off highways, traversing the highly

---

3. As I mentioned in the introduction, I carried out participant-observation at three civil society organizations, including the Porón Foundation, in both its city headquarters and in its Villa Robles Center. (The names of these organizations and locations, as well as those of all employees, volunteers, and clients, have been anonymized in this account.)

heterogeneous landscape of Buenos Aires' suburban rings. Flat fields of mud and grass were interspersed with gigantic shopping centers, informal trash dumps, gated communities, shantytowns, and small-scale centers of light industry. Out of the window of the bus, one could see a parallel dirt road where people would travel on foot, on bicycle, in rickety trucks, and in horse-driven carts. Reaching Porón itself, the bus would exit the highway and deposit its passengers on the muddy shoulder of a service road, across from a gleaming Shell gas station. From there, people scattered as they made the final leg of their journey home. Some hopped into the cars of waiting friends and family. Others dashed under the highway overpass to catch a municipal bus. Still others simply walked off into the distance as cars streaked past them. Near the gas station lay the town of Porón, divided into two very different neighborhoods: Catalinas, home to the founders and most of the volunteers at the Porón Foundation, and Villa Robles, home to the people the foundation sought to help.

The relationships that stretch across these sites are the subject of this chapter, for the Porón Foundation epitomized practices of solidarity in post-crisis Buenos Aires. And the glaring social contrasts to which I have so briefly alluded—between the city center and Porón, between the Porón neighborhoods of Catalinas and Villa Robles, between the beaux arts buildings and the dilapidated city streets, between women in furs and children performing in the streets for small change—were precisely the sorts of socioeconomic differences that the foundation sought to overcome.

The people of the Porón Foundation were not alone in finding inequality troubling. As even the most cursory glance at a newspaper or the most casual of neighborly conversations would indicate, the sorts of socioeconomic differences legible in the landscape I have sketched were the source of considerable anxiety, consternation, and outrage. Poverty and inequality had become the cause of increasing public concern in Argentina over the 1990s. During that decade, a series of structural reforms systematically dismantled the institutions that had once undergirded the claim—never fully realized, of course—that Argentina was a country of equals, a country essentially and paradigmatically middle-class. That claim had long circulated as a matter of routine in newspaper articles and editorials, children's schoolbooks, political speeches, and everyday conversations; just as routinely, it had served as evidence for Argentina's supposed distinction from the rest of Latin America. In the words of one prominent sociologist, "Historically, in our country, the middle classes were considered as a particular feature of the social structure, in comparison with other Latin American countries, and an essential factor in the successive models of social integration" (Svampa 2005, 129). As unemployment forced more and more people into poverty, inequality became encapsulated by the newly invented category of "the new poor." Describing people whose incomes fell beneath the poverty line and who were temporarily or structurally unemployed but who retained other social and cultural markers of the middle class, "the new poor" invoked the critical judgment of a failed national project.[4]

As a result, politicians placed inequality at the very center of their agendas, as did social scientists. Novels, sitcoms, and plays examined the intimate repercussions of a radically unequal society. Discussions of what one might expect for one's children revolved around attempts to imagine the long-term significance of a national economy that seemed to offer less and less room for a financially stable, much less upwardly mobile, middle class. In sum, far from appearing as a natural—if lamentable—feature of society, poverty and socioeconomic inequality stood in the foreground of everyday life for residents of post-crisis Buenos Aires.

First, then, some statistics, not because they speak for themselves or because they sum up the social differences that structured post-crisis Argentina, but because they circulated in that milieu as the shorthand instantiation of a problem that seemed as disturbing as it was self-evident. Between 2003 and 2007, the Argentine economy enjoyed an annual growth rate of nearly 9 percent. Poverty and unemployment fell dramatically following the nadir of the 2001–2002 crisis. And while many people could cite those statistics as proof that things had improved, quick to follow in such an exchange would be statistics that belied any impression of widespread prosperity: In 2007, 24 percent of the population lived in poverty, with 10 percent of the work force unemployed and another 10 percent underemployed (Weisbrot and Sandoval 2007).[5]

By no means was this state of affairs entirely the result of the 2001–2002 economic crisis. Poverty, unemployment, and inequality in the distribution of wealth had all been increasing since at least the late 1970s, when a military dictatorship worked systematically to begin dismantling the institutional heritage of a populist social welfare state. Nonetheless, the statistics were, quite simply, scandalous to most people, hovering as they did at levels unimaginable a generation prior. They routinely appeared in policy reports, news articles, and conversations about "the social question"—the lack of stability and well-being—and stood as proof of an almost unbelievable state of affairs that required continual interrogation and explanation.

---

4. See Minujin and Kessler 1995 and Minujin and Anguita 2004 for discussions of these dynamics among the new poor.

5. As stark as these statistics are, they likely underestimate these indexes. In part, this is because social welfare surveys were difficult and expensive to carry out in the rural regions where poverty and unemployment tended to be highest. It is also because the methodology for measuring unemployment did not take into account the large percentage of Argentine jobs that were inadequate, part-time, unstable, or part of the informal economy.

While any number of situations could elicit this process of examination and interpretation, one exceedingly common occasion for such reflections was the sort of everyday encounter self-described middle-class and ex-middle-class people would have with poor people on the city streets. In those reflections, people taking up a middle-class footing (Goffman 1981) described the encounters in intimate terms that decried a broken social contract by summoning the logics of kinship and resemblance.

Take, for example, the words of a taxi driver, who, upon giving some spare change to children begging at a street corner, muttered, "You never used to see this poverty. Argentina never had this until we all fell for neoliberalism and its false promises. We used to be a country of the middle class. Just look at them—those children could be my grandchildren." Or, the housewife who told me that she began volunteering at a food pantry when she came home one day to find a young girl sleeping in her entry way: "The girl looked just like my daughter, and I just couldn't stand that my daughter had a home and this girl didn't. Look what neoliberalism has done. A country can't go on without its middle class." Or, the man who began volunteering at a local community center because he saw "poorly dressed men looking for food in the trash, men who could have been my father. We're becoming like Bolivia, a country without a middle class, and it's our own fault, having believed in Menem's shitty neoliberal lies."

All of which is to say that the very real ethical and interpersonal outrage occasioned by socioeconomic inequality was shaded by a concern not only with the welfare of particular poor people or even with the enormity of poverty but also with discomfort at the way those facts gave lie to long-standing national mythologies and identities. In this context, then, poor people bore a heavy interpretive burden: They were the particular victims of morally egregious neoliberal reforms for which nearly everyone felt some responsibility. They were the embodiment of a national process of socioeconomic polarization. And, of course, for those people who had maintained some modicum of relative economic security, they were harbingers of one's own potential future.

ENVISIONING SOLIDARITY

The 2001–2002 crisis solidified this understanding of poverty—as evidence of injustice, sign of national disintegration, and omen of things to come. And so, in the years following, poor people were the emblematic target of a variety of social projects aimed at redressing those problems. In earlier historical moments, the obvious solution to poverty and inequality in Argentina had always been employment, generated through some combination of state and market initiatives. Now, however, neither state nor market seemed capable of producing the kinds of stable, well-paying jobs that were so desperately needed.

It was at this time that "solidarity" began appearing in the press and in day-to-day conversations with increasing frequency.[6] With the state unable to guarantee even the semblance of political stability or the circulation of its currency, much less the day-to-day welfare of its citizens, articles abounded detailing the grassroots efforts of people across the country to find short-term solutions to problems of survival. In the words of one newspaper editorial, as "individuals and private organizations to carry out social assistance work, solidarity reveals the vitality and importance of civil society in the resolution of community problems and, at the same time, the enormous failure of the state in this matter."[7] The appeal of solidarity depended on its location in civil society, a realm popularly understood to have somewhat avoided the ossified and corrupt bureaucracies of the state and political parties and the self-interested competition of the market, offering instead the possibility of "transparency" and a "lack of mediation and [outside] influence."[8] Grounded in civil society, then, solidarity offered a way to transform individual practices of self-actualization into interpersonal practices of ethical care and a way to reimagine the nation as a community grounded in egalitarian bonds.

Solidarity building (*fomentar la solidaridad*) thus stood in stark contrast to the work of the *piqueteros*, the unemployed workers who had begun organizing themselves and blockading roads in the mid-1990s. By the 2001–2002 crisis, those blockades had developed into a well-honed technique for pressuring provincial and federal governments into giving *piquetero* organizations money and material resources in exchange for lifting the blockade. *Piquetero* organizations would then redistribute those goods to individuals and families within their communities. Those marginalized and impov-

---

6. In one telling indicator of the appeal of "solidarity," the term (in its noun and adjectival forms) appeared on average approximately five times per day in the three major national newspapers, *Clarín*, *La Nación*, and *Página 12* in 2002—about twice as often as in 2000. Over the following half decade, the term continued to appear with roughly the same frequency. As mentioned in the introduction, I carried out a survey of these three newspapers' content for the seventeen-year period of 1990–2007 in order to chart these sorts of trends in national public discourse.

7. "La ayuda solidaria y los déficit del Estado," *Clarín*, May 18, 2002.

8. "El aporte privado para mejorar la ayuda social," *Clarín*, March 2, 2002. The term *tercer sector* (third sector, i.e., neither the market nor the state) was more common than the synonym *sociedad civil* (civil society). The significance of this distinction lies beyond the scope of this chapter but points to the enduring legacy of Argentina's mid-twentieth-century corporatist model of development. For more on corporatist development in Argentina and elsewhere in Latin America, see Etchemendy and Collier 2007; Klaren and Bossert 1986; and Plotkin 2003d.

erished communities became newly invigorated and vibrant sites for collective life, which revolved around institutions such neighborhood-run cafeterias, schools, and medical facilities. In the years following the crisis, these communities thrived as *piquetero* organizations entered into long-term alliances with political parties and factions, thereby directing a relatively steady stream of state resources into their neighborhoods even in the absence of regular road blockades.[9]

Thus, in the *piqueteros*, we find an extraordinarily successful mode of post-crisis politicking, one that grounded new modes of social life and that promised a renewed future for its members (Svampa and Pereyra 2003). Nonetheless, the *piqueteros* were suspect in the eyes of many people, particularly those who retained some degree of self-identification as middle-class, whatever their current economic condition. *Piquetero* communities depended on the social welfare funds that they received from state and party apparatuses, and, unsurprisingly, they voted overwhelmingly in support of those politicians and parties. In public discourse, that dynamic of material and political support was routinely glossed as "clientelism" or "assistence-ism" (*clientelismo* or *asistencialismo*).

Typically understood as hierarchical system of obligation linking poor voters to their elite political representatives, clientelism had become a central and increasingly visible mode of Argentine politicking during the 1990s and was strongly associated with Menem and his Peronist party even though clientelist relations spanned the partisan spectrum. In the wake of the 2001–2002 crisis, then, many middle-class people saw clientelism as a political ill that was in no small part responsible for the economic mismanagement that had produced the crisis. It was not uncommon during this time to hear fairly vicious rhetoric about the relationship between supposedly conniving party bosses and their allegedly irrational supporters.

One example of this rhetoric—laced with prejudices about class and race—occurred in October 2005, just before congressional elections. A popular news radio station reported that a brawl had broken out between supporters of rival Peronist candidates vying over the right to campaign in the central plaza of a town on the outskirts of Buenos Aires. Two commentators debated the significance of the event for over an hour. One argued that the clash was the result of overly excited party supporters "carried away by their intense loyalty." The other contended that the two factions were "fake" (*truchas*) and that the violence was a staged attempt to mask a secret alliance between the two groups. About forty-five minutes into the debate,

---

9. For analyses of various piquetero organizations over the years, see Alcañiz and Scheier 2007; Delamata 2004; Delfini and Picchetti 2004; Epstein 2009; Golbert 2004; Hanson and Lapegna 2017; Svampa and Pereyra 2003; and Weitz-Shapiro 2006.

a woman called into the show and said, in a tone at once plaintive and furious, "These people are animals! What does this tell us about the Peronist party!?" Later that day, I brought up the event with my neighbors, a young couple with two children. "I'll explain it to you," the husband told me in what I took to be an infuriatingly indulgent and didactic tone of voice, "This is Argentina. Of course they [the party factions] are fake, but the violence is real. The politicians buy their votes with a few bags of food. . . . They [the poor] don't know anything." He went on, "They're poor and uneducated and don't care. It's the corrupt politicians who manipulate everything, and it's us, the middle-class people with an education, people who work hard and try to bring up their children in a decent way, who suffer." Summing up his plaintive account of victimhood at the hands of a conspiracy between the poor and the elite, he told me, "Corruption has destroyed this country."

Explaining clientelism in this way, middle-class people thus thrust responsibility for the crisis on an asymmetrical alliance between the poor and the politicians. In the process, the term "politics" (*la política*) became a synonym for corruption. While this perspective on clientelism and on politics in general was typically middle-class, one could easily find it among the poor as well.[10] Once the *piqueteros* had forged alliances with politicians, then, they too became guilty by association in the eyes of many (Golbert 2004). One longtime unemployed client of the Villa Robles Center, for example, explained to me in 2004 that he refused to attend *piquetero* events or to receive their aid because "they've become all politics, all corruption." It was for that reason, he explained to me, that he went instead to the Villa Robles Center, "where there is real solidarity instead of *piquetero* politics."[11]

The social field of solidarity building was diffuse, but it hinged on the figure of the *piquetero* as its foil, and it was animated by a more or less shared understanding of solidarity that drew on an array of discursive and practical traditions even as it also distinguished itself from those traditions. First, the term "solidarity" conjured certain aspects of leftist modes of political organization, particularly those that emphasized autonomy from the state, such as Argentina's long and robust tradition of anarcho-syndicalism (James 1988). It also referred, more obliquely, to Catholic social dogma and the imperative to "love one's neighbor as oneself" (O'Donnell 2001). It even harnessed a vaguely Durkheimian (1984) attention to the interwoven threads of material interdependence and moral commitment

---

10. For discussions of clientelism and how is seen from the perspective of the client and within poor communities more generally in Argentina throughout the 1990s and 2000s, see Auyero 1999, 2000; Amaral and Stokes 2005; Brusco, Nazareno, and Stokes 2004; Szwarcberg 2008.

11. For related dynamics of the dehumanization of the poor and logics of contagion in politics, see Caldeira 2000.

necessary for social cohesion, an attention that had long found local expression in Peronist politics (Plotkin 2003d). However, solidarity in post-crisis Argentina drew on this varied repertoire to name something else: a utopian mode of explicit, heartfelt, intersubjective commitment that would overcome socioeconomic inequality through carefully calibrated relations of interpersonal commitment. Within this framework, equality would take place through an ethicized process of self-transformation, by which each individual would become committed to the welfare of others. And it was this expanding system of egalitarian mutual commitment that promised to reverse the historical situation of national loss and degeneration that neoliberalism had entailed.

In all these ways, solidarity in post-crisis Argentina bore a strong family resemblance to the ideas of "ethical citizenship" that Muehlebach (2012) has identified as so crucial to the restructuring of civic belonging in neoliberal Italy, as well as to similar organizing tropes in roughly contemporary contexts ranging from England and the Netherlands to Egypt, Turkey, Croatia, Myanmar, and the Philippines.[12] Across these varied contexts, decreased state investments in social welfare and insurance programs have been compensated for (to whatever limited extent) by a reliance on volunteers to care for family, neighbors, and compatriots. In many instances, analysts have shown that this turn to voluntarist social care tends to reproduce or exacerbate existing inequalities, in large part because the capacity to give and to care is distributed differentially.

However, unlike in the cases mentioned above, solidarity workers in post-crisis Argentina were as keenly aware as any anthropologist that the acts of giving and caring have the ability to generate hierarchical relations of obligation, dependence, and authority.[13] Taking up the same suspicious stance and deploying the same arsenal of interpretive techniques familiar from previous chapters, solidarity workers subjected their own practices to relentless, ongoing critique in order to root out any hint of inequality. Take the example of Clara, a supervisor at one of the civil society organizations where I volunteered, who turned down a grant offered by a local community board "because the offer is part of a conspiracy to bind us to the system of favors that is politics." Or, consider the words of Félix, who mentioned in passing that he "worried about [his] motives for volunteering becoming corrupted by the egoistic desire to show off [*fanforronear*]

---

12. See, e.g., Babül 2015; Bautista 2015; Doolan, Cepic, and Walton 2018; Verhoeven and Tonkens 2013; and Watanabe 2014.

13. The anthropological literature on the politics of the gift is enormous. For works that elaborate the dynamics of equality and inequality in gifting, see, e.g., Godelier 1999; Gregory 1982; Mauss 1967; Lévi-Strauss 1987; Parry 1986; Sahlins 1972; Smart 1993; and Weiner 1992.

and be better than the other, whom I should be helping without regard for myself." Roberto, a staff member at Villa Robles, summed it up nicely when he told me that "neoliberalism was the intentional production of a life of corruption, impunity, and egoistic materialism. Because of its legacy, we are all used to manipulating our own moral motives, of pretending to be something we are not." As a result, he asserted, "we risk unknowingly trapping the other in our own self-serving fantasy instead of helping the other become our equal."

Given this suspicious and anxious concern, solidarity workers typically insisted that true solidarity could only exist if the recipient also became, in turn, a gift giver. The transformation of a recipient into a giver would entail a movement from passivity to agency, from dependence to committed interdependence, and from the self to the social as the orienting horizon. The result, workers hoped, would be an open-ended and expanding network of individuals committed to one another and each occupying a structurally equivalent role with respect to one another. The nation would thus be refounded as egalitarian, horizontalist, and voluntarist in nature— complete without the hierarchizing and mediating institutions of state and market. In the field of solidarity building, then, a neoliberal vision of ethicized, supposedly unmediated voluntarism was intertwined uncannily with the avowedly anti-neoliberal vision of radical horizontalist politics that had circulated globally across networks of activists and intellectuals and that found such inspiration in the heady days of protest during the nadir of Argentina's 2001–2002 crisis.[14]

Solidarity programs thus articulated a vision of "generalized" (Sahlins 1972) reciprocity in which the dilemma of the gift was solved by positing a third party and envisioning an infinitely expansive and temporally open-ended mode of sociality. It is this logic of infinite spatiotemporal expansion that goes to the heart of solidarity's utopian promise. In a context of near total disenchantment with extant political and economic institutions, solidarity offered a vision of community defined by horizontal, unmediated, intersubjective commitment through gift exchange. What is more, it made possible the imagination of such a community not only in a locality defined by face-to-face interactions but on a national scale of anonymized generosity.[15]

---

14. See, e.g., Callinicos 2003; Graeber 2002; Hardt and Negri 2004; Lewkowicz 2002; and Sitrin 2006, 2012.

15. The paradigmatic site of solidarity were face-to-gace gifts. However, many solidarity-building organizations experimented with ways of engaging in less personalized and more mediated modes as well, such as online communities linking groups across the nation and beyond, mass media campaigns, and other ways of creating a public that revolved around the dynamics of "distant suffering" (Boltanski 1999).

Staff at the Porón Foundation's Villa Robles Center and other organizations I frequented openly and continuously expressed concerns over how to ensure that gifts of material aid became the medium of this sort of egalitarian commitment. They would worry aloud that their programs risked reproducing the hierarchical logics of charity and clientelistic politics. A computer skills teacher told me, for example, "The essential thing is they're learning to be solidary, to give to the other, to commit themselves actively to the neighborhood, to society. The computer stuff is only the road to that transformation." "Would it be so bad," I asked, "if they only learned 'the computer stuff'?" He corrected me immediately, saying, "They come because they need something, they lack something. . . . But if we only respond to that demand, we leave them in a situation of dependency . . . [and] marginality. And that marginality, that inequality is what neoliberalism has produced in this country."

Solidarity workers thus reconceptualized poverty and inequality as problems of systematic disempowerment and resource distribution that could nonetheless be redressed by realigning interpersonal ethics and motivations and by rejecting the distorting mediation of state and market institutions. They also distinguished two groups of participants and laid out a differential set of demands for each in order to achieve solidarity. For the structurally unemployed and chronically poor, being the beneficiary of an act of material generosity should prompt a subjective transformation from passive dependence to active commitment. The transformation of the middle-class person into someone capable of that initial act of generosity was, however, a different matter. It is to these different demands that I now turn in order to show how attempts to cultivate egalitarian interdependence in a system of generalized reciprocity nonetheless reproduced hierarchies of racialized and classed inequalities.

PROTAGONISM

Housed in a textile factory that had shut down in 1996, the Porón Foundation's Villa Robles Center was run entirely by volunteers, most of whom hailed from the neighborhood of Catalinas, which lay literally across the tracks from the neighborhood of Villa Robles. Given the widespread economic problems of post-crisis Argentina, volunteers from Catalinas faced difficulties of unemployment, a lack of money, and inaccessible health care that were not entirely dissimilar to those faced by their clients. And yet, the Catalinas staff was distinguished from their Villa Robles clients in that, whatever their current incomes, staff took up a middle-class footing in both public and domestic spaces. Relative to their clients, they had more years of schooling, more experience traveling, and a more robust history of employment in the formal economy. They lived in houses that were more solidly built, with costlier furnishings, and located on paved streets. Children from the two neighborhoods tended to go to different schools. Families frequented different shops, parks, and restaurants. Distinctions between volunteer and client were thus profoundly classed. They were also subtly but no less consistently racialized, with volunteers tending to lay explicit claim to their European immigrant progenitors and clients tending to make no such claims.

The largest of the Villa Robles Center's initiatives was called the Youth Protagonism Program. Through work-training sessions and community activities, the program encouraged (in the words of its glossy brochure) "youth protagonism and constant participation in their community. In this way, they [the poor youth] go from being recipients of aid to being active protagonists generating changes in themselves and their surroundings." This fundamental reorientation would (the brochure continued) promote their "social inclusion . . . by helping them recuperate their self-esteem and the possibility of projecting their future." The program thus promised a subjective transformation of the individual impoverished youth from passivity to activity, from marginalization to participation, from presentist paralysis to future-oriented collaboration. Three features are particularly notable about this alchemy: the insistence on eradicating the pernicious condition of material dependency; the assumed co-constitution of psychological well-being and social inclusion; and the ideal of a future grounded in voluntarist engagement. One of the women in charge of the program explained to me the importance of those three features, saying that "just by showing [the young participants] that it is possible to learn skills and find a job, we help them learn a culture of work and . . . build a future. When they realize this is possible, they can stop being dependent and passive."

Each year, some six hundred teenagers participated in the program. Some attended computer classes or workshops on résumé writing and other job-application skills. Others received basic English instruction and remedial tutoring. All were eligible—as was anyone in the municipality—to receive free health care from the foundation's clinic as well as basic foodstuffs from its community pantry. The most involved teens also lent a hand with the foundation's many initiatives by mentoring younger kids, performing administrative office work, working on neighborhood literacy campaigns, or publicizing vaccinations and psychoanalytic care at the foundation's clinic. These modes of participation were all highly informal. Attendance in classes and collaboration on other projects varied from day to day and week to week, in accordance with teenagers' fluctuating interests to be sure, but also due to family demands, such as caring for a younger sibling or taking advantage of a sudden and temporary work opportunity. However, the informality and lack of regimentation was not only a pragmatic concession to the unpredictability of these teenagers' lives. It also manifested a policy on the part of the program's administrators to encourage participation but not to demand reciprocation.

That policy was the practical effect of a paradox in the conceptualization of solidarity at work both in this foundation and more widely. On the one hand, people described solidarity as "spontaneous," "from the heart," and "without coercion." It was "a true commitment to others," one friend told me in an attempt to define the term. Or, in the words of one teenager in the Youth Protagonism Program, "Solidarity is helping others because one wants to, not to receive anything in return." We might seem, then, to be facing an example of what Parry (1986, 467) termed "an ideology of the pure gift," arising out of "an ethicized salvation religion, in which rewards are contingent on conduct [thereby] . . . orienting the ideal goals of social action towards a future existence." However, the very same people were at pains to distinguish solidarity from mere charity. They insisted that solidarity could not exist when one party gave and the other simply received; that was "dependence" and to be avoided at all costs. As a volunteer at a soup kitchen told me, "We don't just give them food. We want to encourage participation and solidarity, a community. Otherwise it's *asistencialismo*." A social psychologist and professor of solidarity studies at an area university made explicit the presumed logic in a 2007 interview: "Unless people become active participants in their communities, aid contributes to the pandemic of political clientelism . . . [and] reproduces social inequality and marginalization." Here, of course, we see the inverse of the pure gift—the poisonous gift (Derrida 1992) that appears unmotivated but in fact captures the recipient in a relation of indebtedness and subordination.

Volunteers and workers at the Youth Protagonism Program and other civil society organizations often expressed these two seemingly contrary imperatives—to give without reciprocation and to give without subordinating—in the same breath. As one young woman told me, "We help them without asking for anything in return. We help them so they don't just continue to receive, in a situation of dependence." Caught between a commitment to the gift as an unreservedly pure act of spontaneous generosity and a finely honed suspicion of the gift as a vehicle for manipulative domination, workers and volunteers in the Youth Protagonism Program responded to their dilemma by continually encouraging the teens to "collaborate," "to help others," "to contribute to the community," or to "involve themselves." Rather than demand direct reciprocation, they urged recipients to give to others and thereby overcome their "social marginalization" by transforming themselves from recipients into givers. It was through giving that poor teens would become productive protagonists capable of projecting not only their own futures but also the future of their community.

The relative success or failure of the Youth Protagonism Program in instilling this virtue in impoverished teens is not especially of interest here. However, one particular case is illuminating for other reasons. Introduced to me as one of the program's success stories, Susana had begun attending computer classes at the center when she was fourteen and went on to participate in a slew of activities throughout and after high school. She had received after-school tutoring and English classes, routine vaccinations and medical care, and took full advantage of the foundation's food pantry, supplementing her family's purchases with regular boxes of rice, pasta, and vegetables. Twenty-two years old when I met her in 2006, she continued to receive those services and volunteered at the foundation nearly every day, helping teenagers in the program, all the while searching for a stable, paid job.

Sitting in a Burger King along the highway near the foundation, Susana described for me her never-ending job search. She had sent out dozens of applications in the last few weeks alone but was pessimistic. Given what seemed to me a discouraging situation, I asked her whether she thought the skills she had learned at the Youth Protagonism Program had been of any help. She rose to the defense of the program. "It's incredible," she said. "People get together and meet each other and share experiences. That's what's essential . . . The training sessions and things like that are important, too. Without training, I probably wouldn't be able to find work." She went on, "Of course, I haven't found work yet. It's really hard. There is no work." Still, she insisted, "I have the opportunity because of the program." "What's essential is the solidarity, the community," she concluded, displaying no overt sign of real disappointment. Asked what she meant by solidarity, she went on: "It means helping without expecting anything. Before, the program helped me and now I collaborate with the program, helping other kids."

Susana's story is telling not because it is representative, nor because it demonstrates the futility of solidarity-building programs in solving the problem of unemployment, impoverishment, and socioeconomic inequality, but because it exemplifies so clearly the form of this program's self-proclaimed "success." Although she deemed important and lamentable her ongoing unemployment and continued reliance on the foundation's food pantry, she declared those concerns to be subsidiary to the fundamental, intersubjective structure of solidarity, within which people shared experiences, felt a sense of community, and learned how to want to give to others. In the terms of the program, she had succeeded; she had cultivated a sense of self-esteem and of herself as a protagonist. She had, it would seem, imbibed a culture of work. It just so happened that she actualized the values of work not through remunerated labor, of which there was almost none, but through unpaid volunteer work and community service.

NARRATIVE INEQUALITY

Ensuring that middle-class volunteers and workers were acting out of a sense of solidarity required something different than what was required with the poor recipients of solidary aid. Within the field of solidarity work, new volunteers or paid employees of organizations would first receive an orientation, usually consisting of a single session with the head of the program in which the person planned to work. As I came to see after participating in and witnessing many such sessions, they almost always consisted of the orienter recounting what had originally brought him or her to focus on solidarity, followed by the orientee offering up a structurally similar narrative. Almost without exception, these personal stories were offered in the genre of a conversion narrative, in which an encounter with a poor person would awaken a sympathetic response and engender an active social commitment.[16] Within the context of an orientation session, these conversion narratives allowed long-standing and new workers to engage in a practice of intersubjective calibration, helping to ensure, in the words of the head of the Villa Robles Center, that "we're here for the right reasons, that we're here out of solidarity."

The following transcript of a December 2004 conversation between Patricia, a Villa Robles worker, and myself is exemplary of these conversion narratives.[17] It took place one sweltering morning in the kitchen of the center. Patricia walked in, prepared *mate*, and slowly worked her way toward the topic of solidarity. Of particular interest are Patricia's temporalization of the narrated event in relation to the narrating event; the play of resemblance and difference that she established between me, a poor man she once encountered on the street, and herself; and the dramatic subjective transformation that she attributed to that encounter.

After a good deal of chitchat, she broached the central question, saying, "As Sergio told you, we meet with all the new volunteers so we can talk about why we are here." Then she went on:

---

16. In using the term "conversion narrative" to characterize narratives of politico-ethical self-transformation, I aim to invoke the large corpus of linguistic anthropological analyses of religious (usually Christian) conversion narratives, e.g., Buckser and Glazier 2003; Gooren 2010; Handman 2011; Keane 2007; Priest 2003; Rafael 1993; and Stromberg 1993.

17. The transcript here is lightly edited for readability. A full Spanish-language transcript appears in the appendix.

> You know, Sarita, solidarity, cooperation—it's essential, in this country above all because before, during the era of neoliberalism . . . we weren't very solidary. We Argentines, we middle-class people, we didn't think about others. . . . Everything changed with the crisis: we woke up. I woke up. I realized that solidarity was missing. . . . At that time, the streets were full of poor people in situations you can't even imagine. . . . You couldn't remain unaware without doing anything.

In these opening remarks, Patricia positions solidarity in opposition to neoliberalism. She disavows her former, neoliberal self and identifies the crisis as a moment of awakening and transformation. Crucially, the crisis here serves as a pivot point not only for her own personal transformation, but also for the subjective transformation of the nation or, at least, the Argentine middle class, at large.

> One day, right in that time of full-blown crisis, I'm going to my parents' house (You know what my parents are like, very middle-class, very proper, very hard-working) Well, so one day, in the middle of the crisis (well, you know how it was), I'm going to the dinner that my parents have every Saturday . . . the whole family gets together . . . I get off the bus (I'm a couple of blocks from the house where I grew up), and do you know what I see? A man, older, the age of my grandfather, and Sarita, I tell you the honest truth: I was captivated. He looked like my grandfather in a way that was so incredible.

Here, Patricia focuses on the event that effected the radical subjective transformation she has already referred to. In focusing her and my attention on her encounter with a man who looked like her grandfather, she switches to the historical present in order to make the encounter as vivid in the here-and-now of the storytelling moment as it was for her when it actually occurred. She also slowed down her speech, stretching out words like "captivated," iconically reenacting the way this sight arrested her own movement.

> I freeze—with my grandfather's light blue eyes, with my grandfather's hair. He's even dressed like my grandfather, very well dressed. And you know how it was that I knew that he was not my grandfather? Because he's eating in the street, looking for food in the trash, a horrible thing. And at that moment, Sarita, I realized—All of a sudden I understood that I couldn't remain quiet, that I had to do something to help the other, that this man could have been my grandfather and he was eating trash.

Still in the historical present, Patricia reaches the key moment in her narrative. This man in the street resembles her grandfather, but someone like her grandfather shouldn't be in the street. It is this jarring dissonance, this disjunctive resemblance, that catalyzes her ethical awakening and subjective transformation.

> Well, I started to live differently. I woke up to what was happening in this country, and within a year, here I was working, cooperating with the people of this neighborhood to improve things. . . . You know, Sarita, that I'm poor. I'm one of those "new poor," if you think about it. And that's why I know what this country needs. I know what we can achieve. And that's what I want to give to the kids in this neighborhood, these kids who never formed part of the national project because they couldn't. . . . That's how I started working here.

Identifying as a member of the "new poor," Patricia grants that identity and structural position a privileged role in reconstituting the national project. In virtue of that position, she asserts, she can bridge the gulf between the truly poor and the middle class. In this way, her own transformation can be replicated in others and, ultimately, at the level of the nation. She then concluded, saying, "So, Sarita, how about you? What brought you to solidarity work?" In this final utterance, she offers me a turn to speak, a turn predicated implicitly on the premise that I, too, would have a story to tell about how I became committed to solidarity.

Throughout her narrative, Patricia recruited me to the role of an interlocutor who was potentially, if not yet fully, on equal footing by asserting that I knew what her parents were like, what the crisis was like, and so on. She thus projected an increasing degree of similarity and even intimacy between us, a projection that culminated at the end of her discourse, when she turned my question back onto me. Patricia knew that I was not Argentine, that I had not been in the country during the crisis itself, that I had not met her parents, and so on. And yet, she addressed me as if we shared a social world in which a great deal of social knowledge could be assumed and pointed to with a simple "you know." She thus laid the groundwork for the intersubjective calibration of motive that was the explicit aim of the discussion.

That calibration hinged on Patricia's narration of her 2002 encounter with the poor man on the street. That encounter stood in for the crisis in general as the catalyst that catalyzed her newfound solidarity. In Patricia's framing, that awakening was personal, but (in a move familiar from numerous examples in previous chapters) it was simultaneously national and middle-class, as in her use of the pronoun "we" to refer ambivalently to both "Argentines" and "middle-class people." Further, that awakening hinged on the supposed resemblance between the poor man and her grandfather. In the Argentine context, the particular qualities that Patricia picked out (light blue eyes and so on) are clearly coded for both class and race; in Patricia's comments, these classed and racialized qualities became, in turn, signs of possible kinship.[18] For this reason, they provoked particular outrage, for, she gives us to understand, one would expect someone of that sort to be attending a family dinner, not picking through the garbage. That dissonance transforms Patricia in a sudden moment, narrated for dramatic emphasis in the historical present, that converted her into a new kind of person, with expanded horizons of action that transcend the self and oriented her toward the good of others.[19]

Altogether, then, the poetics of Patricia's narrative positioned the poor man as a figure of grace, an unexpected gift of ethical and epistemological insight.[20] But he did not figure as an interlocutor. Rather, he was relegated to what Benveniste (1971) calls the grammatical "non-person." He stood as a third-person object that made possible Patricia's subjective transformation into a newly authoritative, speaking "I"—a position that Patricia invited me to take up by opening up a space for me to recount a presumably similar experience of awakening.[21] In this way, Patricia's narrative presumed and privileged a normative middle-class footing even as she declared her commitment to egalitarian solidarity.

Over the course of years of fieldwork, I heard and/or participated in twenty-three full instances of these narratives and abbreviated reference to countless others. However, while Patricia's narrative was utterly commonplace among middle-class volunteers and workers, I never heard a similar one from clients at the Villa Robles Center or any of the other organizations where I spent time. That was not for want of trying on the part of the organizations' staff. In community-building meetings and other semiformal

---

18. The logic of Patricia's recognition thus exemplifies Sahlins's (2013, 28) conceptualization of kinship as "mutuality of being," with an emphasis on the dynamics of yearning and phaticity that Nozawa (2015) explicates in contemporary Japanese anxieties over solitary death.

19. We can understand this recognition of kinship as one of "rhematization" (Gal 2013), the semiotic process by which a particular interpretive framework is deployed so as to allow specific qualities to be picked out in a relationship of resemblance. Here, the recognition of resemblance is also bound up with a process of "dicentization" (Ball 2014), that is, the semiotic process that allows causality to be seen, as Patricia explains that seeing the old man as kin caused her ethical awakening. For more on the metapragmatic processes of rhematization and dicentization, see Gal 2018 and Nakassis 2019. On the semiotics of recognizing race and class and the accompanying anxieties of misrecognition, see Reyes 2017.

20. The encounter thus narrated takes the shape of an event in the Badiouian (2003 and 2013) sense—an eruption into the present that opens up radical new horizons of possibility, regimes of evaluation, and modes of subjectivity. On Christian kinship chronotopes that mobilize this sort of temporal logic of rupture, see Harkness 2015.

21. As Trouillot (2003) insists, this same interactional structure has typically characterized the discipline of anthropology as well as the "savage slot" within which it is situated and which dates at least to the debates between Sepúlveda and de Las Casas.

gatherings, staff would often invite clients to rehearse a story of coming to solidarity. What clients offered in response rarely seemed to satisfy.

The following short transcript comes from a meeting of teenagers in the computer class.[22] Patricia led the meeting and attempted to mold it into a stage for the reenactment of solidary awakenings, but the teenagers, not surprisingly, were guarded in their speech and declined to take up fully the role Patricia offered them.

PATRICIA   Well guys, we're going to talk a little bit about solidarity, about the importance of solidarity, about what solidarity is. What does it mean to be solidary? How do we build it? And why? . . . Who feels like saying something? . . . Ernesto, do you want to begin?

ERNESTO   Yeah, well, I just want to say that by yourself, you can't do anything. By yourself, you can't solve your problems. You need solidarity. Look— all this, everything we've done in this neighborhood, we achieved it through solidarity.

PATRICIA   Yes, and how can we build it? Was it always this way? Were you always solidary? . . . Ernesto, do you want to say something? For you, how is it that the people of this neighborhood learned to be solidary?

ERNESTO   Well, we all know the difficulties we've been through. We never had things easy. We've always had to help each other. But yeah, with the crisis things got worse and we came here. The center helped all of us in the neighborhood survive.

PATRICIA   Hmmmm yes. Does someone else want to comment? . . . OK, well, let's talk about something else: next week's party . . . .

In this short snippet of conversation, Patricia attempted to offer Ernesto and the other teenagers the grounds for an equal footing. She elicited a story of ethical awakening. But Ernesto and the others could not articulate one, not because they did not have their own histories and personal experiences of the crisis and of working in solidarity, but because they understood the crisis to be simply a moment when "things got worse," a more processual temporalization than the one Patricia's story entailed. Ernesto offered a story of gradual, perhaps minimal personal change rather than sudden transformation. As a result, although Patricia assented to Ernesto's narrative ("Hmmmm yes"), it did not give her the discursive resources with which to launch a broader or deeper discussion about solidarity. Instead, she found herself compelled to shift to something else, the following week's party and its logistical questions.

---

22. The transcript is lightly edited for readability. A Spanish-language transcript appears in the appendix.

Even when invited to take up an egalitarian footing, Ernesto could not do so. The events that brought him to the center were taken by all concerned to be fundamentally different from the ones that brought Patricia. Ernesto came to the center to solve material problems of day-to-day survival and, later, to take computer classes, not because of a conversion experience that had transformed his very sense of self and compelled him to seek new ways of forming community. Not only did he continue to live in Villa Robles while Patricia lived across the tracks in Catalinas, not only did he continue to command a dramatically lesser valued set of cultural, political, and economic capital than that which Patricia had at her disposal, but he was also effectively barred from assuming a position of narrative equality within the center.[23]

Removed from their context, transcribed, and dissected, it seems fairly obvious that the genre of the solidarity conversion narrative produced a relation of inequality between staff and clients. However, in the continual flow of daily interactions, that process was not so clear. Staff at these organizations were painfully aware that their interactions with their clients were profoundly unequal—despite their work to establish interpersonal equality, despite their attention to the gift's hierarchizing potential, and despite their self-reflexive critiques of their own complicity in the political-economic processes that had produced massive social inequalities in the first place. Nonetheless, I never heard anyone remark on the role these conversion narratives might have played in reproducing unequal relations. That blindness was not theirs alone; for some time I did not even realize that I had stumbled on the genre. It took some time for me to conclude that, laminated on top of and reinforcing entrenched relations of socioeconomic inequality was a pattern of narrative inequality emerging out of the new dynamics of solidarity building.

The conversion narratives did not only perform the subjective transformation they recounted, they also reanimated the registers of distinction and regimes of value that defined the parameters of that transformation. Such is the work of ritual, which produces that which it displays. As such, these narratives served a dual pedagogical purpose. They guided people as they attempted to reshape their motivational and affective structures according to the ideals of solidarity. However, they also taught people how

---

23. Hymes (1996) coined the term "narrative inequality." I take it up here in a slightly different way in order to name and highlight the differential capacities of people to offer socially legible and valorized genres of narrative. As Stephen Scott (2017, 187) argues with respect to genres of talk among women in El Alto, Bolivia, sympathy and solidarity are "not so much the ground of commiseration as its interactional entailment." Here, Ernesto seemed to say, where commiseration was impossible due to materially different conditions and engrained narratives of self and community, solidarity was not truly possible.

to see classed and racialized distinctions anew in a context where the stability and clarity of those distinctions had come under strain. Despite the social and economic upheavals that residents of Catalinas as well as those of Villa Robles had undergone in recent decades, conversion narratives recontextualized long-standing registers of class and race and made them newy relevant.

In conversion narratives like Patricia's, we can see starkly one way that solidarity, as a mode of ethicized civility, reanimates the very inequalities it would overcome. For Patricia, the encounter with the man on the street was a moment of grace, an unexpected rupture of the everyday that propelled her into a transcendent, ethically and epistemologically valorized space of solidarity. However, Ernesto could not access that grace nor that regime of ethical and epistemological value, because the genre of the conversion narrative is unavailable to the poor. They cannot take up the national and middle-classed "I" and "we." And so, they are grammatically relegated to third-person object and evidence, about whom much can be said, but who are not authorized to assume equal footing in the national conversation.

THE GIFTS OF NEOLIBERALISM

There is much to be said about the ironies and contradictions inherent in cultivating a "culture of work" in a place like Villa Robles, defined as it was by abandoned factories and the near total absence of opportunities for remunerated labor. Argentina's economy enjoyed a tremendous expansion during the post-crisis period. However, this boom depended on a commodity-export driven political economy that produced "widening income inequalities and an increasing trend toward precarious forms of labor" (Svampa 2008, 80).[24] As such, the quality of that expansion left much to be desired, especially for those Argentines, like Susana and Ernesto, with the least social, cultural, and economic capital to sell on the marketplace. Despite this context, solidarity-building initiatives did not abandon a commitment to "the culture of work" as indispensable to the projection of individual and collective futures. Of course, work and futurity are bound up with one another across a host of traditions of political, economic, and social philosophy, and the twenetieth-century chronotope of progress always hinged on the mechanism of productive labor.[25] In this sense, the field of

24. This "commodities consensus" (Svampa 2013) also had devastating environmental consequences and ran roughshod over the rights of indigenous communities in the rural interior.

25. Summing up nicely that widespread intuition are the words of two Argentine sociologists who mobilized a constellation of Arendtian-sounding ideas about productivity as they wrote

solidarity building was an attempt to reanimate that modern chronotope even in the absence of the kinds of employment that had once undergirded it. Crucially, that attempt at resuscitation hinged not primarily on material or institutional change but first and foremost on subjective transformation: if only gifts could be given and received in the right spirit, equality could be achieved and horizons of a new national future could be projected.[26]

Of course, to discern the spirit animating an action requires constant vigilance and anxious self-examination. And so, suspicious critiques of self and other blossomed in solidary endeavors. The critiques generated a constant drumbeat of concerns about the difficulties of subjective transformation in a world overdetermined by the relentless systems of the neoliberal world order. Ultimately, though attempts to regiment that subjective transformation through the alignment of conversion narratives reaffirmed existing inequalities and made it all the more difficult to imagine structural transformation.[27]

Given the unavoidable monetary loss and sense of historical exhaustion that defined the post-crisis Buenos Aires middle class, it is not surprising that demands for a radically different political-economic system did not abound within the field of solidarity building. Those sentiments entailed shrinking horizons for action to the scale of the individual. The idea of solidarity was a creative attempt to counteract that nearly paralyzing set of restrictions by elaborating a form of futurity that extended beyond the individual precisely by constructing new forms of selfhood that would avoid the corrupting taint of state and market institutions.

As a gift-based model of society, solidarity thus rejected certain strains of

---

anxiously about the changing terrain of work in post-crisis Argentina: "The emancipatory task of work consists in the possibility of the exercise of power [and for this reason] we understand that assistence practices [*prácticas asistencialistas*] proliferate in social spaces where the transformational capacity of human beings is negated and where there is no space for critical reason" (Schvarstein and Leopold 2005, 21). For a remarkably consonant account of the changing conditions of possibility for productivity (in her terms, "*vita activa*"), see Arendt 1958.

26. This idealist and "productionist" approach to the gift that dominated solidarity-building efforts thus contrasts sharply with the more materialist approaches to gifts, community belonging, and "anti-productionist" futures that Ferguson (2015) explores in his discussion of the politics of distribution in an era of mass unemployment and that Kropotkin (1906), whose words stand as the epigraph for this chapter, articulated.

27. In the third of her Neapolitan novels, Ferrante (2014, 46) paints a similar dynamic between leftist university students and the workers whose consciousnesses they aim to raise. "Lila noticed how easy it was to distinguish the faces of the students from those of the workers, the fluency of the leaders from the stuttering of the followers. And she quickly became irritated. . . . The refrain, besides, was always the same: We're here to learn from you, meaning from the workers, but in reality they were showing off ideas that were almost too obvious about capital, about exploitation, about the betrayal of social democracy, about the modalities of the class struggle."

liberalism, such as the abstract, proceduralist logics of a commodity-based economy and representative democracy. However, it grounded community membership and material well-being in affective, voluntarist relations that dovetailed with neoliberal understandings of the transformative power of "civil society" and "social capital" to solve all manner of social ills.[28] What sets solidarity apart in this context is the emphasis on the spontaneity, immediacy, and transparency of one's intentions, an emphasis that calls forth continual suspicion. As a result, the utopianism of solidarity building was deeply anxious, plagued by the looming sense of its own impossibility. In the words of one employee at a community health center, "That is how we are. We must work toward a more moral Argentina; a solidary Argentina; an Argentina defined by the virtues of education, work, and commitment; an Argentina that the middle class once thought it had achieved but which we never will."

In the end, solidarity building was a rare example of an explicitly future-oriented form of sociality in post-crisis, middle-class Buenos Aires. However, it was predicated on the capacity of the event of crisis to awaken critical insight and compel subjective transformation, with narratives of that ennobled self serving as inspiration and catalyst for the similar transformation of other selves. Because their generic requirements demanded a particular kind of speaker, with a particular biography and place in the social world, those narratives of solidarity were not only differentially distributed, they also reanimated a disavowed regime of class and racial difference. What is more, unable to avoid the nagging suspicion that their very selves had been corrupted and that their motives could never be sufficiently purified, solidarity workers found themselves compelled to be constantly, anxiously vigilant. In solidarity, then, the moralized perspective on social history that is so familiar from modern accounts of historical time was introjected into the individual. There, it could not but falter.

---

28. The work of Putnam (2000) exemplifies the utopian promise that civil society has recently come to hold for so many. On this point, see Comaroff and Comaroff 1999 and Muehlebach 2012; see also Paley 2001 for an extended critique.

ARGENTINE AFTERWORD

"Crisis is becoming the new normal," the president of the Rockefeller Foundation, Judith Rodin, recently declared. Responding to a world in which catastrophes of all sorts—economic, ecological, terrorist, and so on—are becoming ever more frequent, she argues that we must "build greater resilience."[1] Only in this way will we be able to withstand the systemic shocks that are inevitably to come.

My aim in this book has been not to dispute that assessment but rather to interrogate its conditions of possibility, to ask what it blinds us to in the contemporary moment, and to underscore the constraints that it puts on the horizons of the imaginable. What a reduced vision of the future, to assume that it will consist of an infinite series of disasters and recoveries! Where the assumption of progressive modernity has become obsolete, to replace it with the assumption of routine crisis would be to abandon the possibility of imagining different kinds of flourishing and to reconcile ourselves to a grim ethic of resignation.

Over the last five chapters, I have traced the causes and consequences of routine crisis, this disillusioned configuration of crisis, critique, and historical time, as they appear in Argentina. By design, my analysis has not proceeded according to the logic of revelation that is so intimately tied up with modern understandings of crisis and historical time. To do so would have been to laminate one more layer of suspicious critique on top of those of my interlocutors and therefore to risk echoing and even amplifying their sentimental stance of disillusion. Instead, I have asked the reader to accompany me in attending to the practices and folk categories that produced that disillusion and to allow for the possibility that, in so doing, our own

---

1. Stephen Moss, "Judith Rodin's Warning for the World: 'Crisis Is Becoming the New Normal,'" *Guardian*, January 27, 2015.

analytic categories and sentimental dispositions might themselves be productively unsettled.

At one level, this approach offers insight into the dramatic polarization that has characterized Argentine politics in recent years. During the 2003–2007 period that is at issue in this book, the recent crisis served as a collective touchstone that allowed a broad swath of society to reach a consensus about its significance. However, in the years thereafter, a stark contrast emerged between the avowedly progressive political project of Cristina Fernández de Kirchner and her allies on the one hand and, on the other hand, a newly consolidated oppositional bloc—frequently stylized as "the middle class"—that denounced that project as a web of populist lies and wishful thinking. This ongoing conflict—usually called *la grieta* ("the crevasse")—has regularly produced dramatic moments of confrontation, such as street protests, accusations of coups and conspiracies, and nationwide strikes. Within Argentina, it is commonplace to treat this political rift as the inevitable outcome of a long tradition of middle-class antagonism toward Peronism. However, by looking more closely at the historical, ethical, and social sensibilities of the post-crisis Buenos Aires middle class, it is possible to see *la grieta* not as inevitable but as the understandable product of those sensibilities. The broadly felt sense of disillusion, suspicion, and exhausted possibilities made it difficult for many in the middle class to envision not merely how but even *whether* a legitimate national project was possible, especially one driven by a state that had been so thoroughly discredited. Within the chronotope of routine crisis—with its set of characters, plausible plotlines, imaginable temporalities, horizons of possibility, and regimes of value—such a project was inconceivable, even absurd.

More broadly, the approach I have taken speaks to the melancholic nostalgia now widely shared amongst leftists and liberals alike for the "mass utopias" (Buck-Morss 2000) of the nineteenth and twentieth centuries. When we look around the world today and feel dismay at the rising tide of fascism, how can we avoid the grim conclusion that we must simply ride it out? Imagining another response requires that we go beyond simply reiterating Arendt or Benjamin or any other post–World War II critique, insightful and to the point though they may be. Those critiques have not inoculated us and they will not save us. What is more, like the suspicious critiques of the post-crisis Buenos Aires middle class, they operate today as a badge of honor, an iterable (and highly predictable) performance, and an insignia and mark of distinction. That distinction easily feeds into holding patterns of political inaction. We need to forge different kinds of engagement and envision decidedly different futures that do not reinscribe, in however roundabout a way, the regimes of value that have undergirded past mass utopias. To do so, we must ask what obsolete commitments we need jettison, however painful their loss may be.

In dwelling on the impasses, disappointments, and double-binds of the post-crisis Buenos Aires middle class, my aim in the preceding chapters has been to feel out where some of those obsolete commitments may be and to open them up to interrogation and challenge. My approach has thus differed from the emphasis on finding hope in "precarity" (Allison 2015, Tsing 2015) or in "vulnerability in resistance" (Butler 2016). Instead, I have attended above all to negativity, and this in two related senses of the word.

In one sense, the book's attention to negativity is an attention to frustrated hopes, to things going wrong, and to worlds coming undone. Attending to those dynamics allows us to register things that go unnoticed if we insist on foregrounding hope and newness. In this regard, I have been inspired by Adorno's entreaty to forego finding comfort in "the negation of the negation" and instead to witness the open-ended, unpredictable, and frequently disappointing movement of negative dialectics: "The thesis that the negation of a negation is something positive can only be upheld by one who presupposes positivity—as all-conceptuality—from the beginning" (1994, 160).

The second and related sense of negativity that the book has emphasized is also conjured by the above quotation. As Adorno is at pains to emphasize, negativity is not simply disappointment but also the impossibility of conceptuality—ideas, interpretations, descriptions, theories—to fully grasp the world as it is. For Adorno, that impossibility is not merely a constraint but also an opening, for it means that the world exceeds our representations and that unimaginable things can happen. The world—and we ourselves—can truly surprise us. And it is here, I think, that we might find tools for imagining a different kind of future.

Adorno is not alone in emphasizing the irreconcilable distance between object and concept. Such an emphasis is also prominent in Montaigne's (1991) spirit of playful anthropological inquiry and provocation, as well as in Hume's (1993) insistence on the insufficiency of categories of knowledge and in Peirce's (1932) attention to the open-endedness of semiosis. This foregrounding of a permanent friction between the world and our ideas leaves conceptual schema permanently changeable, such that one must voice critique in the interrogative or hypothetical rather than in the declarative mood. Dimensions of Boltanski's (2011) critical engagement with critique resonate with that friction, as do Tambar's (2017) attention to uncanny media of critique, Rutherford's (2012) call for a "kinky empiricism" and Asad's questioning of the "the limits of critical inquiry itself" and "whether and in what way intellectualizing is important" (Bardawil and Asad 2016,

158, 159). By knitting together a genealogy of thought that is skeptical of its own import (rather than suspicious of the world of appearances), we can allow the world and our own thoughts to surprise us once again.

Chapter 2 concluded with a brief description of a bit of graffiti that declared, "NOTHING NEW." That phrase captured a widespread historical stance within the Buenos Aires middle class in the years following the 2001–2002 Argentine crisis. It also captures a widespread historical stance within the transnational middle classes following the 2008 global financial crisis. Our shared challenge is to recognize that stance for what it is and to construct something else in its place.

ACKNOWLEDGMENTS

For nearly a decade, I was resigned to the fact that this book would never come into being. In 2011, I was the stay-at-home mother of two children under the age of two. I had just defended my dissertation after a long struggle, had no job prospects, and assumed that the career I had long wanted was an impossibility. The existence of this book is incredible to me, and I can claim only a sliver of responsibility for it. It is a truism that all books are the visible product of the distributed labors of a mostly invisible network of people. However, more than most, this book is the doing of people other than myself: people whose generosity and rigorous engagement buoyed the project and carried me along with it.

The questions that animate this book were forged at the University of Chicago, where my experience was one of nearly unbridled intellectual excitement and discovery. A handful of classes—Systems I with Michel-Rolph Trouillot; Language and Culture with Susan Gal and Michael Silverstein; The Anthropology of Value with Danilyn Rutherford; and Self, Culture, and Society with Moishe Postone—changed my thinking in the most profound ways and sparked an entirely new set of intellectual obsessions. My committee members, John Comaroff, Susan Gal, Claudio Lomnitz, Joseph Masco, and Elizabeth Povinelli, all offered encouragement as I pursued those obsessions. And, as will come as no surprise to anyone who knows anything about the Department of Anthropology at Chicago, Anne Ch'ien was the deeply kind, competent, and reassuring bulwark without whom I, like so many other students, might well never have completed my degree.

More than anything else, however, it was the community of students who defined my time at Chicago. Now that we are all flung to the far corners of the earth, they have become my "invisible college" (a term I and many others learned from Michael Silverstein; it was coined by Crane 1972 and cited in Gal 2018, 5). My memories of casual conversations, workshop comments, and long nights in the Regenstein continue to spur my thinking, and the work my erstwhile peers have done since our time together at Chicago is an ongoing inspiration, as are the sadly infrequent occasions for renewed face-to-face conversation. While I can't name everyone, I must extend my deepest appreciation to Gretchen Bakke, Andrew Bauer, Greg Beckett, Rob Blunt, Mike Cepek, Nusrat Chowdhury, Erin Debenport, Cassie Fennell, Mark Gheraghty, Drew Gilbert, Andy Graan, Jessica Greenberg, Courtney Handman, Elina Hartikainen, Brian Horne, Zoe Humphreys, Paul Kockelman, Steve Kosiba, Rocío Magaña, Simon May, Sean Mitchell, Andrea Muehlebach, Shunsuke Nogawa, Nitzan Shoshan, James Slotta, Jeremy Walton, Hylton White, Hannah Woodroofe, and Rihan Yeh.

The core of this far-flung web of relationships forged at Chicago consists of Joe Hankins, Kelda Jamison, and Kabir Tambar. The three of them read every word of this book, multiple times over, and they were indispensable in helping me locate its center of gravity and hone its arguments. Kelda copyedited the entire manuscript at its early stage, correcting innumerable infelicities and improving it in every way. For two decades now, they have been the most devoted of friends and the most serious of interlocutors. Without them, I could not have managed, and this book would never have seen the light of day. And they well know that this is not hyperbolic praise.

In New York City, I have beeen lucky to be included in a patchwork of lively, engaged, intellectual circles. My colleagues in the City University of New York, both at City College and at the Graduate Center, are model scholars, interlocutors, and coworkers from whom I continue to learn how to construct an academic path that responds to the often conflicting intellectual, political, and pedagogical demands we all face. For this, I am indebted to Asale Angel-Ajani, Jillian Cavanaugh, Leo Coleman, John Collins, Miki Makihara, Jeff Maskovsky, Matthew Reilly, Angela Reyes, Andrew Rich, Asha Samad-Matías, Jane Schneider, Irina Carlota (Lotti) Silber, Julie Skurski, and Stanley Thangaraj. I hope to conntinue learning from them for many years to come. I am similarly grateful to have had the opportunity to work alongside Nadia Abu el-Haj, Severin Fowles, Brian Larkin, Lesley Sharp, and Paige West while at Barnard College. There, I also had the extraordinary fortune to get to know Gökçe Günel, Chelsea Kivland, and Stephen Scott, whose keen intellects and warm support I continue to rely on. Beyond my own institutional homes, the Oikos Working Group at New York University's Institute for Public Knowledge, the Unpayable Debt Working Group at Columbia University's Center for the Study of Social Difference, and the more informal Anthropology Writing Workshop at Columbia University have all provided generative spaces that have furthered my scholarship immeasurably. Within these spaces, I am particularly grateful to Lily Chumley, Nicholas D'Avella, Cassie Fennell, Sean Mitchell, Frances Negrón-Muntaner, Gustav Peebles, Michael Ralph, Erica Robles-Anderson, Jessie Shipley, and Caitlin Zaloom. Without their relentlessly provocative thinking, my own would be so much the poorer.

The research that undergirds this book was funded by the Fulbright-Hays Doctoral Dissertation Research Abroad Fellowship as well as the Tinker Field Research Grant, the Leiffer Fellowship, the Orin Williams Grant, the Doolittle-Harrison Grant, the Lichstern Grant, the University of Chicago Dissertation Teaching and Research Fellowship, and the Markovitz Dissertation Fellowship for Research on Social and Economic Behavior. However, that research was only possible because of the patience, hospitality, and charity of people I met while living in Buenos Aires. Most of those people will necessarily go unnamed, but I must especially thank Sergio Abad, Carlos Báez Silva, Laura Benbenaste, Marcelo Cespedes, Álvaro del Villar, Liliana Devoto, Karina Lencina, and Lizzie Wanger. I am also grateful for the time in Buenos Aires spent with Mireille Abelin, Leticia Barrera, Karen Faulk, Carolyn Merritt, and Noa Vaisman as well as for ongoing engagements with Enrique Garguin, Sergio Visacovsky, and Ariel Wilkis—all scholars of Argentina whose work informs my own in innumerable ways.

Priya Nelson has been the kind of editor an author doesn't dare dream of. Clear-eyed, patient, and insightful, she has shepherded this book through the publication process with grace and generosity. What is more, she has a fabulous sense of humor. I am amazed at my good luck in having had this opportunity to work with her.

Among the innumerable helpful and inspired things that Priya has done for this book was to collaborate with the editors for the Chicago Series in Studies in Practices of Meaning at the University of Chicago Press to workshop the manuscript. The experience of sitting in Wilder House and listening to the animated critiques of Susan Gal, Andreas Glaeser, William Mazzarella, and Lisa Wedeen will always be one of the highlights of my academic life. Their interventions made the book smarter, pithier, and better in every way. The anonymous reviewers Priya recruited provided similarly charitable and productive feedback; I only wish I could thank them by name. For all their detailed, thoughtful, and careful work, I am also grateful to the entire editorial team at the University of Chicago Press, especially Tristan Bates, Jenni Fry, Dylan Montanari, Kristen Raddatz, Mary Tong, and Kyle Wagner.

Finally, my family. If ten years ago it seemed to me that family was one reason this book wouldn't come into existence, in retrospect it's clear that the book owes them everything. My two children, Matilda and Calum, are now getting big, and I see in them the courage, kindness, and wit that I would like to have. Susan and Tom Muir have always been exemplary parents. I can't begin to describe how grateful I am for their patience, love, and support throughout my academic travails, and I only wish I could live up to their example. Finally, since the day I met him, David Giles has been an indefatigable enabler of my scholarly work. He has introduced me to philosophers, novelists, musicians, filmmakers, and poets I would not otherwise have known. He has debated and challenged me with an acumen I can never quite muster. He has read, edited, and commented on my writing. He has solo-parented for days and weeks on end while I travel. He has enriched my life in every sense. And he has not once made me feel that his support was a favor or an indulgence, but always that it was a matter of course. Thank you.

APPENDIX

The following transcription conventions are adapted from Stromberg 1993, xvi:

Underlining indicates spoken emphasis
: indicates extended sound
.... indicates a noticeable pause too short to be accurately timed
..... indicates a pause of 0.5 second; each dot represents one-tenth of a second
(()) bounds transcriber's comments
bounds quickly spoken speech
? indicates rising intonation
, indicates falling intonation
= indicates short transition time
[...] indicates an omitted section of transcript

CHAPTER 1 TRANSCRIPTS

TAXI DRIVER   fue una crisis, ... una crisis de veras y nada va a ser igual, ... nunca. ... cuando el pueblo salió a la calle y hubo un caos?. ... cuando el presidente huyó y la policía perdió control? .... cuando ni pudiste retirar tu pro:pia pla:ta de los bancos? .... allí nos despertamos, y vimos que nada estuvo bien, que muchísimo estuvo injusto e ilegítimo, que no hubo un futu:ro para un país como lo nuestro, ... fue una crisis verdadera, ... profunda, y creo que nosotros. ... nosotros los argentinos. ... nosotros de la clase media. ... nos vimos por primera vez, ... y pensamos que todo iba a cambiar, pero no va a cambiar nunca, nada va a cambiar nunca, ... siempre hemos estado caóticos, siempre vamos a estar caóticos

MANUEL   los noventa? .... fue una época del bien-estar. ... de la productividad. ... de la confianza y de la esperanza, por fin formamos parte del primer mundo, #bueno casi# ((pauses to sip mate)). .... nosotros la clase media trabajabamos arduamente por el futuro y por nuestra dedicación? viajamos. ... y vivimos bien ((pauses to sip mate)). .... #claro que hubo mucha corrupción de parte de los políticos# y todo eso se mostró en 2001, cuando se puso el corralito, eso fue la gran corrupción, quisieron destruir la clase media, robarnos todo para los politicos y las grandes empresas aquí y fuera ((pauses to sip *mate*)). . . . . . . No tuvimos opción sino reclamar nuestros derechos, no se #pusieron los cacerolazos porque nos tocó el bolsillo# como se dice todo el mundo, sino para demandar nuestros derechos, para exigir el principio de la ley, para hacernos un país de leyes, la clase media, nosotros quisimos ((bangs table with right index finger)) defender el país contra tal ((bangs table with right index finger)) impunidad, #pero no importó# ((waves right hand dismissively)) fue la clase media la que la crisis golpó tan fuerte, sufrimos pésimamente, fue un trauma insólito, pero? nunca hará justicia, el país esta arruinado y no hay remedio. . . . somos un pueblo egoista, tenemos una profunda contradicción entre el egoismo y los valores y #así no se supera eso#. . . . ahora se sabe. . . . algo así #no podría pasar# en un país en serio, #no podría pasar# ((points right index finger at me)) en los Estados Unidos, verdad? es ((pounds fist on table)) muy argentino esta incapacidad de ver las cosas como son,

A N A   durante los noventa todo el mundo fue a Miami, compró electrónicos y ropa de lujo, pretendió #formar parte del primer mundo,# pero fue un sueño, una ilusión, y eso? porque millones de argentinos #estaban siendo marginali-zados y empobrecidos# ((looks out window and sighs)). . . . . y fuimos cómplices en eso, los políticos controlaron todo? pero #nosotros la clase media# fuimos todos cómplices en permitirlo, porque quisimos ir a Miami, a los shoppings, a cenar fuera y pretender estar en otro mundo ((looks out window)). . . . . pensamos que construyéramos algo? que creciéramos? pero el país estaba perdiendo todo, ... sólo el corra-lito despertó a la gente y la hizo ver lo que pasó durante los noventa, ... el pueblo salió a la calle porque se había tocado el bolsillo, ((lights ciga-rette)). . . . . los pobres siempre han sido pobres, pero eso fue un verdadero trauma para nosotros, pero también fuimos a la calle porque nosotros la clase media nos dimos cuenta de que #habíamos permitido que se ocurriera algo horrible,# porque quisimos poner fin a #una cultura de impunidad#, de corrupción, quisimos crear ((gestures with air quotes)) un país en serio, fomentar la solidaridad en vez del egoismo, ... pero esto también fue un sueño, somes muy egoistas como para construir un futuro verdadero. . . . hay que seguir a construir lo que pueda pero este país está fundado en la mentira la corrupción, y la avaricia, y eso es casi imposible cambiar porque al fondo? no tenemos ganas, ... hemos sido enseñados por mucho tiempo preocuparnos por nosotros mismos, ... es una patología inducida, como la de un nene maltratado que al hacerse mayor? ((wags left index finger back and forth)) se maltrata a simismo y no piensa en los demás

E D U A R D O   yo crecí durante los noventa, durante el uno a uno, y no #se me ocurrió que cambiara,# fue la ley ((shrugs, throws up hands)). . . . . #no ganamos lo mismo que la gente del primer mundo# pero ((shrugs)). . . . . . . pensamos que #compartimos del mismo mundo,# que la Argentina #finalmente iba a ser lo que aprendimos en la escuela que pretendió,# un país de la clase media, el bienestar y la productividad y la paz y poco a poco despacito el progreso que dejara por detrás todo lo feo de la dictadura y los autos de mierda y las villas ((shrugs, throws up hands, drums fingers on table)). . . . . estábamos todos equivocados, ((points to the side)) los políticos lo sabían, ((points to the side)) los empresarios y los con muchos recursos lo sabían, ((points to the side)) los Estados Unidos y la UE lo sabían, pero ((places hand on chest)) nosotros, la gente común, la gente de clase media estábamos soñando, soñabamos con nuestro sueño más profundo, el vínculo inconsciente al primer mundo, un sueño que fue inducido por la anestesia, por la clase dirigente que nos mantenó dormidos durante todo los noventa, mientras las cosas se desarmaban poco a poco ((strokes chin)). la crisis, el corralito, fue como la desaparición de repente de la anestesia, de repente todos nos despertamos y vimos que nos habían robado, pero ya fue muy tarde ((rolls up sleeves)). . . . . algunos dicen que hemos aprendido de todo eso, que no soñamos más con el primer mundo pero no lo sé, ... creo que todavía tenemos una dedicación profunda a la #fantasía de pertenecer al primer mundo,# así fue para siempre por la Argentina, por la clase media de acá, es lo que ha conducido el bienestar de la clase media pero tambien lo que nos causó a perder todo, ... no creo que la podamos dejar ((strokes chin, grins)). . . . . por eso me voy a Europa, capaz que allá suene otra cosa

CHAPTER 2 TRANSCRIPTS

LETICIA   de repente? no tener ni la plata como para comprar la leche? fue cuando me dí cuenta de que nunca hubo sido un futuro en este país de mierda, ... [. . .] antes fingimos inocencia, pero aún después #de la crisis más profunda de todas#? nosostros la clase media todavía no podemos abandonar nuestros vínculos a las fantasías consumistas, ... [. . .] siempre vamos a estar en crisis

HÉCTOR   ver el riesgo país va pa'rriba, pa'rriba, pa'rriba todos los días? [. . .] me desperté y yo ví que nunca íbamos a ser el país en el cual pensamos que nos convertiríamos, hemos pasado por muchas crisis, pero por fin nos despertó a esta verdad, ... pero nosotros ((places hand on chest)) la clase media todavía negamos renunciar nuestros sueños con el primer mundo, ... y eso es el problema

MARTA   fue un shock, ... nosotros la clase media? . . . . perdimos mucho pero lo bueno es que entendimos que #nunca hemos estado en el camino al futuro,# pero ya? no fue un verdadero shock, con nuestra historia de crisis trás crisis, ... [. . .] todos supimos lo que fue cuando occurieron los saqueos [. . .] somos un pueblo falso, una nación trucha, vivimos en una crisis perpetua de nuestra propia fabricación, pero ya? qué más es el capitalismo?

MABEL   intentamos entender como es que una crisis tras otra nos ha definido. . . . cómo podemos dejar que esta pobreza y esta desigualdad? ((points to the side)) esta corrupción total ((points to the side)) continue? hay que criticar todo, ... pero no va a cambiar, ojalá los argentinos nosotros de la clase media aprendamos, ... pero no se puede desarmar el deseo como no se puede desarmar el complejo de Edipo, ... así que avanzamos, participando a sabiendas en nuestra propia trajedia, el sistema del capitalismo global asegura otra crisis, y nosotros somos cómplices

CHAPTER 3 TRANSCRIPTS

ARTURO   todo eso me hace enfermo, ... es que una persona que ((points at himself)). . . . . una persona ((continues pointing at himself)) que trabaja desde abajo hacia encima y eso te trae desde encima hacia abajo. . . . la verdad es? lo que me pasó a mí pasó a muchas, pero muchas familias argentinas. . . . . no hablo de los ricos ((waves hand dismissively)), los muy ricos. . . . somos ((points to himself)) trabajado-res. . . . . no soy el hombre de antes. . . . fue una mentira, #se pasó todo, para siempre,# pero #no lo voy a dejar,# es el principio de la justicia, el principio de la ley

CHAPTER 4 TRANSCRIPTS

ALICIA solo la clase dirigente y la gente humilde que vende el voto para sobrevivir, ... no entiendo #el verdadero valor# del voto. . . . hoy los #valores de la clase media# no tienen importancia,. . . . soy de una familia de clase media pero ahora no. . . . es una pena pero no nos compadezcas, ... nosotros somos los corruptos, ... aquí hay un lema, todo país? tiene el presidente que merezca, ... merecíamos a Menem y merecemos a los políticos que tenemos ahora, ... son de nosotros. . . . de todos nosotros. . . . no existen en un lugar afuera, son de aquí, y nos reflejan

CHAPTER 5 TRANSCRIPTS

PATRICIA AND SARAH

S1 Y. . . . cómo fue que empezaste a trabajar aquí?

P1 Trabajar? mejor colaborar. . . . porque no es un laburo, ... un puesto así no más, ... es un trabajo de colaboración, ... sabés?

S2 Mmm y para vós? . . . . la colaboración? . . . . qué es? cómo la describís?

P2 La colaboración es el trabajo solidario, ... es el trabajo del corazón ((gestures toward her heart)). . . . el trabajo que surge del compromiso, de la solidaridad. . . .

S3 mm mmm

P3 Y vos sabés. . . . Sarah. . . . la solidaridad. . . . la colaboración es esencial. . . . sobre todo en este país. . . . porque antes? . . . . durante todo lo de. . . . la época del neoliberalismo. . . . durante los noventa. . . . con todo lo del menemato. . . . no éramos muy solidarios, ... nosotros los argentinos nosotros de la clase media. . . . no pensábamos en los demás,. . . . en el otro

S4 mm

P4 Con la crisis cambió todo, ((sweeps hand in front of her as if clearing the table)). . . . nos despertamos, ... me desperté. . . . me dí cuenta de que hacía falta la solidaridad. . . . la colaboración. . . . empecé a pensar en el otro. . . . empecé a colaborar para mejorar las cosas. . . . para ayudar al otro,

S5 Y. . . . bueno. . . . fue así que te diste cuenta de =

P5 = Sí. . . . te lo explico, ... fijate, ((points at me)). . . . . . te voy a contar como fue, ... en aquel momento las calles? estaban llenas de pobres de personas en situaciones que ni te podés imaginar, ... horrible. . . . No podías quedarte ignorante. . . . quedarte. . . . sin hacer nada

S6 mm mm

P6 Un día.... justo en aquel momento de plena crisis.... yo estoy yendo a lo de mis papás.... vos <u>sabés</u> como son mis papás

S7 mmm

P7 <u>muy</u> ((waves hand in upward motion)) de la clase media muy ((waves hand in upward motion)) <u>correctos</u>.... muy ((waves hand in upward motion)) <u>traba</u><u>jadores</u>...... bueno, así que un <u>día</u>.... en medio <u>crisis</u> con <u>todo</u>.... bueno vos <u>sabés</u> como fue, =

S8 = ah =

P8 = bueno uno día estoy yendo a la cena que hacen mis padres <u>todos</u> los sábados.... la cena que hacen desde que soy chica.... que hacen siempre,.... nos juntamos toda la <u>familia</u>.... mis papás mis hermanos mis primos mis tíos mis abuelos.... bueno,.... como digo toda la familia, =

S9 = mm mm =

P9 = y bajo del colectivo.... estoy a unas cuadras de la casa.... unas cuadras de la casa donde <u>yo crecí</u>.... y <u>sabés</u> lo que <u>veo</u>? un hombre,.... mayor,.... de la edad de mi abuelo,.... y Sara te digo la <u>pu:ra</u> verdad,.... me quedé <u>cau:ti:vada</u> ((grabs the corners of the table)).... se <u>parece</u> a mi abuelo

S10 ahhh

P10 de una manera tan.... <u>i:ncreí:ble</u>.... me quedo <u>pa:ra:da</u>, mirandolo.... con los ojos celestes de mi <u>abuelo</u>.... con el cabello de mi <u>abuelo</u>.... incluso esta vestido de manera de mi abuelo muy bien vestido

S11 mm mm

P11 Y <u>sabés</u> como fue que supe que <u>no</u> era mi abuelo? porque esta comiendo en la <u>ca:lle</u> ((points to the side)).... buscando comida en la <u>basu:ra</u>.... un <u>horror</u>....

S12 mmm

P12 Y en este momento.... Sarita.... me dí cuenta.... #de repente entendí que no ((pats chest)) me podía ((pats chest)) quedar callada que tenía que hacer <u>algo</u># para ayudar al otro.... que este hombre podría haber sido mi <u>abuelo</u> y estaba comiendo <u>basu:ra</u>.... en la <u>ca:lle</u>.... no lo podía soportar....

S13 ah ha

P13 Con esto, empecé a vivir.... de otra manera.... me desperté a lo que estaba pasando en este país.... y dentro de un año #aquí estaba trabajando <u>colaborando</u> con la gente de este barrio para mejorar las cosas para que nos <u>comprometamos</u> todos el uno con el otro#

S14 mm mm

P14 Y podés ver Sarita lo que estoy haciendo.... #los pibes de este barrio que están aprendiendo poco a poco a ser solidarios a colaborar# y eso? <u>eso</u> es todo....... es lo que importa.... es la posibilidad de un futuro para <u>todos</u> para todos que somos de este país tan.... tan.... vos sabés.... <u>imposible</u>

S15 Ah entonces para vos tiene que ver con la posibilidad de un futuro....

P15 Y <u>sí</u> vos sabés Sarita que yo ((points toward her chest)).... bueno.... yo soy pobre.... soy de esos nuevos <u>pobres</u> si lo pensás <u>bien</u>.... y por eso yo <u>sé</u> lo que falta en este país.... yo <u>sé</u> lo que podemos lograr.... y eso es lo que quiero dar a los pibes de este barrio. . . . a estos chicos que <u>nunca</u> se sumaron al proyecto nacional porque no <u>podían</u>. . . . porque siempre fueron marginalizados, y bueno así es. . . . es así que empecé a trabajar aquí. . . . y vos Sara? para vos cómo es? que te trajo al trabajo solidario?

S16   mmmmmmmquieroentendermejorcomosevacambiandoloqueesserdeclase media en la Argentina y espero que trabajar acá con ustedes me ayude a ver esos cambios

P16   ah, así que vos también ves la importancia de la solidaridad

PATRICIA AND ERNESTO

P1   bueno chicos. . . . vamos a hablar un poquito sobre la solidaridad. . . . sobre la importancia de la solidaridad. . . . de lo que es la solidaridad. . . . que significa ser solidario? . . . . como fomentar<u>la</u>? . . . . . y porqué? . . . . <u>para</u> que? . . . . alguien tiene ganas comentar? alguien quiere empezar? . . . . sí? Ernesto? ((gestures toward Ernesto with open hand)) vos querés empezar?

E1   y si ((rubs chin)) bueno yo quiero nada más decir que <u>sólo</u> no se puede hacer nada ((looks down and fidgets)). . . . sólo no podés resolver tus problemas. . . . hace falta la solidaridad. . . . mirá. . . . todo eso? ((looks up and gestures broadly with open hand)). . . . todo lo que hicimos en este barrio? lo logramos por la solidaridad

P2   sí. . . . y cómo la podemos fomentar? . . . . tomemos este barrio por ejemplo. . . . cómo es que ustedes son solidarios? . . . . siempre fue así? siempre fueron solidarios?. . . . . nadie?. . . . . Ernesto? vos querés comentar algo?

E2   . . . . y bueno ((shrugs shoulders)). . . . . . . todos sabemos lo que pasó en este barrio. . . . todos recordamos las dificultades que hemos vivido. . . . . . nunca teníamos. . . . . nosotros en este barrio. . . . las cosas nunca fueron fáciles. . . . siempre tuvimos que ayudar el uno al otro, ... pero sí con la crisis las cosas se empeoraron. . . . y sí tuvimos que venir pa'ca no? tuvimos que buscar una manera de sobrevivir. . . . y nos ayudó un montón. . . . . . el Centro nos ayudo a todos en este barrio

P3   hmmm mmmm sí. . . . . alguien más tiene ganas? . . . . . . OK, bueno, hablemos de algo un poco más concreto ((smiles)). . . . cómo vamos a arreglar todo para la fiesta la semana que viene?

REFERENCES

Abelin, Mireille. 2012. "'Entrenched in the BMW': Argentine Elites and the Terror of Fiscal Obligation." *Public Culture* 24, no. 2: 329–56.

Ablard, Jonathan D. 2003. "Law, Medicine, and Confinement to Public Psychiatric Hospitals in Twentieth-Century Argentina." In *Argentina on the Couch: Psychiatry, State, and Society, 1880 to the Present*, edited by Mariano Ben Plotkin, 87–112. Albuquerque: University of New Mexico Press.

Adamovsky, Ezequiel. 2009. *Historia de la clase media argentina: Apogeo y decadencia de una ilusión, 1919–2003*. Buenos Aires: Planeta.

Adorno, Theodor. 1967–68. "Sociology and Psychology." *New Left Review*, 46–47.

———. 1994. *Negative Dialectics*. New York: Continuum.

Adorno, Theodor, and Max Horkheimer. 1990. *The Dialectic of Enlightenment*. Translated by John Cumming. New York: Continuum.

Agha, Asif. 2007. "Recombinant Selves in Mass-Mediated Spacetime." *Language and Communication* 27, no. 3: 320–35.

Aguiar de Medeios, Carlos. 2009. "Asset-Stripping the State: Political Economy of Privatization in Latin America." *New Left Review* 55:109–32.

Aguinis, Marcos. 2001. *El atroz encanto de ser argentinos*. Buenos Aires: Planeta.

Alberto, Paulina, and Eduardo Elena, eds. 2016. *Rethinking Race in Modern Argentina*. New York: Cambridge University Press.

Alcañiz, Isabella, and Melissa Scheier. 2007. "New Social Movements with Old Party Politics: The MTL Piqueteros and Communist Party in Argentina." *Latin American Perspectives* 34, no. 2: 157–71.

Allen, Lori. 2013. *The Rise and Fall of Human Rights: Cynicism and Politics in Occupied Palestine*. Stanford, CA: Stanford University Press.

Allison, Anne. 2015. *Precarious Japan*. Durham, NC: Duke University Press.

Allon, Fiona. 2016. "The Wealth *Affect*: Financial Speculation as Everyday Habitus." In *Bodies and Affects in Market Societies*, edited by Anne Schmidt and Christoph Conrad, 109–25. Tubingen: Mohr Siebeck.

Allon, Fiona, and Guy Redden. 2012. "The Global Financial Crisis and the Culture of Continual Growth." *Journal of Cultural Economy* 5, no. 4: 375–90.

Alonso, Ana María. 1994. "The Politics of Space, Time and Substance: State Formation, Nationalism, and Ethnicity." *Annual Review of Anthropology* 23:379–405.

Altamirano, Héctor, and Graciela DiMarco. 2003. *Movimientos sociales en la Argentina: Asambleas, la politicización de la sociedad civil*. Buenos Aires: Jorge Baudino UNSM.

Althusser, Louis. 2001. "Ideology and Ideological State Apparatuses (Notes Toward an Investigation)." In *Lenin and Philosophy and Other Essays*. Translated by Ben Brewster, 85–132. New York: Monthly Review Press.

Amaral, Samuel, and Susan C. Stokes. 2005. "La democracia local y la calidad de la democracia." In *Democracia local: Clientelismo, capital social e inovación política en la Argentina*, edited by Samuel Amaral and Susan C. Stokes, 11–35. Buenos Aires: Universidad Nacional de Tres de Febrero.

Andermann, Jens, Philip Derbyshire, and John Kraniauskas. 2002. "Introduction to *Cacerolazos*: People, Class and Multitude—A Dossier." *Journal of Latin American Cultural Studies* 11, no. 2: 135–36.

Anders, Gerhard. 2008. "The Normativity of Numbers: World Bank and IMF Conditionality." *Political and Legal Anthropology Review* 31, no. 2: 187–202.

Anguita, Eduardo, and Alberto Minujin. 2005. *El futuro: El mundo que nos espera a los argentinos*. Buenos Aires: Edhasa.

Ansell, Aaron. 2014. *Zero Hunger: Political Culture and Antipoverty Policy in Northeast Brazil*. Chapel Hill: University of North Carolina Press.

Appadurai, Arjun. 2015. *Banking on Words: The Failure of Language in the Age of Derivative Finance*. Chicago: University of Chicago Press.

Apter, Andrew. 1999. "IBB=419: Nigerian Democracy and the Politics of Illusion." In *Civil Society and the Political Imagination in Africa: Critical Perspectives*, edited by Jean Comaroff and John L. Comaroff, 267–307. Chicago: University of Chicago Press.

Arendt, Hannah. 1958. *The Human Condition*. Chicago: University of Chicago Press.

Armony, Ariel C., and Víctor Armony. 2005. "Indictments, Myths, and Citizen Mobilization in Argentina: A Discourse Analysis." *Latin American Politics and Society* 47, no. 4: 27–54.

Armony, Víctor, and Gabriel Kessler. 2004. "Imágenes de una sociedad en crisis: Cuestión social, pobreza y desempleo." In *La historia reciente: Argentina en democracia*, edited by Marcos Novaro and Vicente Palermo, 91–113. Buenos Aires: Edhasa, 2004.

Astarita, Martín. 2014. "Los usos políticos de la corrupción en la Argentina en los años noventa: Una perspectiva histórica." *Revista Estado y Políticas Públicas* 3: 171–90.

Austen, Ralph. 1993. "Moral Economy of Witchcraft: An Essay in Comparative History." In *Modernity and Its Malcontents: Ritual and Power in Postcolonial Africa* edited by Jean Comaroff and John L. Comaroff, 89–110. Chicago: University of Chicago Press.

Auyero, Javier. 1999. "'From the Client's Point(s) of View': How Poor People Perceive and Evaluate Political Clientelism." *Theory and Society* 28, no. 2: 297–334.

———. 2000. "Cultura política, destitución social y clientelismo político en Buenos Aires: Un estudio etnográfico." In *Desde abajo: La transformación de las identidades sociales*, edited by Maristella Svampa, 181–208. Buenos Aires: Biblos.

Auyero, Javier, and Timothy Patrick Moran. 2007. "The Dynamics of Collective Violence: Dissecting Food Riots in Contemporary Argentina." *Social Forces* 85, no. 3: 1341–67.

Avelar, Idelbar. 1999. *The Untimely Present: Postdictatorial Latin America and the Task of Morning*. Durham, NC: Duke University Press.

Babül, Elif. 2015. "The Paradox of Protection: Human Rights, the Masculinist State, and the Moral Economy of Gratitude in Turkey." *American Ethnologist* 42, no. 1: 116–30.

Badiou, Alain. 2003. *Saint Paul: The Foundation of Universalism*. Stanford, CA: Stanford University Press.

———. 2013. *Being and Event*. New York: Bloomsbury Academic.

Bähre, Erik. 2005. "How to Ignore Corruption: Reporting on the Shortcomings of Development in South Africa." *Current Anthropology* 46, no. 1: 107–13.

Bakhtin, Mikhail M. 1982. *The Dialogic Imagination: Four Essays*, edited by Michael Holquist. Translated by Caryl Emerson and Michael Holquist. Austin: University of Texas Press.

———. 1986. *Speech Genres and Other Late Essays*, edited by Caryl Emerson and Michael Holquist. Translated by Vern McGee. Austin: University of Texas Press.

Balán, Manuel. 2011. "Competition by Denunciation: The Political Dynamics of Corruption Scandals in Argentina and Chile." *Comparative Politics* 43, no. 4: 459–78.

Ball, Christopher. 2014. "On Dicentization." *Journal of Linguistic Anthropology* 24, no. 2: 151–73.

Bardawil, Fadi A., and Talal Asad. 2016. "The Solitary Analyst of Doxas: An Interview with Talal Asad." *Comparative Studies of South Asia, Africa, and the Middle East* 36, no. 1: 152–73.

Barrera, Leticia. 2013. "Performing the Court: Public Hearings and the Politics of Judicial Transparency in Argentina." *Political and Legal Anthropology Review* 26, no. 2: 326–40.

Barros, Rodolfo. 2005. *Fuimos: Aventuras y desventuras de la clase media.* Buenos Aires: Aguilar.

Basualdo, Eduardo. 2011. *Sistema político y modelo de acumulación: Tres ensayos sobre la Argentina actual.* Buenos Aires: Atuel.

Bass, Jeffrey D. 2000. "In Exile from the Self: Identity, Politics, and Psychoanalysis in Buenos Aires." Ph.D. diss., University of California, San Diego.

Bataille, Georges. 1991. *The Accursed Share, Volume III: Sovereignty.* Translated by Robert Hurley. New York: Zone Books.

Bauman, Richard. 1986. *Story, Performance, and Event: Contextual Studies of Oral Narrative.* New York: Cambridge University Press.

Bauman, Richard, and Charles Briggs. 1990. "Poetics and Performance as Critical Perspectives on Language and Social Life." *Annual Review of Anthropology* 19:59–88.

Bautista, Julius. 2015. "Export-Quality Martyrs: Roman Catholicism and Transnational Labor in the Philippines." *Cultural Anthropology* 30, no. 3: 424–47.

Bayart, Jean-François, Stephen Ellis, and Béatrice Hibou. 1999. *The Criminalization of the State in Africa.* Translated by Stephen Ellis. Bloomington, IN: International African Institute.

Beccaria, Luis. 2002. "Empleo, remuneraciones y diferenciación social en el último cuarto del siglo XX." In *Sociedad y sociabilidad en la Argentina de los 90*, edited by Luis Beccaria, 27–54. Buenos Aires: Biblos.

Beckett, Gregory. 2019. *There Is No More Haiti: Between Life and Death in Port-au-Prince.* Berkeley: University of California Press.

Behringer, Wolfgang. 2004. *Witches and Witch-Hunts: A Global History.* New York: Polity.

Benjamin, Walter. 1968. "Theses on the Philosophy of History," *Illuminations: Essays and Reflections*, edited by Hannah Arendt. Translated by Harry Zohn, 254–57. New York: Schocken Books.

———. 2003. *The Origin of German Tragic Drama.* Translated by John Osborne. New York: Verso.

Benveniste, Emile. 1971. *Problems in General Linguistics.* Coral Gables, FL: University of Miami Press.

Blanco, Luisa, and Robin Grier. 2013. "Explaining the Rise of the Left in Latin America." *Latin American Research Review* 48, no. 1: 68–90.

Bleichmar, Silvia. 2002. *Dolor País.* Buenos Aires: Zorzal.

Bloch, Maurice, and Jonathan Parry. 1989 "Introduction: Money and the Morality of Exchange." In *Money and the Morality of Exchange*, edited by Maurice Bloch and Jonathan Parry, 1–32. New York: Cambridge University Press.

Blommaert, Jan. 2015. "Chronotopes, Scales, and Complexity in the Study of Language in Society." *Annual Review of Anthropology* 44:105–16.

Blunt, Robert. 2004. "'Satan Is an Imitator': Kenya's Recent Cosmology of Corruption." In *Producing African Futures: Ritual and Reproduction in a Neoliberal Age*, edited by Brad Weiss, 294–328. Boston: Brill.

Blustein, Paul. 2005. *And the Money Kept Rolling In (and Out): Wall Street, the IMF, and the Bankrupting of Argentina.* New York: Public Affairs.

Boltanski, Luc. 1999. *Distant Suffering: Morality, Media, and Politics.* New York: Columbia University Press.

———. 2011. *On Critique: A Sociology of Emancipation.* New York: Wiley.

———. 2014. *Mysteries and Conspiracies: Detective Stories, Spy Novels, and the Making of Modern Culture.* Translated by Catherine Porter. Malden, MA: Polity Press.

Bombal, Inés González. 2002. "Sociabilidad en clases medias en descenso: Experiencias en el trueque." In *Sociedad y sociabilidad en la Argentina de los 90*, edited by Luis Beccaria, Silvio Feldman, and Paula Bartley, 97–136. Buenos Aires: Biblos.

Bombal, Inés González, and Mariana Luzzi. 2006. "Middle-Class Use of Barter Clubs: A Real Alternative or Just Survival?" In *Broken Promises? The Argentine Crisis and Argentine Democracy*, edited by Edward Epstein and David Pion-Berlin, 141–60. Oxford: Lexington Books.

Bourdieu, Pierre. 1977. *Outline of a Theory of Practice*. Translated by Richard Nice. Cambridge, MA: Harvard University Press.

———. 1984. *Distinction: A Social Critique of the Judgement of Taste*. Translated by Richard Nice. Cambride, MA: Harvard University Press.

———. 1987. "The Biographical Illusion." In *Working Papers and Proceedings of the Center for Psychosocial Studies #14*.

———. 1989. "Social Space and Symbolic Power." *Sociological Theory* 71, no. 1: 14–25.

———. 1991. *Language and Symbolic Power*. Translated by Gino Raymond and Matthew Adamson. Cambridge, MA: Harvard University Press.

Boyer, Dominic. 2006. "Conspiracy, History, and Therapy at a Berlin *Stammtisch*." *American Ethnologist* 33, no. 3: 327–39.

Bratsis, Peter. 2003. "The Construction of Corruption, or Rules of Separation and Illusions of Purity in Bourgeois Societies." *Social Text* 77:9–34.

Briggs, Charles L. 2004. "Theorizing Modernity Conspiratorially: Science, Scale, and the Political Economy of Public Discourse in Explanations of a Cholera Epidemic." *American Ethnologist* 31, no. 2: 164–87.

Briggs, Charles L., and Richard Bauman. 1995. "Genre, Intertextuality, and Social Power." In *Language, Culture, and Society* edited by Ben Blount, 567–608. Prospect Heights, IL: Waveland.

Briones, Claudio, Ricardo Fava, and Ana Rosan. 2004. "Ni todos, ni alguien, ni uno: La politicización de los indefinidos como clave para pensar la crisis argentina." In *La cultura en las crisis latinoamericanas*, edited by Alejandro Grimson, 81–106. Buenos Aires: CLACSO.

Brooks, Peter. 1984. *Reading for the Plot: Design and Intention in Narrative*. New York: Knopf.

Brown, Wendy. 2001. "Futures: Specters and Angels: Benjamin and Derrida." In *Politics Out of History*, 138–73. Princeton, NJ: Princeton University Press.

Brusco, Valeria, Marcelo Nazareno, and Susan C. Stokes. 2004. "Vote Buying in Argentina." *Latin American Research Review* 39, no. 2: 66–88.

Buck-Morss, Susan. 2000. *Dreamworld and Catastrophe: The Passing of Mass Utopia in East and West*. Cambridge, MA: MIT Press.

Buckser, Andrew, and Stephen D. Glazier, eds. 2003. *The Anthropology of Religious Conversion*. Lanham, MD: Rowman & Littlefield.

Burnham, John. C. 1982. "The Reception of Psychoanalysis in Western Cultures: An Afterword on Its Comparative History." *Comparative Studies in Society and History* 24, no. 4: 603–10.

Butler, Judith. 2016. "Rethinking Vulnerability and Resistance." In *Vulnerability in Resistance*, edited by Judith Butler, Zeynep Gambetti, and Leticia Sabsay, 12–27. Durham, NC: Duke University Press.

Cafiero, Mario, and Javier Llorens. 2002. *La Argentina robada: El corralito, los bancos y el vaciamiento del sistema financiero*. Buenos Aires, Macchi Grupo.

Caimari, Lila. 2003. "Psychiatrists, Criminals, and Bureaucrats: The Production of Scientific Biographies in the Argentine Penitentiary System (1907–1945)." In *Argentina on the Couch: Psychiatry, State, and Society, 1880 to the Present*, edited by Mariano Ben Plotkin, 113–40. Albuquerque: University of New Mexico Press.

Caldeira, Teresa. 2000. *City of Walls: Crime, Segregation, and Citizenship in São Paulo*. Berkeley: University of California Press.

Calhoun, Craig. 2011. "From the Current Crises to Possible Futures." In *The Deepening Crisis: Governance Challenges after Neoliberalism*, edited by Craig Calhoun and Georgi Derluguian, 9–42. New York: New York University Press.

Callinicos, Alex. 2003. "State of Discontent: A Mass Movement's Strategy Toward the State is Vital to Its Success." *Socialist Review* 272, http://socialistreview.org.uk/272/state-discontent.

Canetti, Elias. 1984. *Crowds and Power*. Translated by Carol Stewart. New York: Farrar, Straus, and Giroux.

Canitrot, Adolfo. 1994. "Crisis and Transformation of the Argentine State (1978–1992)." In *Democracy, Markets, and Structural Reform in Latin America*, edited by William C. Smith, Carlos H. Acuña, and Eduardo A. Gamarra, 75–95. New Brunswick: Transaction Publishers.

Carr, E. Summerson, and Michael Lempert, eds. 2016. *Scale*. Berkeley: University of California Press.

Carrió, Alicia. 2002. "Contrato Moral." http://www.ccari.org.ar.

Chakrabarty, Dipesh. 2000. *Provincializing Europe: Postcolonial Thought and Historical Difference.* Princeton, NJ: Princeton University Press.

Chatman, Seymour. 1978. *Story and Discourse: Narrative Structure in Fiction and Film.* Ithaca, NY: Cornell University Press.

Chatterjee, Partha. 2004. *Politics of the Governed: Reflections on Popular Politics in Most of the World.* New York: Columbia University Press.

Cody, Francis. 2015. "Populist Publics: Print Capitalism and Crowd Violence beyond Liberal Frameworks." *Comparative Studies of South Asia, Africa, and the Middle East* 35, no. 1: 50–65.

Comaroff, Jean, and John L. Comaroff, eds. 1999. Introduction to *Civil Society and the Political Imagination in Africa: Critical Perspectives*, 1–43. Chicago: University of Chicago Press.

Condorcet, Jean-Antoine-Nicolas de Caritat. 1955. *Sketch for a Historical Picture of the Progress of the Human Mind.* Translated by June Barraclough. London: Weidenfeld and Nicolson.

Corbin, John. 2004. "*Interés*, Morality, and Legality in Southern Spain." In *Between Morality and the Law: Corruption, Anthropology, and Comparative Society*, edited by Italo Pardo, 19–32. Burlington, VT: Ashgate.

Coronil, Fernando. 1997. *The Magical State: Nature, Money, and Modernity in Venezuela.* Chicago: University of Chicago Press.

Corradi, Juan E. 1985. *The Fitfull Republic: Economy, Society, and Politics in Argentina.* Boulder, CO: Westview.

Corrigan, Philip, and Derek Sayer. 1985. *The Great Arch: State Formation as Cultural Revolution.* New York: Blackwell.

Costa, Flavia. 2002. "Entre la desobediencia y el éxodo, reportaje a Paulo Virno." *Archipiélago* 54; reposted at http://ar.groups.yahoo.com/group/listasociologia/message/2690.

Crane, Diana. 1972. *Invisible Colleges.* Chicago: University of Chicago Press.

Crapanzano, Vincent. 1984. "Life Histories." *American Anthropologist* 86, no. 4: 953–60.

———. 1996. "'Self'-Centering Narratives." In *Natural Histories of Discourse*, edited by Michael Silverstein and Greg Urban, 106–29. Chicago: University of Chicago Press.

Dagfal, Alejandro. 2009. "Paris-London-Buenos Aires: The Adventures of Kleinian Psychoanalysis between Europe and South America." In *The Transnational Unconscious: Essays in the History of Psychoanalysis and Transnationalism*, edited by Joy Damousi and Mariano Ben Plotkin, 179–88. New York: Palgrave.

D'Avella, Nicolas. 2014. "Ecologies of Investment: Crisis Histories and Brick Futures in Argentina." *Cultural Anthropology* 29, no. 1: 173–99.

Dean, Jodi. 1998. *Aliens in America: Conspiracy Cultures from Outerspace to Cyberspace.* Ithaca, NY: Cornell University Press.

———. 2002. *Publicity's Secret.* Ithaca, NY: Cornell University Press.

Debenport, Erin. 2015. *Fixing the Books: Secrecy, Literacy, and Perfectibility in Indigenous New Mexico.* Santa Fe, NM: School for Advanced Research Press.

Delamata, Gabriela. 2004. *Los barrios desbordados: Las organizaciones de desocupados del Gran Buenos Aires.* Buenos Aires: Eudeba.

Delaney, Jean H. 2002. "Imagining *El Ser Argentino*: Cultural Nationalism and Romantic Concepts of Nationhood in Early Twentieth-Century Argentina." *Journal of Latin American Studies* 34, no. 3: 625–58.

Deleuze, Gilles, and Félix Guattari. 1983. *Anti-Oedipus: Capitalism and Schizophrenia.* Minneapolis: University of Minnesota Press.

Delfini, Marcelo, and Valentina Picchetti. 2004. "De la fábrica al barrio y del barrio a las calles: Desempleo y construcción de identidades en los sectores populares desocupados del conurbano bonaerense." In *El trabajo frente al espejo: Continuidades y rupturas en los procecos de construcción identitaria de los trabajadores*, edited by Osvaldo Battistini, 269–90. Buenos Aires: Prometeo.

della Paolera, Gerardo, and Alan M. Taylor. 2003a. Introduction to *A New Economic History of Argentina*, edited by Gerardo della Paolera and Alan M. Taylor, 1–18. New York: Cambridge University Press.

———, eds. 2003b. *A New Economic History of Argentina*, New York: Cambridge University Press.

Derrida, Jacques. 1992. *Given Time: Counterfeit Money*. Translated by Peggy Kamuf. Chicago: University of Chicago Press.

———. 1994. *Specters of Marx: The State of the Debt, the Work of Mourning, and the New International*. Translated by Peggy Kamuf. New York: Routledge.

Dinerstein, Ana. 2002. "The Battle of Buenos Aires: Crisis, Insurrection, and the Reinvention of Politics of Argentina." *Historical Materialism* 10, no. 4: 5–38.

———. 2003. "*¡Que Se Vayan Todos!* Popular Insurrection and the *Asambleas Barriales* in Argentina." *Bulletin of Latin American Research* 22, no. 2: 187–200.

Doolan, Karin, Drazen Cepic, and Jeremy Walton. 2018. "Charity's Dilemmas: An Ethnography of Gift-Giving and Social Class in Croatia." *Journal of Organizational Ethnography* 8, no. 1:11–24, https://doi.org/10.1108/JOE-03-2018-0015.

Drake, Paul W., ed. 1994. *Money Doctors, Foreign Debts, and Economic Reforms in Latin America from the 1890s to the Present*. Wilmington, DE: Scholarly Resources.

Durkheim, Emile. 1984. *The Division of Labor in Society*. Translated by W. D. Halls. New York: Free Press.

Eigen, Peter. 2004. *Las redes de la corrupción: La sociedad civil contra los abusos de poder*. Translated by Mireia Bartels, Natalia French, and David Sánchez. Buenos Aires: Editorial Planeta.

Eisenstadt, S. N., and L. Roniger. 1984. *Patrons, Clients, and Friends: Interpersonal Relations and the Structure of Trust in Society*. Cambridge: Cambridge University Press.

Elias, Norbert. 1982. *The Civilizing Process*. Translated by Edmund Jephcott. New York: Pantheon.

Elyachar, Julia. 2005. "Comments on 'How to Ignore Corruption' by Erik Bähre." *Current Anthropology* 46, no. 1: 107–20.

Epstein, Edward C. 2009. "Perpetuating Social Movements amid Declining Opportunity: The Survival Strategies of Two Argentine *Piquetero* Groups." *Revista europea de estudios latinoamericanos y del Caribe* 86:3–19.

Epstein, Edward C., and David Pion-Berlin, eds. 2006. *Broken Promises? The Argentine Crisis and Argentine Democracy*. Lexington, UK: Lanham.

Escudé, Carlos. 2006. "From Captive to Failed State: Argentina under Systemic Populism, 1975–2006." *Fletcher Forum of World Affairs* 30, no. 2: 125–47.

Etchemendy, Sebastián, and Ruth Berins Collier. 2007. "Down but Not Out: Union Resurgence and Segmented Neocorporatism in Argentina (2003–2007)." *Politics and Society* 35, no. 3: 363–401.

Evans-Pritchard, E. E. (1937) 1976. *Witchcraft, Oracles, and Magic among the Azande*. New York: Oxford University Press.

Faubion, James D. 1999. "Deus Absconditus: Waco, Conspiracy (Theory), Millennialism, and (the End of the) Twentieth Century." In *Paranoia Within Reason: A Casebook on Conspiracy as Explanation*, edited by George E. Marcus, 375–404. Chicago: University of Chicago Press.

Faulk, Karen. 2012. *In the Wake of Neoliberalism: Citizenship and Human Rights in Argentina*. Stanford, CA: Stanford University Press.

Feitlowitz, Marguerite. 1998. *A Lexicon of Terror: Argentina and the Legacies of Torture*. New York: Oxford University Press.

Fennell, Catherine. 2015. *Last Project Standing: Civics and Sympathy in Post-Welfare Chicago*. Minneapolis: University of Minnesota Press.

Ferguson, James. 1999. *Expectations of Modernity: Myths and Meanings of Urban Life on the Zambian Copperbelt*. Berkeley: University of California Press.

———. 2015. *Give a Man a Fish: Reflections on the New Politics of Distribution*. Durham, NC: Duke University Press.

Ferme, Mariane. 2001. *The Underneath of Things: Violence, History, and the Everyday in Sierra Leone*. Berkeley: University of California Press.

Ferrante, Elana. 2014. *Those Who Leave and Those Who Stay*. Translated by Ann Goldstein. New York: Europa Editions.

Fiorucci, Flavia. 2005. "Fascinated by Failure: The 'Bestseller' Explanations of the Crisis." In *The Argentine Crisis at the Turn of the Millennium: Causes, Consequences, and Explanations*, edited by Flavia Fiorucci and Marcus Klein, 150–72. Amsterdam: Alesant.

Flandreau, Marc, ed. 2003. *Money Doctors: The Experience of International Financial Advising, 1850–2000*. New York: Routledge.

Flores-Macías, Gustavo A. 2012. *After Neoliberalism? The Left and Economic Reforms in Latin America*. New York: Oxford University Press.

Foucault, Michel. 1992. *The Use of Pleasure*. Vol. 2: *The History of Sexuality*. Translated by Robert Hurley. New York: Penguin.

Franco, Jean. 2002. *The Decline and Fall of the Lettered City*. Cambridge, MA: Harvard University Press.

Freud, Sigmund. 1957. "Mourning and Melancholia." In *On the History of the Psychoanalytic Movement*. Translated and edited by James Strachey, 237–58. London: Hogarth.

——. 1960. *Group Psychology and the Analysis of the Ego*. Translated by James Strachey. New York: Bantam.

——. 1966. "Transference." In *Introductory Lectures on Psychoanalysis*. Translated and edited by James Strachey, 536–56. New York: W. W. Norton.

——. 1989. "The Sense of Symptoms." In *Introductory Lectures on Psychoanalysis*. Translated and edited by James Strachey, 318–37. New York: W. W. Norton.

——. 1990. *Beyond the Pleasure Principle*. Translated by James Strachey. New York: W. W. Norton.

Gago, Verónica. 2017. *Neoliberalism from Below: Popular Pragmatics and Baroque Economies*. Durham, NC: Duke University Press.

Gago, Verónica, and Diego Sztulwark. 2002. "Argentina según el autor de Imperio: Antonio Negri (entrevista)," *Revista Tres Puntos*, Buenos Aires, August. Accessed January 2008. http://colectivoph.com.ar.

Gal, Susan. 2002. "A Semiotics of the Public/Private Distinction." *differences: A Journal of Feminist Cultural Studies* 13, no. 1: 77–95.

——. 2013. "Tastes of Talk: Qualia and the Moral Flavor of Signs." *Anthropological Theory* 13, nos. 1/2: 31–48.

——. 2018. "Registers in Circulation: The Social Organization of Interdiscursivity." *Signs and Society* 6, no. 1: 1-24.

Gal, Susan, and Judith Irvine. 2000. "Language Ideology and Linguistic Differentiation." In *Regimes of Language: Ideologies, Polities, and Identities*, edited by Paul V. Kroskrity, 35–84. New York: SAR Press.

Gal, Susan, and Kathryn A. Woolard. 1995. "Constructing Languages and Publics: Authority and Representation." *Pragmatics* 5, no. 2: 129–38.

Gandsman, Ari. 2009. "'A Prick of a Needle Can Do No Harm': Compulsory Extraction of Blood in the Search for the Children of Argentina's Disappeared." *Journal of Latin American and Caribbean Anthropology* 14, no. 1: 162–84.

García, Germán. 2005. *El psicoanálisis y los debates culturales: Ejemplos argentinos*. Buenos Aires: Paidós.

García Allegrone, Verónica, Florencia Partenio, and María Inés Fernández Álvarez. 2004. "Los procesos de recuperación de fábrica: una mirada retrospectiva." In *El trabajo frente al espejo: Continuidades y rupturas en los procesos de construcción identitaria de los trabajadores*, edited by Osvaldo R. Battistini, 329–44. Buenos Aires: Prometeo.

García-Heras, Raúl. 2009. "Economic Stability and Sustainable Development in Argentina." *Latin American Research Review* 44, no. 1: 278–90.

Garguin, Enrique. 2009. "'Los argentinos descendemos de los barcos': Articulación racial de la identidad de clase media en Argentina (1920–1960)." In *Moralidades, economías e identidades de clase media: Estudios históricos y etnográficos*, edited by Sergio Visacovsky and Enrique Garguin, 61–94. Buenos Aires: Editorial Antropofagia.

Gellner, Ernst. 1983. *Nations and Nationalism*. Ithaca, NY: Cornell University Press.

Germain, Randall. 2009. "Financial Order and World Politics: Crisis, Change, and Continuity." *International Affairs* 85, no. 4: 669–87.

Geschiere, Peter. 1997. *The Modernity of Witchcraft: Politics and the Occult in Postcolonial Africa.* Charlottesville: University of Virginia Press.

———. 2013. *Witchcraft, Intimacy, and Trust.* Chicago: University of Chicago Press.

Gilbert, Andrew. 2019. "Beyond Nostalgia: Other Historical Emotions." *History and Anthropology* 30, no. 3: 293-312.

Glaeser, Andreas. 2010. *Political Epistemics: The Secret Police, the Opposition, and the End of East German Socialism.* Chicago: University of Chicago Press.

Glaeser, Edward L., Rafael di Tella, and Lucas Llach. 2018. "Introduction to Argentine Exceptionalism." *Latin American Economic Review* 27, no. 1: 1-22.

Gledhill, John. 2003. "Introduction: Old Economy, New Economy; Old Corruption, New Corruption." *Social Analysis* 47, no. 3: 130-35.

Goddard, Victoria. 2006. "This Is History: Nation and Experience in Times of Crisis—Argentina 2001." *History and Anthropology* 17, no. 3: 267-86.

Godelier, Maruice. 1999. *The Enigma of the Gift.* Translated by Nora Scott. Chicago: University of Chicago Press.

Goffman, Erving. 1981. "Footing." *Forms of Talk*, 124-159. Philadelphia: University of Pennsylvania Press.

Golbert, Laura. 2004. *Derecho a la inclusión o paz social? Plan Jefas y Jefes de Hogar Desocupados.* Serie Políticas Sociales 84. Santiago de Chile: CEPAL.

Goldberg, Sarah Bess. 2016. "Entertaining Culture: Mass Culture and Consumer Society in Argentina, 1898-1946." Ph.D. diss., Columbia University.

Goldsmith, Arthur A. 1999. "Slapping the Grasping Hand: Correlates of Political Corruption in Emerging Markets." *American Journal of Economics and Sociology*, 58, no. 4: 865-83.

González, Francisco. 2012. *Creative Destruction: Economic Crises and Democracy in Latin America.* Baltimore, MD: Johns Hopkins University Press.

González, Horacio. 2004. *Filosofía de la conspiración: Marxistas, peronistas y carbonarios.* Buenos Aires: Ediciones Colihue.

Goodman, Jane E., Matt Tomlinson, and Justin B. Richland. 2014. "Citational Practices: Knowledge, Personhood, and Subjectivity." *Annual Review of Anthropology* 43:449-63.

Goodrich, Diana Sorensen. 1996. *Facundo and the Construction of Argentine Culture.* Austin: University of Texas Press.

Gooren, Henri. 2010. "Conversion Narratives." In *Studying Global Pentecostalism: Theories and Methods*, edited by Allan Anderson, Michael Bergunder, and Andre F. Droogers, 93-112. Berkeley: University of California Press.

Gordillo, Gastón. 2014. *Rubble: The Afterlife of Destruction.* Durham, NC: Duke University Press.

Gordillo, Gastón, and Silvia Hirsch. 2003. "Indigenous Struggles and Contested Identities in Argentina." *Journal of Latin American Anthropology* 8, no. 3: 4-30.

Graeber, David. 2002. "The New Anarchists." *New Left Review* 13:61-73.

Granovetter, Mark. 2007. "The Social Construction of Corruption." In *On Capitalism*, edited by Richard Swedberg, 152-172. Stanford, CA: Stanford University Press.

Greenberg, Jessica. 2014. *After the Revolution: Youth, Democracy, and the Politics of Disappointment in Serbia.* Stanford, CA: Stanford University Press.

Gregory, C. A. 1982. *Gifts and Commodities.* London: Academic Press.

———. 1996. *Savage Money: The Anthropology and Politics of Commodity Exchange.* Amsterdam: Taylor and Francis.

Grimson, Alejandro. 2004. *La cultura en las crisis latinoamericanas.* Buenos Aires: CLACSO.

Grondona, Mariano. 2001. *La realidad: El despertar del sueño argentino*, Buenos Aires: Planeta.

Guano, Emanuela. 2003. "A Color for the Modern Nation: The Discourse on Class, Race, and Education in the *Porteño* Middle Class." *Journal of Latin American Anthropology* 8, no. 1: 148-71.

———. 2004. "The Denial of Citizenship: 'Barbaric' Buenos Aires and the Middle-Class Imaginary." *City and Society* 16, no. 1: 69-97.

Gupta, Akhil. 1995. "Blurred Boundaries: The Discourse of Corruption, the Culture of Politics, and the State." *American Ethnologist* 22, no. 2: 375-402.

———. 2014. *Red Tape: Bureaucracy, Structural Violence, and Poverty in India*. Durham, NC: Duke University Press.

Gürpinar, Dogan. 2013. "Historical Revisionism vs. Conspiracy Theories: Transformations of Turkish Historical Scholarship and Conspiracy Theories as a Constitutive Element in Transforming Turkish Nationalism." *Journal of Balkan and Near Eastern Studies* 15, no. 4: 412–33.

Guyer, Jane. 1995. "The Currency Interface and Its Dynamics." In *Money Matters: Instability, Values, and Social Payments in the Modern History of West Africa*, edited by Jane Guyer, 1–26. Portsmouth, NH: Heinemann.

———. 2007. "Prophecy and the Near Future: Thoughts on Macoeconomic, Evangelical, and Punctuated Time." *American Ethnologist* 34, no. 3: 409–21.

———. 2012. "Soft Currencies, Cash Economies, New Monies: Past and Present." *Proceedings of the National Academy of Sciences of the United States of America* 109, no. 7: 2214–21.

Habermas, Jürgen. 1975. *Legitimation Crisis*. Boston: Beacon Press.

———. 1991. *The Structural Transformation of the Public Sphere: An Inquiry into a Category of Bourgeois Society*. Translated by Thomas Burger. Cambridge, MA: MIT Press.

———. 1996. *Between Facts and Norms: Contribution to a Discourse Theory of Democracy*. Translated by William Rehg. Cambridge, MA: MIT Press.

Hage, Ghassan. 2015. *Alter-Politics: Critical Anthropology and the Radical Imagination*. Melbourne: Melbourne University Press.

Hollander, Nancy Caro. 1990. "Buenos Aires: Latin Mecca of Psychoanalysis." *Social Research* 57, no. 4: 889–919.

Halperín Donghi, Tulio. 1964. *Argentina en el callejón*. Montevideo: ARCA.

———. 1994. *La larga agonía de la Argentina peronista*. Buenos Aires: Ariel.

Handman, Courtney. 2011. "Israelite Genealogies and Christian Commitment: The Limits of Language Ideologies in Guhu-Samane Christianity." *Anthropological Quarterly* 84, no. 3: 655–78.

Hankins, Joseph D. 2014. *Working Skin: Making Leather, Making a Multicultural Japan*. Berkeley: University of California Press.

———. 2015. "The Ends of Anthropology: 2014 in U.S. Anthropology." *American Anthropologist* 117, no. 3: 1–12.

———. n.d. "Publics of Coercion: Buraku Politics and the Cultivation of Attention." Unpublished manuscript.

Hanson, Rebecca, and Pablo Lapegna. 2017. "Popular Participation and Governance in the Kirchners' Argentina and Chávez's Venezuela: Recognition, Incorporation, and Supportive Mobilization." *Journal of Latin American Studies* 50, no. 1: 1–30.

Harkness, Nicholas. "Basic Kinship Terms: Christian Relations, Chronotopic Formulations, and a Korean Confrontation of Language." *Anthropological Quarterly* 88, no. 2: 305-336.

Hardt, Michael, and Antonio Negri. 2001. *Empire*. Cambridge, MA: Harvard University Press.

———. 2004. *Multitude: War and Democracy in the Age of Empire*. New York: Penguin, 2004.

Hart, Keith. 1986. "Heads or Tails? Two Sides of the Same Coin." *Man* 21:637–56.

———. 2000. *The Memory Bank: Money in an Unequal World*. London: Profile Books.

Hartog, François. 2003. *Regimes of Historicity: Presentism and Experiences of Time*. Translated by Saskia Brown. New York: Columbia University Press.

Harvey, David. 1990. *The Condition of Postmodernity*. Malden, MA: Blackwell.

———. 2000. *Spaces of Hope*. Berkeley: University of California Press.

———. 2010. *The Enigma of Capital and the Crises of Capitalism*. New York: Oxford University Press.

Hasty, Jennifer. 2005. "The Pleasures of Corruption: Desire and Discipline in Ghanaian Political Culture." *Cultural Anthropology* 20, no. 2: 271–301.

Heiman, Rachel. 2015. *Driving After Class: Anxious Times in an American Suburb*. Berkeley: University of California Press.

Heiman, Rachel, Carla Freeman, and Mark Liechty, eds. 2012. *The Global Middle Classes: Theorizing through Ethnography*. Santa Fe, NM: School for Advanced Research.

Hertz, Robert. 1974. "The Preeminence of the Right Hand: A Study in Religious Polarity." In *Right and Left: Essays on Dual Symbolic Classification*, edited by Rodney Needham, 1–31. Chicago: University of Chicago Press.

Herzfeld, Michael. 1997. *Cultural Intimacy: Social Poetics in the Nation-State*. New York: Routledge.

Herzovich, Guido Roman. 2015. "The Task of Inequality: Literary Criticism and the Mass Expansion of Publishing in Argentina (1950–1960)." Ph.D. diss., Columbia University.

Hetherington, Keith. 2011. *Guerrilla Auditors: The Politics of Transparency in Neoliberal Paraguay*. Durham, NC: Duke University Press.

Hill, Jane. 1995. "The Voices of Don Gabriel: Responsibility and Self in a Modern Mexicano Narrative." In *The Dialogic Emergence of Culture*, edited by Dennis Tedlock and Bruce Mannheim, 94–147. Urbana: University of Illinois Press.

Hirtz, Natalia Vanesa, and Marta Susana Giacone. 2013. "The Recovered Companies Workers' Struggle in Argentina: Between Autonomy and New Forms of Control." *Latin American Perspectives* 40, no. 4: 88–100.

Hofstadter, Richard. 1979. "The Paranoid Style in American Politics," In *The Paranoid Style in American Politics and Other Essays*, 3–40, Chicago: University of Chicago Press.

Hubert, Henri, and Marcel Mauss. 1964. *Sacrifice*. Translated by W. D. Halls. Chicago: University of Chicago Press.

Hume, David. 1993. *An Enquiry Concerning Human Understanding*. New York: Hackett.

———. 2003. *A Treatise of Human Nature*. New York: Dover Publications.

Humphrey, Caroline. 2001. "Rethinking Bribery in Contemporary Russia." In *Bribery and Blat in Russia: Negotiating Reciprocity from the Middle Ages to the 1990s*, edited by Alena Ledeneva, 216–41. New York: Palgrave.

Hutton, Ronald. 2004. "Anthropological and Historical Approaches to Witchcraft: Potential for New Collaboration?" *Historical Journal* 47, no. 2: 413–34.

Hymes, Dell. 1996. *Ethnography, Linguistics, Narrative Inequality: Toward an Understanding of Voice*. New York: Taylor and Francis.

Inoue, Miyako. 2004. "Introduction: Temporality and Historicity in and through Linguistic Ideology." *Journal of Linguistic Anthropology* 14, no. 1: 1–5.

Jackson, Jennifer. 2009. "To Tell It Directly or Not: Coding Transparency and Corruption in Malagasy Political Oratory." *Language and Society* 38:47–69.

Jaffee, Alexandra, ed. 2009. *Stance: Sociolinguistic Perspectives*. New York: Oxford University Press.

Jakobson, Roman. 1990. "Shifters and Verbal Categories." *On Language*, edited by Linda R. Waugh and Monique Monville-Burston, 386–392. Cambridge, MA: Harvard University Press.

James, Daniel. 1988. *Resistance and Integration: Peronism and the Argentine Working Class, 1946–1976*. New York: Cambridge University Press.

Jauretche, Arturo. 1966. *El medio pelo en la sociedad argentina: Apuntes para una sociología nacional*. Buenos Aires: Lillo.

Joseph, Galen. 1999. "Civilizing the Nation: Argentine Narratives of Education, Race, and Democracy." Ph.D. diss., University of California, Santa Cruz.

Keane, Webb. 2002. "Sincerity, 'Modernity,' and the Protestants." *Cultural Anthropology* 17, no. 1: 65–92.

———. 2003. "Semiotics and the Social Analysis of Material Things." *Language and Communication* 23, no. 3-4: 409–25.

———. 2007. *Christian Moderns: Freedom and Fetish in the Mission Encounter*. Berkeley: University of California Press.

———. 2008. "Market, Materiality, and Moral Metalanguage." *Anthropological Theory* 8:27–42.

———. 2018. "On Semiotic Ideology." *Signs and Society* 6, no. 1: 64–87.

Kedar, Claudia. 2013. *The International Monetary Fund and Latin America: The Argentine Puzzle in Context*. Philadelphia: Temple University Press.

Kessler, Gabriel. 2000. "Redefinición del mundo social en tiempos de cambio: Una tipología para la experiencia de empobrecimiento." In *Desde abajo: La transformación de las identidades sociales* edited by Maristella Svampa, 35-50. Buenos Aires: Biblos.

Kindleberger, Charles P., and Robert Aliber. 2005. *Manias, Panics, and Crashes: A History of Financial Crises*. 5th ed. New York: Wiley.

Klappenbach, Hugo. 2003. "La globalización y la enseñanza de la psicología en Argentina." *Psicologia em Estudo* 8, no. 2: 3–18.

Klaren, Peter F., and Thomas A. Bossert, eds. 1986. *The Promise of Development: Theories of Change in Latin America*. New York: Routledge.

Klein, Naomi. 2008. "Synopsis." *The Take*. Accessed April 25, 2020. http://thetake.org/index.cfm?page_name=synopsis.

Kockelman, Paul. 2004. "Stance and Subjectivity." *Journal of Linguistic Anthropology* 14, no. 2: 127–50.

———. 2010. "Value Is Life under an Interpretation: Existential Commitments, Instrumental Reasons, and Disorienting Metaphors." *Anthropological Theory* 10:149–62.

———. 2016. "Meeting the Universe Two-Thirds of the Way or Witchful Thinking: Matters of (and Off) Course." *Signs and Society* 4, no. 2: 1–29.

Kockelman, Paul, and Anya Bernstein. 2012. "Semiotic Technologies, Temporal Reckoning, and the Portability of Meaning, or Modern Modes of Temporality—Just How Abstract Are They?" *Anthropoloical Theory* 12, no. 3: 320–48.

Koelble, Thomas A., and Edward Lipuma. 2007. "The Effects of Circulatory Capitalism on Democratization: Observations from South Africa and Brazil." *Democratization* 13, no. 4: 605–31.

Koselleck, Reinhart. 1988. *Critique and Crisis: Enlightenment and the Pathogenesis of Modern Society*. Cambridge, MA: MIT Press.

———. 2004. "'Space of Experience' and 'Horizon of Expectation.'" *Futures Past: On the Semantics of Historical Time*, 255–76. Translated by Keith Tribe. New York: Columbia University Press.

Kovensky, Martín. 2002. *Limbo: Argentina 2002, Un relato en imagenes*. Buenos Aires: Fondo de Cultura Económica.

Kropotkin, Pëter. 1906. *The Conquest of Bread*. https://theanarchistlibrary.org/library/petr-kropotkin-the-conquest-of-bread.

Kunkel, Benjamin. 2014. *Utopia or Bust: A Guide to the Present Crisis*. New York: Verso.

Lacan, Jacques. 1977. "Aggressivity in Psychoanalysis." In *Ecrits: A Selection*, translated and edited by Alan Sheridan, 9–29. New York: W. W. Norton.

Lakoff, Andrew. 2006. *Pharmaceutical Reason: Knowledge and Value in Global Psychiatry*. New York: Cambridge University Press.

Landaburu, Jorge. 2001. *Argentina: El imperio de la decepción*. Buenos Aires: Editorial Sudamericana.

Larsen, Neil. 2003. "'Theory-Risk': Reflections on 'Globalization Theory' and the Crisis in Argentina." *CR: The New Centennial Review* 3, no. 2: 23–40.

Latour, Bruno. 1988. *Science in Action: How to Follow Scientists and Engineers through Society*. Cambridge, MA: Harvard University Press.

———. 2004. "Why Has Critique Run Out of Steam? From Matters of Fact to Matters of Concern." *Critical Inquiry* 30:225–48.

Lazar, Sian. 2005. "Citizens Despite the State: Everyday Corruption and Local Politics in El Alto, Bolivia." In *Corruption: Anthropological Perspectives*, edited by Dieter Haller and Cris Shore, 212–28. London: Pluto Press.

Lempert, Michael, and Sabina Perrino. 2007. "Entextualization and the Ends of Temporality." *Language and Communication* 27:205–11.

Levack, Brian. 1987. *The Witch-Hunt in Early Modern Europe*. New York: Routledge.

Lévi-Strauss, Claude. 1963. "The Sorceror and His Magic." In *Structural Anthropology*, translated by Claire Jacobson, 167–185. New York: Basic Books.

———. 1968. *Savage Thought*. Chicago: University of Chicago Press.

———. 1987. *Introduction to the Work of Marcel Mauss*. Translated by Felicity Baker. New York: Routledge.

Levitsky, Steven, and María Victoria Murillo. 2006. "Building Castles in the Sand? The Politics of Institutional Weakness in Argentina." In *Argentina Democracy: The Politics of Institutional Weakness*, edited by Steven Levitsky and María Victoria Murillo, 21–44. University Park: Penn State University Press.

Lewkowicz, Ignacio. 2002. *Sucesos argentinos: Cacerolazo y subjetividad postestatal*. Buenos Aires: Paidós.

Liechty, Mark. 2003. *Suitably Modern: Making Middle-Class Culture in a New Consumer Society*. Princeton, NJ: Princeton University Press.

Lim, Linda Y. C.. 1999. "Free Market Fancies: Hong Kong, Singapore, and the Asian Financial Crisis." In *The Politics of the Asian Economic Crisis*, edited by T. J. Pempei. Ithaca, NY: Cornell University Press.

LiPuma, Edward, and Benjamin Lee. 2004. *Financial Derivatives and the Globalization of Risk*. Durham, NC: Duke University Press.

Llach, Lucas. 2004. "¿Dos décadas perdidas? Desafíos, respuestas y resultadosde la política económica de la democracia." In *La historia reciente: Argentina en democracia*, edited by Marcos Novaro and Vicente Palermo, 133–54. Buenos Aires: Edhasa.

Lomnitz, Claudio. 1995. "Ritual, Rumor, and Corruption in the Constitution of Polity in Modern Mexico." *Journal of Latin American Anthropology* 1, no. 1: 20–47.

———. 2001. *Deep Mexico, Silent Mexico: An Anthropology of Nationalism*. Minneapolis: University of Minnesota Press.

———. 2003. "Times of Crisis: Historicity, Sacrifice, and the Spectacle of Debacle in Mexico City." *Public Culture* 15, no. 1: 127–47.

Lomnitz, Larissa. 1971. "Reciprocity of Favors in the Urban Middle Class of Chile." In *Studies in Economic Anthropology*, edited by George Dalton, 93–106. Washington, DC: American Anthropological Association.

López, Argemio. 2005. *La devaluación: Efectos sociales persistentes tras la salida de la convertibilidad*. Buenos Aires: Aurelia.

López, Argemio, and Martín Romero. 2005. *La declinación de la clase media argentina*. Buenos Aires: Equis.

Lukács, Georg. 1971. "Reification and the Consciousness of the Proletariat." In *History and Class Consciousness: Studies in Marxist Dialectics* 83–149. Cambridge, MA: MIT Press.

Mann, Geoff. 2017. *In the Long Run We Are All Dead: Keynesianism, Political Economy, and Revolution*. New York: Verso.

Maradona, Diego Armando. 2000. *Yo soy el Diego*. Buenos Aires: Editorial Planeta.

Marazzi, Christian. 2010. *The Violence of Financial Capitalism*. New York: Semiotexte.

Marcus, George E. 1999. "Introduction: The Paranoid Style Now." In *Paranoia Within Reason: A Casebook on Conspiracy as Explanation*, edited by George E. Marcus, 1–11. Chicago: University of Chicago Press.

Marsilli-Vargas, Xochitl. 2016. "The Off-Line and On-Line Mediatization of Psychoanalysis in Buenos Aires." *Sign and Society* 4, no. 1: 135–53.

Martínez-Echazábal, Lourdes. 1998. "*Mestizaje* and the Discourse of National/Cultural Identity in Latin America 1845–1959." *Latin American Perspectives* 25, no. 3: 21–42.

Martínez Estrada, Ezequiel. 1933. *Radiografía de la Pampa*. Buenos Aires: Losada.

Marx, Karl. 1978. "Crisis Theory." In *The Marx-Engles Reader*, 2nd ed., edited by Robert C. Tucker, 443–65. New York: W. W. Norton.

———. 1992. *Capital*. Vol. 1, *A Critique of Political Economy*, translated by Ben Fowkes. New York: Penguin.

———. 1994. *The 18th Brumaire of Louis Bonaparte*. New York: International Publishers.

Masco, Joseph P. 2017. "The Crisis in Crisis." *Current Anthropology* 58, no. S15: S65–S76.

Maurer, Bill. 2005. *Mutual Life, Limited: Islamic Banking, Alternative Currencies, Lateral Reason*. Princeton, NJ: Princeton University Press.

———. 2006. "The Anthropology of Money." *Annual Review of Anthropology* 35:15–36.

Mauss, Marcel. 1967. *The Gift: The Forms and Functions of Exchange in Archaic Societies*. Translated by Ian Cunnison. New York: W. W. Norton.

Mazzarella, William. 2006. "Internet X-Ray: E-Governance, Transparency, and the Politics of Immediation in India." *Public Culture* 18, no. 3: 473–505.

Mbembe, Achille. 2001. *On the Postcolony*. Berkeley: University of California Press.

Mbembe, Achille, and Janet Roitman. 1995. "Figures of the Subject in Times of Crisis." *Public Culture* 7:323–52.

Melley, Timothy. 2000. *Empire of Conspiracy: The Culture of Paranoia in Postwar America*. Ithaca, NY: Cornell University Press.

Milanesio, Natalia. 2010. "Peronists and *Cabecitas*: Stereotypes and Anxieties at the Peak of Social Change." In *The New Cultural History of Peronism*, edited by Matthew Karush and Oscar Charmosa, 53–84. Durham, NC: Duke University Press.

Minujin, Alberto. 1995."Squeezed: The Middle Class in Latin America." *Environment and Urbanization* 7, no. 2: 153–65.

Minujin, Alberto, and Eduardo Anguita. 2004. *La clase media: Seducida y abandonada*. Buenos Aires: Edhasa.

Minujin, Alberto, and Gabriel Kessler. 1995. *La nueva pobreza en la Argentina*. Buenos Aires: Editorial Planeta.

Montaigne, Michel de. 1991. "On the Cannibals." In *Michel de Montaigne: The Complete Essays*. Translated by M. A. Screech, 228–42. New York: Penguin.

Montesquieu, Charles-Louis de Secondat. 1989. *The Spirit of the Laws*. New York: Cambridge University Press.

Morris, Rosalind. 2000a. "Modernity's Media and the End of Mediumship? On the Aesthetic Economy of Transparency in Thailand." *Public Culture* 12, no. 2: 457–75.

———. 2000b. *In the Place of Origins: Modernity and Its Mediums in Northern Thailand*. Durham, NC: Duke University Press.

———. 2004. "Intimacy and Corruption in Thailand's Age of Transparency." In *Intimacy and Ethnography in the Age of Public Culture*, edited by Andrew Shryock, 225–43. Stanford, CA: Stanford University Press.

Muehlebach, Andrea. 2012. *The Moral Neoliberal: Welfare and Citizenship in Italy*. Chicago: University of Chicago Press.

Muir, Sarah. 2015. "The Currency of Failure: Money and Middle-Class Critique in Post-Crisis Buenos Aires." *Cultural Anthropology* 30, no. 2: 310–35.

———. 2016. "On Historical Exhaustion." *Comparative Studies in Society and History* 58, no. 1: 129–58.

———. 2021. "La corrupción como categoría clave para pensar la clase media argentina." In *Argentina y sus clases medias: Panoramas de la investigación empírica en ciencias sociales*, edited by Enrique Garguin and Sergio Visacovsky. Buenos Aires: Biblos.

Muir, Sarah, and Akhil Gupta. 2017. "Rethinking the Anthropology of Corruption." *Current Anthropology* 59, no. S18: S4–S15.

Muir, Sarah, and Marianinna Villavicencio. 2015. "The Currency of Failure: Money and Middle-Class Critique in Post-Crisis Buenos Aires: Supplemental Material [Interview with Marianinna Villavicencio]." Society for Cultural Anthropology, May 1. Accessed April 25, 2020. https://culanth.org/fieldsights/the-currency-of-failure-money-and-middle-class-critique-in-post-crisis-buenos-aires-supplemental-material.

Munck, Ronaldo. 1997. "Introduction: A Thin Democracy." *Latin American Perspectives* 24, no. 6: 5–21.

———. 2001. "Argentina, or the Political Economy of Collapse." *International Journal of Political Economy* 31, no. 3: 67–88.

———. 2003. "Neoliberalism, Necessitarianism, and Alternatives in Latin America: There is No Alternative (TINA)?" *Third World Quarterly* 24, no. 3: 495–511.

Munn, Nancy. 1986. *The Fame of Gawa: A Symbolic Study of Value Transformation in a Massim (Papua New Guinea) Society*. Durham, NC: Duke University Press.

Nakassis, Constantine V. 2016. "Linguistic Anthropology in 2015: Not the Study of Language." *American Anthropologist* 118, no. 2: 330–45.

Neiburg, Federico. 2010. "Sick Currencies and Public Numbers." *Anthropological Theory* 10, no. 1–2: 96–102.

Novaro, Marcos, and Vicente Palermo. 2004. "Las ideas de la época entre la invención de una tradición y el eterno retorno de la crisis." In *La historia reciente: Argentina en democracia*, edited by Marcos Novaro and Vicente Palermo, 11–34. Buenos Aires: Edhasa.

Nozawa, Shunsuke. 2015. "Phatic Traces: Sociality in Contemporary Japan." *Anthropological Quarterly* 88, no. 2: 373-400.

Oakdale, Suzanne. 2002. "Creating a Continuity Between Self and Other: First Person Narration in an Amazonian Ritual Context." *Ethos* 30, nos. 1/2: 158-75.

Ochs, Elinor, and Lisa Capps. 1996. "Narrating the Self." *Annual Review of Anthropology* 25:19-43.

Olivier de Sardan, J. P. 1999. "A Moral Economy of Corruption in Africa?" *Journal of Modern African Studies* 37, no. 1: 25-52.

O'Donnell, Guillermo. 1973. *Modernization and Bureaucratic-Authoritarianism: Studies in South American Politics*. Berkeley: University of California Press.

———. 1988. *Bureaucratic Authoritarianism: Argentina, 1966–1973, in Comparative Perspective*. Translated by James McGuire and Rae Flory. Berkeley: University of California Press.

———. 1994. "Delegative Democracy." *Journal of Democracy* 5, no. 1: 55-69.

———. 2007. *Dissonances: Democratic Critiques of Democracy*. Notre Dame, IN: University of Notre Dame Press.

O'Donnell, Pacho. 2001. *El prójimo: La revolución de los solidarios*. Buenos Aires: Planeta.

O'Dougherty, Maureen. 2002. *Consumption Intensified: The Politics of Middle-Class Daily Life in Brazil*. Durham, NC: Duke University Press.

Oliveto, Guillermo. 2014. *Argenchip*. Buenos Aires: Atlántida.

Osburg, John. 2013. *Anxious Wealth: Money and Morality among China's New Rich*. Stanford, CA: Stanford University Press.

Ouviña, Hernán. 2008. "Las asambleas barriales y la construcción de lo 'público no estatal': La experiencia en la Ciudad Autónoma de Buenos Aires." In *La política en movimiento: Identidades y experiencias de organización en América Latina*, edited by Bettina Levy and Natalia Gianatelli, 65-102. Buenos Aires: CLACSO.

Painceira, Juan Pablo. 2012. "Developing Countries in the Era of Financialisation: From Deficit-Accumulation to Reserve-Accumulation." In *Financialisation in Crisis*, edited by Costas Lapavitsas, 185-216. Boston: Brill.

Palermo, Vicente. 2012. "Entre la memoria y el olvido: Represión, guerra y democracia en la Argentina." *Journal of Iberian and Latin American Research* 10, no. 2: 131-48.

Paley, Julia. 2001. "The Paradox of Participation: Civil Society and Democracy in Chile." *Political and Legal Anthropology Review* 24, no. 1: 1-12.

Parmentier, Richard. 2007. "It's About Time: On the Semiotics of Temporality." *Language and Communication* 27, no. 3: 272-77.

Parry, Jonathan. 1986. "*The Gift*, the Indian Gift, and the 'Indian Gift.'" *Man* 21:453-73.

Pedersen, David. 2002. "The Storm We Call Dollars: Determining Value and Belief in El Salvador and the United States." *Cultural Anthropology* 17, no. 3: 431-59.

Peebles, Gustav. 2011. *The Euro and Its Rivals: Currency and the Construction of a Transnational City*. Bloomington: Indiana University Press.

Peirce, Charles Sanders. 1932. *Collected Papers of Charles Sanders Peirce*. Vols. 1 and 2: *Principles of Philosophy and Elementary Logic*. Edited by Charles Hartshorne and Paul Weiss. Cambridge, MA: Harvard University Press.

Pereyra, Sebastián. 2012. "La política de los escándolos de corrupción desde los años 90." *Desarrollo Económico* 42, no. 206: 25-284.

Pérez, Germán J., Martín Armelino, and Federico M. Rossi. 2005. "Entre el autogobierno y la representación: La experiencia de las asambleas en la Argentina." In *Tomar la palabra: Estudios sobre protesta social y acción colectiva en la Argentina contemporánea*, edited by Francisco Naishtat, Federico L. Schuster, Gabriel Nardacchione, et al., 387-413. Buenos Aires: Prometeo.

Piccato, Pablo. 2010. "Public Sphere in Latin America: A Map of the Historiography." *Social History* 35, no. 2: 165-92.

Piketty, Thomas. 2014. *Capital in the Twenty-First Century*. Translated by Arthur Goldhammer. Cambidge, MA: Harvard University Press.

Piot, Charles. 2010. *Nostalgia for the Future: West Africa after the Cold War*. Chicago: University of Chicago Press.

Pizzi, Alejandro, and Ignasi Brunet Icart. 2014. "Autogestión obrera y movilización social: El caso de las fábricas recuperadas argentinas en la Ciudad de Buenos Aires y Provincia de Buenos Aires." *Latin American Research Review* 49, no. 1: 39–61.

Plotkin, Mariano Ben. 2001. *Freud in the Pampas: The Emergence and Development of a Psychoanalytic Culture in Argentina*. Stanford, CA: Stanford University Press.

———, ed. 2003a. *Argentina on the Couch: Psychiatry, State, and Society, 1880 to the Present*. Albuquerque: University of New Mexico Press.

———. 2003b. Introduction to *Argentina on the Couch: Psychiatry, State, and Society, 1880 to the Present*, edited by Mariano Ben Plotkin, 1–24. Albuquerque: University of New Mexico Press.

———. 2003c. "Psychiatrists and the Reception of Psychoanalysis, 1910s-1970s." In *Argentina on the Couch: Psychiatry, State, and Society, 1880 to the Present*, edited by Mariano Ben Plotkin, 175–210. Albuquerque: University of New Mexico Press.

———. 2003d. *Mañana Es San Perón: A Cultural History of Perón's Argentina*. Translated by Keith Zahniser. Wilmington, DE: SR Books.

———. 2009. "Psychoanalysis, Transnationalism, and National Habitus: A Comparative Approach to the Reception of Psychoanalysis in Argentina and Brazil (1910s-1940s)." In *The Transnational Unconscious: Essay sin the History of Psychoanalysis and Transnationalism*, edited by Joy Damousi and Mariano Ben Plotkin, 145–77. New York: Palgrave.

Pocock, J. G. A. 1975. *The Machiavellian Moment: Florentine Political Thought and the Atlantic Republican Tradition*. Princeton, NJ: Princeton University Press.

Poovey, Mary. 2008. *Genres of the Credit Economy: Mediating Value in Eighteenth- and Nineteenth-Century Britain*. Chicago: University of Chicago Press.

Postone, Moishe. 1993. *Time, Labor, and Social Domination: A Reinterpretation of Marx's Critical Theory*. New York: Cambridge University Press.

Priest, Robert J. 2003. "'I Discovered My Sin!' Aguaruna Evangelical Conversion Narratives." In *The Anthropology of Religious Conversion*, edited by Andrew Buckser and Stephen D. Glazier, 95–108. New York: Rowman & Littlefield.

Putnam, Robert. 2000. *Bowling Alone: The Collapse and Revival of American Community*. New York: Simon and Schuster.

Quiroga, Hugo. 2005. *La Argentina en emergencia permanente*. Buenos Aires: Edhasa.

Rafael, Vicente. 1993. *Contracting Colonialism: Translation and Christian Conversion in Tagalog Society under Early Spanish Rule*. Durham, NC: Duke University Press.

Ramella, Susana. 2004. *Una Argentina racista: Historia de las ideas acerca de su pueblo y su población (1930–1950)*. Cuyo: Universidad de Cuyo.

Rancière, Jacques. 2009. *Dissensus: On Politics and Aesthetics*. London: Continuum.

Rawls, John. 2005. *A Theory of Justice*. New York: Oxford University Press.

Reyes, Angela. 2017. "Inventing Postcolonial Elites: Race, Language, Mix, Excess." *Journal of Linguistic Anthropology* 27, no. 2: 210–31.

Ricœur, Paul. 1970. *Freud and Philosophy: An Essay on Interpretation*. Translated by Denis Savage. New Haven, CT: Yale University Press.

Riggirozzi, Pía. 2009. "After Neoliberalism in Argentina: Reasserting Nationalism in an Open Economy." In *Governance After Neoliberalism in Latin America*, edited by Jean Grugel, 89–111. New York: Palgrave MacMillan.

Robischeaux, Thomas. 2009. *The Last Witch of Langenburg: Murder in a German Village*. New York: W. W. Norton.

Rock, David. 1985. *Argentina 1516–1987: From Spanish Colonization to Alfonsín*. Berkeley: University of California Press.

———. 2002. "Racking Argentina." *New Left Review* 17:54–86.

Roitman, Janet. 2005. *Fiscal Disobedience: An Anthropology of Economic Regulation in Central Africa*. Princeton, NJ: Princeton University Press.

———. 2014. *Anti-Crisis*. Durham: Duke University Press.

Romero, Luís Alberto. 2002. *A History of Argentina in the Twentieth Century*. Translated by James P. Brennan. University Park: Penn State University Press.

———. 2004. "Veinte años después: Un balance." In *La historia reciente: Argentina en democracia*, edited by Marcos Novaro and Vicente Palermo, 271–82. Buenos Aires: Edhasa.

Rose, Jacqueline. 2003. *On Not Being Able to Sleep: Psychoanalysis and the Modern World*. Princeton, NJ: Princeton University Press.

Roubini, Nouriel, and Stephan Mihm. 2010. *Crisis Economics: A Crash Course in the Future of Finance*. New York: Penguin.

Russo, Jane. 2009. "The Lacanian Movement in Argentina and Brazil: The Periphery becomes the Center." In *The Transnational Unconscious: Essays in the History of Psychoanalysis and Transnationalism*, edited by Joy Damousi and Mariano Ben Plotkin, 199–226. New York: Palgrave.

Rutherford, Danilyn B. 2012. "Kinky Empiricism." *Cultural Anthropology* 27, no. 3: 465–79.

———. 2015. "Introduction: About Time." *Anthropological Quarterly* 88, no. 2: 241–49.

Sabatini, Christopher, and Eric Farnsworth. 2006. "The Urgent Need for Labor Law Reform." *Journal of Democracy* 17, no. 4: 51.

Sader, Emir. 2008. "The Weakest Link? Neoliberalism in Latin America." *New Left Review* 52:5–31.

Sahlins, Marshall. 1972. "The Spirit of the Gift." In *Stone Age Economics*, 149–84. Hawthorne, NY: Aldine de Gruyter.

———. 1995. *Islands of History*. Chicago: University of Chicago Press.

———. 2013. *What Kinship Is—And Is Not*. Chicago: University of Chicago Press.

Salvatore, Ricardo D. 2008. "The Unsettling Location of a Settler Nation: Argentina, from Settler Economy to Failed Developing Nation." *South Atlantic Quarterly* 107, no. 4: 757–91.

Sanders, Todd. 2003. "Invisible Hands and Visible Goods: Revealed and Concealaed Economies in Millennial Tanzania." In *Transparency and Conspiracy: Ethnographies of Suspicion in the New World Order*, edited by Todd Sanders and Harry West, 148–74. Durham, NC: Duke University Press.

Sarlo, Beatriz. 1988. *Una modernidad periférica*. Buenos Aires: Ediciones Nueva Visión.

Sarmiento, Domingo. (1845) 2003. *Facundo: Civilization and Barbarism*. Translated by Kathleen Ross. Berkeley: University of California Press.

Sautu, Ruth. 2004. *Católogo de prácticas corruptas: Corrupción, confianza y democracia*. Buenos Aires: Lumière.

Scalabrini Ortiz, Raúl. 2005. *El hombre que está sólo y espera: una biblia porteña*. Buenos Aires: Biblos.

Scarre, Geoffrey, and John Callow. 2001. *Witchcraft and Magic in Sixteenth- and Seventeenth-Century Europe*. New York: Palgrave.

Schaumberg, Heike. 2008. "In Search of Alternatives: The Making of Grassroots Politics and Power in Argentina." *Bulletin of Latin American Research* 27, no. 3: 368–87.

Schijman, Agustina, and Guadalupe Dorna. 2012. "Clase media y clase media vulnerable: Evidencia empírica de la volatilidad intrageneracional de los sectores medios en Argentina (1996-mitad de 2007)." *Desarollo Económico* 52, no. 206: 179–202.

Schneider, Jane C., and Peter T. Schneider. 2003. *Reversible Destiny: Mafia, Antimafia, and the Struggle for Palermo*. Berkeley: University of California Press.

Schumpeter, Joseph A. 1983. *The Theory of Economic Development: An Inquiry into Profits, Capital, Credit, Interest, and the Business Cycle*. New Brunswick, NJ: Transaction Press.

Schvarstein, Leonardo, and Luis Leopold. 2005. Introducción to *Trabajo y subjetividad: Entre lo existente y lo necesario*, edited by Leonardo Schvarstein and Luis Leopold, 19–27. Buenos Aires: Paidós.

Scott, David. 2004. *Conscripts of Modernity: The Tragedy of Colonial Enlightenment*. Durham, NC: Duke University Press.

———. 2014. *Omens of Adversity: Tragedy, Time, Memory, Justice*. Durham, NC: Duke University Press.

Scott, Stephen Kingsley. 2017. "The Politics of Commiseration: On the Communicative Labors of 'Co-Mothering' in El Alto." *Journal of Linguistic Anthropology* 27, no. 2: 171–89.

Seoane, María. 2003. *El saqueo de la Argentina*. Buenos Aires: Sudamericana.

———. 2005. *Nosotros*. Buenos Aires: Sudamericana.

Sewell, William H., Jr. 2005. *Logics of History: Social Theory and Social Transformation*. Chicago: University of Chicago Press.

———. 2008. "The Temporalities of Capitalism." *Socio-Economic Review* 6:517–37.

———. 2012. "Economic Crises and the Shape of Modern History." *Public Culture* 24, no. 2: 303–27.

Shore, Cris. 2005. "Culture and Corruption in the EU: Reflections on Fraud, Nepotism, and Cronyism in the European Commission." In *Corruption: Anthropological Perspectives*, edited by Dieter Haller and Cris Shore, 131–55. London: Pluto Press.

Shumway, Nicolas. 1993. *The Invention of Argentina*. Berkeley: University of California Press.

Siegel, James. 2006. *Naming the Witch*. Stanford, CA: Stanford University Press.

Silverstein, Michael. 1998. "The Uses and Utility of Ideology: A Commentary." In *Language Ideologies: Practice and Theory*, edited by Bambi B. Schiefflelin, Kathryn A. Woolard, and Paul V. Kroskrity, 123–45. New York: Oxford University Press.

———. 2003. "Indexical Order and the Dialectics of Sociolinguistic Life." *Language and Communication* 23:193–229.

———. 2005. "Axes of Evals: Token vs. Type Interdiscursivity." *Journal of Linguistic Anthropology* 15, no. 1: 6–22.

Silverstein, Michael, and Greg Urban, eds. 1996. *Natural Histories of Discourse*. Berkeley: University of California Press.

Simonetti, José M. 2002. *El fin de la inocencia: Ensayos sobre la corrupción y la ilegalidad del poder*. Quilmes: Universidad Nacional de Quilmes.

Sitrin, Marina. 2006. *Horizontalism: Voices of Popular Power in Argentina*. New York: AK Press.

———. 2012. *Everyday Revolutions: Horizontalism and Autonomy in Argentina*. New York: Zed Books.

Skurski, Julie. 1994. "The Ambiguities of Authenticity: Doña Bárbara and the Construction of National Identity." *Poetics Today* 15, no. 4: 605–42.

Smart, Alan. 1993. "Gifts, Bribes, and Guanxi: A Reconsideration of Bourdieu's Social Capital." *Cultural Anthropology* 8, no. 3: 388–408.

Smart, Alan, and Josephine Smart. n.d. "Experiencing Crisis: Constructing Sequence in Series of Crises." Unpublished manuscript.

Smith, Daniel Jordan. 2008. *A Culture of Corruption: Everyday Deception and Popular Discontent in Nigeria*. Princeton, NJ: Princeton University Press.

Smith, Sean. 2008. "From Charitable to Public Assistance: Late Eighteenth-Century Transformations of Assistance in Buenos Aires, Lima, and Madrid." Ph.D. diss., University of Chicago.

Smulovitz, Catalina. 2006. "The Judicialization of Protest in Argentina: The Case of the *Corralito*." In *Enforcing the Rule of Law: Social Accountability in the New Latin American Democracies*, edited by Enrique Peruzzuti and Catalina Smulovitz, 55–74. Pittsburgh, PA: Pittsburgh University Press.

Soros, George. 2003 *The Alchemy of Finance*. New York: Wiley.

Spinoza, Benedictus de. 2007. *Theological-Political Treatise*. Edited by Jonathan Israel. Translated by Michael Silverthorne and Jonathan Israel. New York: Cambridge University Press.

Stasch, Rupert. 2011. "Ritual and Oratory Revisited: The Semiotics of Effective Action." *Annual Review of Anthropology* 40:159–74.

Stewart, Kathleen, and Susan Harding. 1999. "Bad Endings: American Apocalypsis." *Annual Review of Anthropology* 28:285–310.

Stromberg, Peter G. 1993. *Language and Self-Transformation: A Study of the Christian Conversion Narrative*. New York: Cambridge University Press.

Sutton, Barbara. 2008. "Contesting Racism: Democratic Citizenship, Human Rights, and Antiracist Politics in Argentina." *Latin American Perspectives* 35, no. 6: 106–21.

Svampa, Maristella. 2001. *Los que ganaron: La vida en los countries y barrios privados*. Buenos Aires: Biblos.

———. 2005. *La sociedad excluyente: La Argentina bajo el signo del neoliberalismo*. Buenos Aires: Taurus.

———. 2008. "The End of Kirchnerism." *New Left Review* 53:79–95.

———. 2011. "Argentina, una década después: Del 'que se vayan todos' a la exacerbación de lo nacional-popular." *coyuntura* 235:17–34.

———. 2013. "'Consenso de los *commodities*' y lenguajes de valoración en América Latina." *Nueva Sociedad* 244: 30–46.

Svampa, Maristella, and Damián Corral. 2006. "Political Mobilization in Neighborhood Assemblies: The Cases of Villa Crespo and Palermo." In *Broken Promises? The Argentine Crisis and Argentine Democracy*, edited by Edward Epstein and David Pion-Berlin, 117–40. Oxford: Lexington.

Svampa, Maristella, and Sebastián Pereyra. 2003. *Entre la ruta y el barrio: La experiencia de las organizaciones piqueteras*. Buenos Aires: Biblos.

Swinehart, Karl, and Anna Browne Ribeiro. 2019. "When Time Matters." *Signs and Society* 7, no. 1: 1–5.

Szwarcberg, Mariela. 2008. "Feeding Loyalties: Political Clientelism in Argentina, an Analysis of the Case of the Manzaneras." Ph.D. diss., University of Chicago

Taguieff, Pierre-André. 2000. *L'effacement de l'avenir*. Paris: Galilée.

Tambar, Kabir. 2009. "Secular Populism and the Semiotics of the Crowd in Turkey." *Public Culture* 21, no. 3: 517–37.

———. 2017. "The Uncanny Medium: Semiotic Opacity in the Wake of Genocide." *Current Anthropology* 58, no. 6: 762–74.

Taussig, Michael. 1999. *Defacement: Public Secrecy and the Labor of the Negative*. Stanford, CA: Stanford University Press.

Teunissen, Jan Joost, and Age Akkerman, eds. 2003. *The Crisis that Was Not Prevented: Lessons for Argentina, the IMF, and Globalisation*. The Hague: Forum on Debt and Development.

Tocqueville, Alexis de. 1969. *Democracy in America*. Translated by George Lawrence, edited by J. P. Mayer. New York: Harper Collins, 1969.

Treisman, Daniel. 2004. "Stabilization Tactics in Latin America: Menem, Cardoso, and the Politics of Low Inflation." *Comparative Politics* 36, no. 4: 399–419.

Trevor-Roper, Hugh. 1969. *The European Witch-Craze of the Sixteenth and Seventeenth Centuries*. New York: Penguin.

Trouillot, Michel-Rolph. 1997. *Silencing the Past: Power and the Production of History*. Boston: Beacon.

———. 2003. *Global Transformations: Anthropology and the Modern World*. New York: Palgrave Macmillan.

Turkle, Sherry. 1992. *Psychoanalytic Politics: Jacques Lacan and Freud's French Revolution*. London: Guilford Press.

Turner, Victor. (1957) 1996. *Schism and Continuity in an African Society: A Study of Ndembu Village Life*. London: Berg.

Ulanovsky, Carlos. 2004. *Cómo somos: Trapitos argentinos al sol*. Buenos Aires: Sudamericana.

UNDP (United Nations Development Programme). 2009. *Assessment of Development Results: Argentina*. New York: UNDP.

Urban, Greg. 1989. "The 'I' of Discourse." In *Semiotics, Self, and Society*, edited by Benjamin Lee and Greg Urban, 27–52. New York: Mouton de Gruyter.

Verhoeven, Imrat, and Evelien Tonkens. 2013. "Talking Active Citizenship: Framing Welfare State Reform in England and the Netherlands." *Social Policy and Society* 12, no. 3: 315–426.

Vezzetti, Hugo. 1996. *Aventuras de Freud en el país de los argentinos: De José Ingenieros a Enrique Pichón-Rivière*. Buenos Aires: Paidós.

———. 2002. *El Lanús: Memoria y política en la construcción de una tradición psiquiátrica y psicoanalítica argentina*. Buenos Aires: Alianza Editorial.

———. 2004. "Los comienzos de la psicología como disciplina universitaria y profesional: Debates, herencias y proyecciones sobre la sociedad." In *Intelectuales y expertos: La constitución del conocimiento social en la Argentina*, edited by Federico Neiburg and Mariano Plotkin, 293–326. Buenos Aires: Paidós.

Visacovsky, Sergio Eduardo. 2009a. "Origin Stories, Invention of Genealogies, and the Early Diffusion of Lacanian Psychoanalysis in Argentina and Spain (1960–1980)." In *The Transnational Unconscious: Essays in the History of Psychoanalysis and Transnationalism*, edited by Joy Damousi and Mariano Ben Plotkin, 227–56. New York: Palgrave.

———. 2009b. "La Constitución de un sentido práctico del malestar cotidiano y el lugar del psicoanálisis in la Argentina." *Cuilcuilco* 16, no. 45: 51–79.

———. 2009c. "Imágenes de la 'clase media' en la prensa escrita argentina durante la llamada 'crisis del 2001–2002.'" In *Moralidades, economías e identidades de clase media: Estudios históricos y etnográficos*, edited by Sergio Visacovsky and Enrique Garguin, 247–78. Buenos Aires: Editorial Antropofagia.

———. 2018. "The Days Argentina Stood Still: History, Nation, and Imaginable Futures in the Public Interpretations of the Argentine Crisis at the Beginning of the Twenty-First Century." *Horizontes antropológicos* 24, no. 52: 311–41.

Visacovsky, Sergio Eduardo, and Enrique Garguin. 2009. Introducción to *Moralidades, economías e identidades de clase media: Estudios históricos y etnográficos*, edited by Sergio Visacovsky and Enrique Garguin, 11–59. Buenos Aires: Editorial Antropofagia.

Vološinov, V. N. 1986. *Marxism and the Philosophy of Language*. Translated by Ladislav Matejka and I. R. Titunik. Cambridge, MA: Harvard University Press.

Wagner-Pacifici, Robin. 2017. *What Is an Event?* Chicago: University of Chicago Press.

Wallerstein, Immanuel. 2004. *World-Systems Analysis: An Introduction*. Durham, NC: Duke University Press.

Warner, Michael. 2002. *Publics and Counterpublics*. New York: Zone.

Watanabe, Chika. 2014. "Muddy Labor: A Japanese Aid Ethic of Collective Intimacy in Myanmar." *Cultural Anthropology* 29, no. 4: 648–71.

Weber, Max. 1949. "Objectivity in Social Science and Social Policy." In *The Methodology of the Social Sciences*, edited by E. A. Shils and H. A. Finch. New York: Free Press.

Wedeen, Lisa. 2008. *Peripheral Visions: Publics, Power, and Performance in Yemen*. Chicago: University of Chicago Press.

Weiner, Annette. 1992. *Inalienable Possessions: The Paradox of Keeping-While-Giving*. Berkeley: University of California Press.

Weisbrot, Mark, and Luis Sandoval. 2007. *Argentina's Economic Recovery: Policy Choices and Implications*. Washington DC: Center for Economic and Policy Research.

Weitz-Shapiro, Rebecca. 2006. "Partisanship and Protest: The Politics of Workfare Distribution in Argentina." *Latin American Research Review* 41, no. 3: 122–47.

West, Harry. 2005. *Kupilikula: Governance and the Invisible Realm in Mozambique*. Chicago: University of Chicago Press.

White, Hayden. 1990. *The Content of the Form: Narrative Discourse and Historical Representation*. Baltimore, MD: Johns Hopkins University Press.

White, Luise. 1990. *The Comforts of Home: Prostitution in Colonial Nairobi*. Chicago: University of Chicago Press.

Wilkis, Ariel. 2018. *The Moral Power of Money: Morality and Economy in the Life of the Poor*. Stanford, CA: Stanford University Press.

Williams, Raymond. 1977. "Structures of Feeling." In *Marxism and Literature*, 128–35. Oxford: Oxford University Press.

Wilson, Monica. 1951. "Witch Beliefs and Social Structure." *American Journal of Sociology* 56, no. 4: 307–13.

Wirtz, Kristina. 2016. "The Living, the Dead, and the Immanent: Dialogue across Chronotopes." *Hau* 6, no. 1: 343–69.

Wortham, Stanley. 2000. "Interactional Positioning and Narrative Self-Construction." *Narrative Inquiry* 10, no. 1: 157–84.

Wortman, Ana. 1999. Introducción to *Pensar las clases medias: Consumos culturales y estilos de vida urbanos en la Argentina de los noventa*, 15–21. Buenos Aires: La Crujía.

Yeh, Rihan. 2017. *Passing: Two Publics in a Mexican Border City*. Chicago: University of Chicago Press.

Yurchak, Alexei. 2005. *Everything Was Forever until It Was No More*. Princeton, NJ: Princeton University Press.

Zelizer, Viviana A. 1997. *The Social Meaning of Money: Pin Money, Paychecks, Poor Relief, and Other Currencies*. Princeton, NJ: Princeton University Press.

———. 2005. *The Purchase of Intimacy*. Princeton, NJ: Princeton University Press.

Žižek, Slavoj. 1989. *The Sublime Object of Ideology*. New York: Verso.

INDEX

address, 36, 38, 43, 56, 135. *See also* "I," speaking; public; "we," speaking
Adorno, Theodor W., 13, 46, 145
ahorristas, 68, 70–78
Alfonsín, Raúl, 17, 111
ambivalence, 5–9, 62–63, 76–77, 84, 105–6
antimaterialism, 85–86
anxiety, 19–20, 35, 51–52
Asad, Talal, 145
asambleas barriales/neighborhood assemblies, 3, 70
aspiration, 45, 72, 87. *See also* hope
autobiography, 34, 108; and history, 17–27, 102. *See also* address; history; "I," speaking; narration; narrative; "we," speaking

Bakhtin, Mikhail M., 9n, 32, 55
barter. See *trueque*/barter
Bataille, Georges, 109
Benjamin, Walter, 46, 61
Benveniste, Emile, 136
Boltanski, Luc, 57, 145
Bourdieu, Pierre, 36, 41, 46, 90
Bretton Woods Accords, 79
Brown, Wendy, 8–9

cacerolazos, 20, 22, 69–70, 152
capital: cultural, 27, 41, 43, 45, 54, 138, 139; economic, 138, 139; educational, 84; foreign, 78, 80; political, 138; social, 43, 45, 84, 139, 141
capital flight, 19, 50, 69
capitalism, 98, 114; and crisis, 3–4, 45–46, 48, 49, 62
Cavallo, Domingo, 17, 18, 20, 80
chronotope, 9n, 11, 17n, 32–33, 49n, 60–61,

67, 81, 83, 128, 136n20, 139–40, 144. *See also* future/futurity; history; narrative; past, engagement with; present and presentism
citizenship, 26, 58, 86n27, 127
classism, 138–39. *See also* inequality; middle class; narrative; poverty; race and racism; unemployment
clientelism, 95–96, 125–26, 131. *See also* corruption
complicity, 7, 24, 28, 29, 55, 58, 62, 83–84, 92, 94–95, 96, 101, 103, 113, 115, 134, 138
confession, 92, 96, 98, 100–110, 134, 138
consensus, 16, 22–36, 47, 59–60, 74, 92
conspiracy and conspiracy theories, 21, 24, 28, 30–31, 33, 37, 52, 54–56, 58–60, 76–77, 82, 85, 92, 100–101, 125–26. *See also* crisis talk; critique; interpretation; psychoanalysis and psychoanalytic theories; representational economy; revelation; truth
conversion: and devaluation, 86–87; of dollars into pesos, 21–22, 69; to solidarity, 133–36, 138–39; of value, 95–96
corralito, 19, 69, 80
corralón, 69, 80
corruption, 5, 7, 11–12, 18, 25, 28, 30n18, 33, 55, 62, 92–116, 118, 126, 128. *See also* clientelism
counterfeit, 48, 84–85, 96
coups d'état, 5, 49–50, 54, 84n, 113, 144
crisis, 2–12, 14–16, 17–28, 29–34, 41, 45–52, 54, 56–58, 61–62, 68–70, 75–77, 84, 88, 113, 134, 141, 143; routine, 4, 11–12, 45–52, 61, 143–44. *See also* chronotope
crisis talk, 17, 30n18, 32–33, 36–37, 51–52, 77, 102, 111–12, 135

critical theory. *See* critique

critique, 4, 7–8, 10–12, 16, 27–36, 38, 40, 41, 46, 48, 52–60, 62, 67–69, 74–75, 77–78, 82, 87, 90, 93–94, 102, 105–6, 122, 127–28, 140–41, 145. *See also* conspiracy and conspiracy theories; crisis; crisis talk; interpretation; psychoanalysis and psychoanalytic theories; representational economy; revelation; ritual; suspicion

currency, 21, 50, 66, 78, 79, 83. *See also* conversion; currency peg; devaluation; dollar; money; peso; value

currency peg, 17, 19, 21, 23, 78–79, 81, 83, 84–87. *See also* conversion; currency; devaluation; dollar; money; peso; value

debt, 5, 17–19, 21, 69, 75, 79, 80, 84n, 110, 111, 131

deception, 30, 37, 84, 118. *See also* disillusion

de la Rúa, Fernando, 2, 18, 20, 21, 23, 30

Deleuze, Gilles, 82

democracy, 47, 70, 110–13, 140

Descartes, René, 57

devaluation, 2, 5, 11, 19, 21–22, 30, 47, 66–90, 92, 110. *See also* conversion; currency; currency peg; dollar; money; peso; value

dicentization, 136, 138n

dictatorship, 29, 30, 53, 71, 97n8, 110–11, 122

disappointment, 9, 40, 62, 88, 132, 145. *See also* disillusion

disillusion, 3, 11, 30, 40, 40n, 41, 45, 60–63, 88, 112n19, 118, 143–44

disinvestment, 18, 112–13. *See also* future/futurity; investment; value

distinction, 87, 102, 121, 130, 138–39. *See also* capital; classism; inequality; middle class; race and racism

dollar, 17, 19, 21–22, 66, 67, 69, 72, 78–80, 83, 89. *See also* conversion; money; peso

dream, 7, 26, 28–30, 35, 37, 48, 72, 74, 79, 81, 84. *See also* disillusion

Duhalde, Eduardo, 21–22, 30, 78

Durkheim, Emile, 118, 126

egoism, 28, 92, 94, 96, 99, 109, 114; solidarity as inverse, 118, 127–28. *See also* antimaterialism; solidarity

el pueblo, 43–44. *See also* classism; inequality; public

epistemology, 32–33, 36, 56, 87, 88, 131, 136, 139

equality. *See* inequality

escraches, 71

ethics, 56, 85, 87, 88, 103–6, 127–29, 134–37, 139

Europe/European Union, 4, 8, 14, 18, 26, 29, 35, 43, 49, 54, 57, 77, 80–82, 97, 102, 112–14, 130. *See also* first world; United States

evaluation, 62n28, 87, 94, 105, 136n20. *See also* devaluation; revaluation; value

fábricas recuperadas, 70

failure, 3, 9, 13, 23, 26, 33, 35, 51, 66–69, 75, 77, 79, 83–84, 87–89, 106, 111, 122, 127–28, 132

fantasy, 7, 23, 29–31, 33, 40, 48, 58, 66–67, 74–75, 77, 81, 84–85, 89, 128. *See also* disillusion

Ferguson, James, 47

first world, 27–29, 37, 48, 73, 77–78, 80–81, 83, 87. *See also* chronotope; Europe/European Union; modernity; progress; United States

Freud, Sigmund, 59, 81

future/futurity, 7, 40, 42, 47–48, 80–81, 93, 130–31, 139–41. *See also* chronotope; history; narrative; past, engagement with; present and presentism

Gal, Susan, 51, 52

genre, 17, 30–31, 33, 38, 55–56, 60, 62, 70, 76, 103, 110, 133, 138–39. *See also* narration; narrative

Geschiere, Peter, 99n10, 109

gift, 58, 108, 118–19, 127–29, 131, 136, 139–41. *See also* reciprocity; solidarity

Greenberg, Jessica, 62n27

Guattari, Félix, 82

Habermas, Jürgen, 46

Hage, Ghassan, 8

Hankins, Joseph D., 9

history, 9n, 33–34, 39–63, 68, 78–79, 82, 86, 87, 89, 92–98, 109–14; and autobiography, 16, 17, 23–27, 33–34, 36, 71–74, 77 (*see also* autobiography; "I," speaking; "we," speaking); exhaustion of, 114–16. *See also* chronotope; future/futurity; narrative; past, engagement with; public

hope, 2–3, 7, 9–10, 15, 22, 24, 27, 30, 35, 40, 61, 72, 109, 128, 145. *See also* future/futurity; utopia

horizontalism, 70, 75, 128. *See also* solidarity

Hume, David, 145

Hymes, Dell, 138n

ideology, 34–35, 43, 51, 113, 131

illegitimacy. *See* legitimacy

immediacy, 118, 141. *See also* mediation; transparency

immigration. *See* migration

immorality. *See* ethics; morality

impasse, 119, 145. *See also* future/futurity

individualism, 54, 97–98. *See also* antimaterialism; egoism; solidarity

inequality, 3, 42, 62, 75, 84, 111–13, 115, 119, 122–24, 127, 129, 131–32; narrative, 133–39. *See also* classism; poverty; race and racism; unemployment

inflation, 50, 76, 78–79, 85, 111, 114

International Monetary Fund (IMF), 2, 18, 19, 21, 82

interpretation, 6, 34, 36–38, 40–41, 51, 56–58, 75, 77, 81–83, 87, 96, 102, 123, 127, 145. *See also* representational economy; semiosis

intimacy, 82, 106, 135

investment, 7–9, 17–22, 26, 36, 50, 57, 72–73, 80–81, 85, 111–12, 127. *See also* disinvestment; future/futurity; value

irony, 3, 9, 108, 139

"I," speaking, 33–34, 37–38, 48, 101–2, 136, 139. *See also* address; public; "we," speaking

kinship, 99, 123, 136

Kirchner, Cristina Fernández de, 5, 144

Kirchner, Néstor, 4–5, 42, 70, 113

kirchnerismo, 5n. *See also* Kirchner, Cristina Fernández de; Kirchner, Néstor

Koselleck, Reinhart, 8, 46

labor, 5, 11, 35, 75, 86, 96, 133, 139. *See also* unemployment; work

Lacan, Jacques, 59

Latour, Bruno, 8, 31

legitimacy, 14, 18, 37, 45, 51, 54, 60, 70–71, 75, 78, 92–97, 99–100, 105–6, 108, 110, 115–16, 144

liberalism, 4, 57, 89, 102, 113, 144. *See also* neoliberalism

Lomnitz, Claudio, 47, 98, 99

Lukács, Georg, 46

Macri, Mauricio, 5

Maradona, Diego, 94, 106–11, 115

markets, financial, 4, 68, 74, 76–77, 79, 85. *See also* capitalism: and crisis; disinvestment; investment; neoliberalism

Marx, Karl, 9n, 45–46

materialism, 14, 25, 54, 85, 87, 118, 128. *See also* egoism; neoliberalism; solidarity

Maurer, William, 67, 88–89

media, 10, 23, 30, 37, 42, 45, 51, 57–58, 77, 111–12, 121, 124n6, 125–26. *See also* immediacy; mediation

mediation, 19, 34, 41–42, 67, 81, 85n, 102, 118, 124, 128, 129. *See also* immediacy; media; transparency

Menem, Carlos Saúl, 18, 23, 72, 78–80, 95, 111–12, 114–15

mestizaje, 113. *See also* race and racism

middle class, 41–46. *See also* classism; distinction; "I," speaking; public; race and racism; "we," speaking

migration, 34, 49, 72, 73, 77, 87, 119, 120, 130

mistrust, 58, 67, 80, 85–86, 92–94, 96–97, 99, 106, 118. *See also* corruption; legitimacy; transparency

modernity, 8, 35, 37, 51, 81, 83, 89, 93, 114, 143. *See also* chronotope; first world; normality; progress

money, 66–69, 74–75, 78, 83, 88–90. *See also* conversion; currency; devaluation; dollar; peso; value

Montaigne, Michel de, 145

morality, 24, 34, 38n26, 85–87, 89, 92, 93, 97, 100–102, 111, 118–19, 126–27, 141. *See also* ethics

Muehlebach, Andrea, 127

Munn, Nancy, 3, 99

narration, 9, 30, 33, 34n, 36, 38, 42, 46, 48–49, 63, 71, 101, 133, 135–36. *See also* narrative

narrative, 9, 32–34, 36–38, 40–41, 47, 49, 57, 60, 72–73, 93, 99, 102, 114, 133–41. *See also* address; genre; history; inequality: narrative; "I," speaking; narration; plot; "we," speaking

negativity, 3, 9–10, 59, 61n23, 88, 92, 95–100, 103, 110, 113, 115, 145. *See also* corruption; disillusion; impasse; witchcraft

neighborhood assemblies. See *asambleas barriales*/neighborhood assemblies

neoliberalism, 2–3, 47, 74–75, 77, 83–84, 114, 118–19, 123, 128–29, 134, 139–41. *See also* liberalism

normality, 8, 24, 29, 40, 60–61, 75, 83, 85, 87, 93, 143. *See also* norms

norms, 40, 61n26, 94, 97, 99, 103–5, 109, 115. *See also* ethics; normality

nostalgia, 30, 144

past, engagement with, 3–7, 36, 45–48, 50–51, 54, 61–62, 68, 72, 75, 97, 114, 144. *See also* chronotope; future/futurity; history; narrative; present and presentism

pedagogy, 51, 59, 102, 128

Peirce, Charles Sanders, 145

peso, 17, 19, 66–69, 70, 72, 77–80, 83, 89. *See*

peso (*continued*)
  also conversion; currency; currency peg; devaluation; dollar; money; value
piqueteros, 18, 20, 70n4, 124–26. *See also* labor; poverty; solidarity; unemployment; work
pleasure, 60, 62, 75, 81–82
plot, 33, 51, 60–62, 72, 78, 110–14, 144. *See also* narrative
Pocock, J. G. A., 99
poetics, 32, 136
Postone, Moishe, 49
poverty, 15, 18, 22–23, 35, 42, 67, 74, 81, 84, 92, 95, 100, 102, 107, 115, 119–39. *See also* classism; distinction; inequality; race and racism
present and presentism, 6–7, 12, 45–48, 51, 54, 56, 61, 67–69, 72, 81, 83, 102, 118, 130, 134, 136n20. *See also* chronotope; crisis: routine; future/futurity; history; narrative; past, engagement with
productivity, 27–30, 92, 95, 100, 131–32, 139–40. *See also* distinction; labor; solidarity; work
progress, 4, 8, 30, 47–48, 51, 60–62, 72, 80, 84, 93, 102, 106, 110, 113–14, 139–40, 143–44. *See also* chronotope; first world; modernity
psychoanalysis and psychoanalytic theories, 10, 30, 31, 33, 48, 52–54, 56n, 58–60, 76, 81–82, 84, 86, 92–94. *See also* conspiracy and conspiracy theories; crisis talk; critique; interpretation; representational economy; revelation; truth
public, 2, 10–11, 16–17, 23, 27n16, 44–45, 53, 56–57, 75, 81, 86, 89, 94–95, 106, 110, 128n15; autobiographical, 36–38; intellectual, 45

race and racism, 8, 11, 35–36, 38n26, 43–44, 54, 93, 102, 106, 110, 113–15, 125, 129–30, 136, 138–39, 141. *See also* classism; distinction; inequality; poverty
Rancière, Jacques, 16
reciprocity, 85, 96, 99–100, 118–19, 128–29, 131. *See also* gift
recognition and misrecognition, 4, 6, 9, 14–17, 27, 29, 32, 37, 48, 51–52, 56, 71, 75, 81, 88–89, 94, 99, 106, 115, 136, 146. *See also* resemblance
representational economy, 76, 87–90. *See also* interpretation; semiosis; value
resemblance, 38, 48, 51–52, 123, 127, 133–36. *See also* recognition and misrecognition; rhematization
revaluation, 87. *See also* currency; currency

peg; devaluation; dollar; money; peso; value
revelation, 9, 11, 33, 47, 56–57, 59, 67, 75–76, 89, 94, 101, 108–10, 115, 143. *See also* critique; disillusion; interpretation; suspicion
rhematization, 49n, 136n19. *See also* recognition and misrecognition; resemblance
Ricœur, Paul, 56–57, 58
ritual, 11, 27–36, 51, 106, 138. *See also* crisis talk; critique; poetics; semiosis
routine crisis. *See* crisis: routine
Rutherford, Danilyn, 145

Sahlins, Marshall, 136n18. *See also* kinship; reciprocity
scale, 6, 19, 36, 40, 82, 128, 140. *See also* chronotope
semiosis, 16–17, 49n, 51–52, 67, 76, 88n30, 106n, 136n19, 145. *See also* interpretation
sentiment, 2, 12, 16, 41, 47, 62–63, 75, 113, 115, 119, 140, 143–44
Sewell, William H., Jr., 49
solidarity, 12, 28, 67, 85n, 86–87, 118–46. *See also* ethics; gift; inequality; morality; reciprocity
spatiotemporal. *See* chronotope
stance, 8, 16, 38n28, 46, 56, 62, 68–69, 85, 93–94, 114, 127, 143, 146
style, 25–26, 35, 40, 42, 53–56, 74, 76–77
suspicion, 4, 11–12, 16, 20, 25, 39–61, 67–69, 76–78, 85–90, 106, 116, 118n, 127–28, 131, 140–41, 143–44, 146. *See also* critique; interpretation; revelation

Tambar, Kabir, 17n, 44n9, 145
time/temporality, 3–4, 7–9, 11–12, 16, 32, 39, 46, 48–49, 51, 56–63, 66–67, 81, 83, 96, 112, 128, 133, 136n20, 137, 141, 143–44. *See also* chronotope; future/futurity; history; narrative; past, engagement with
transparency, 57n, 80, 97–98, 113, 118, 124, 141. *See also* corruption; immediacy; mediation
Trouillot, Michel-Rolph, 7n, 9, 136n21
trueque/barter, 3, 22, 24, 66, 70, 84–85, 118
trust. *See* mistrust
truth, 4, 13–14, 31, 45, 48, 54–59, 74, 76, 82, 89, 100, 103, 107, 134. *See also* critique; representational economy; revelation

unemployment, 2, 5–6, 15, 18, 22, 35, 44, 57, 69–70, 75, 84, 86, 92, 113, 119, 121–22, 124,

126, 129, 132, 140n26. *See also* classism; labor; *piqueteros*; poverty; race and racism; solidarity; work

United States, 4, 14, 18–19, 24, 36, 80–82, 101–2, 114. *See also* dollar; Europe/European Union; first world

utopia, 8, 10, 12, 26, 118–19, 127–28, 141, 144–45. *See also* chronotope; hope

value, 11, 21–22, 25–26, 28, 30, 32, 35, 45, 49, 54, 62, 65–69, 71, 74–77, 82–89, 96, 99, 101–3, 109, 119, 133, 138–39, 144. *See also* conversion; currency; devaluation; dollar; ethics; money; morality; peso; revaluation; virtue

virtue, 84, 92, 100, 102, 110, 118, 132, 135, 141. *See also* ethics; morality; value

voluntarism, 12, 86, 118, 127–28, 130, 141. *See also* solidarity

Washington Consensus, 2, 17–18, 50

"we," speaking, 33, 48, 102, 135. *See also* address; "I," speaking; public

White, Hylton, 9n

Wirtz, Kristina, 32

witchcraft, 98–100. *See also* corruption; negativity

work, 3, 7, 11, 15, 19, 22, 24–26, 28, 34, 40, 43–44, 46, 57, 68–70, 72–74, 77–78, 81, 85–86, 96, 100–102, 109, 119–20, 122, 124, 126, 128–41. See also *fábricas recuperadas*; labor; *piqueteros*; solidarity; unemployment; voluntarism

World Bank, 18

Žižek, Slavoj, 59, 88–89

Lightning Source UK Ltd.
Milton Keynes UK
UKHW022213060821
388325UK00002B/140